Overcoming Fragmentation in Teacher Education Policy and Practice

Edited by **Brian Hudson**

CAMBRIDGE
UNIVERSITY PRESS

University Printing House, Cambridge CB2 8BS, United Kingdom

One Liberty Plaza, 20th Floor, New York, NY 10006, USA

477 Williamstown Road, Port Melbourne, VIC 3207, Australia

4843/24, 2nd Floor, Ansari Road, Daryaganj, Delhi – 110002, India

79 Anson Road, #06–04/06, Singapore 079906

Cambridge University Press is part of the University of Cambridge.

It furthers the University's mission by disseminating knowledge in the pursuit of education, learning and research at the highest international levels of excellence.

www.cambridge.org
Information on this title: www.cambridge.org/9781316640791

First published 2017

20 19 18 17 16 15 14 13 12 11 10 9 8 7 6 5 4 3 2 1

Printed and bound in Great Britain by CPI Group (UK) Ltd, Croydon CR0 4YY

A catalogue record for this publication is available from the British Library

ISBN 978-1-31664079-1 Paperback

Contents

Series editors' preface

The manifold dimensions of the field of teacher education are increasingly attracting the attention of researchers, educators, classroom practitioners and policymakers, while awareness has also emerged of the blurred boundaries between these categories of stakeholders in the discipline. One notable feature of contemporary theory, research and practice in this field is consensus on the value of exploring the diversity of international experience for understanding the dynamics of educational development and the desired outcomes of teaching and learning. A second salient feature has been the view that theory and policy development in this field need to be evidence-driven and attentive to diversity of experience. Our aim in this series is to give space to in-depth examination and critical discussion of educational development in context with a particular focus on the role of the teacher and of teacher education. While significant, disparate studies have appeared in relation to specific areas of enquiry and activity, the Cambridge Education Research Series provides a platform for contributing to international debate by publishing within one overarching series monographs and edited collections by leading and emerging authors tackling innovative thinking, practice and research in education.

The series consists of three strands of publication representing three fundamental perspectives. The Teacher Education strand focuses on a range of issues and contexts and provides a re-examination of aspects of national and international teacher education systems or analysis of contextual examples of innovative practice in initial and continuing teacher education programmes in different national settings. The International Education Reform strand examines the global and country-specific moves to reform education and particularly teacher development, which is now widely acknowledged as central to educational systems development. Books published in the Language Education strand address the multilingual context of education in different national and international settings, critically examining among other phenomena the first, second and foreign language ambitions of different national settings and innovative classroom pedagogies and language teacher education approaches that take account of linguistic diversity.

We are delighted to include Brian Hudson's edited collection in the series. This book is a comprehensive and important overview of teacher education in Europe. It begins with the local – from case studies of the national contexts of Ireland, Finland, Poland, Sweden and Scotland – and moves on to the European and then global level. The importance of local contexts as well as international movements is clearly demonstrated in chapters written by contributors with a deep-rooted, informed and influential position in shaping these agendas. The second key organizing principle is a focus on career-long teacher education. The full spectrum is debated from initial teacher education to induction and continuing professional development. The important aspects and influences on teacher education are also focused upon, including teacher identity and role conception as well as role enactment, and the processes that facilitate teacher learning such as mentoring. The fragmentation refers to the current tensions, pushes and pulls in the educational landscape. The debates around the place of subject knowledge and pedagogical knowledge; the relationship between research and practice and the wider or narrower purposes of teacher education are all represented within these pages. This book is also a fine companion to the recently published text edited by Bob Moon and focused on the role of universities, based around the world, in teacher education.

Colleen McLaughlin and Michael Evans

Acknowledgements

Dedication:

To my parents

Gerard Hudson (20.12.1921–23.05.1997) and
Ellen Hudson (née Flynn) (07.06.1929–)

Firstly, I would like to acknowledge the essential and invaluable support of academic colleagues who contributed to the peer review process. The members of the TEPE Board at that time who contributed to the process of peer review are listed below:

Dr Francesca Caena, University of Venice, Italy; Dr Eve Eisenschmidt, Tallinn University, Estonia; Dr Judith Harford, University College Dublin, Eire; Dr Erika Löfström, University of Helsinki, Finland; Professor Joanna Madalinska-Michalak, University of Warsaw, Poland; Professor Teresa Moran, University of Dundee, Scotland; Professor Hannele Niemi, University of Helsinki, Finland; Dr Marina Vasylenko, CREF University Pais Ouest Nanterre, France; Dr Vlasta Vizek Vidovic, Institute of Social Research, Zagreb, Croatia; Professor Pavel Zgaga, University of Ljubljana, Slovenia; Dr Björn Åstrand, Karlstad University, Sweden.

Also I would like to acknowledge the invaluable contribution to the process of peer review from the anonymous reviewer and also from the series editors at the book proposal stage.

I would also like to thank the following colleagues for their essential support with the editorial process:

For his English language editing and proof reading at the first stage of the editorial process, I would like to acknowledge Murray Bales for his expert support. In addition, I would like to acknowledge Paul Sloman and his team at Cambridge University Press for their expert support with proofreading, page layout and oversight of the final publication and also to thank Paul Sloman especially for his patience and support throughout this process.

Professor Brian Hudson, Sussex, April 2017

Notes on contributors

Dr Kwame Akyeampong is Professor of International Education and Development at the Centre for International Education in the School of Education and Social Work at the University of Sussex. His research interests are in teacher education policy and practice, complementary basic education for out-of-school children and impact evaluation of education programmes. He has worked on a wide range of research projects and reform programmes for UNESCO, JICA, DFID and the World Bank. In 2001, he was a Senior Fulbright Research Scholar at Georgia State University, USA, and in 2002, he served as a Visiting Professor at the Centre for the Study of International Co-operation in Education (CICE) at Hiroshima University, Japan. From 2011 to 2013, he was appointed Senior Policy Analyst with UNESCO's Global Monitoring Report team (GMR) in Paris. He is currently the Co-Chair of the Teacher Alliance of the Global Education and Skills Forum (GESF).

Dr Francesca Caena's professional background, research interests and publications focus on European education policies, comparative studies, teacher education, virtual teaching/learning environments and foreign-language teaching. She has worked as an education research consultant for the European Commission for five years (2011–15), supporting the Working Groups 'Professional Development of Teachers' and 'School Policy'. She has also given contributions on the topic of teacher policy as an expert for OECD and UNESCO. She has substantial experience in ITE as a teacher educator and lecturer (University of Venice), as well as in EFL teaching and continuous training. In 2010 she successfully defended her PhD thesis at Padua university (a comparative mixed-method study on European teacher education in four national contexts). She explored additional insights into this policy field as co-ordinator of an Erasmus LLL project for a European Joint Master's teacher education curriculum, involving eight higher-education institutions across Europe.

Anthony Finn, CBE was Chief Executive of the General Teaching Council for Scotland (GTCS), the world's first independent, self-regulating professional body for teaching, until his retirement from this post in October 2013. Currently Professor of Teacher Education and Professionalism at the University of Glasgow and Chair of the Board of the new Scottish College for Educational Leadership, he contributes regularly to the understanding and development of professionalism and leadership, and of wider educational issues; and he is a frequent contributor to national and international conferences. Originally a Modern Languages teacher, he spent much of his career working in schools, including 18 years as head teacher of a successful secondary school. Before taking up his post with GTCS, he was Senior Manager (Deputy Director) for Education in Fife. He has received a number of awards, including, in 2014, the UK award of CBE for services to education.

Dr Peter Gray is research adviser at the Faculty of Social Science and Technology Management, Norwegian University of Science and Technology, Trondheim. He has worked on several European projects including S-TEAM (Science-Teacher Education Advanced Methods) and is currently coordinator of the TEQUILA (Teacher Education Quality through Integrating Learning and Research) network, coordinator of the VISconti project on vocational education, and a partner in the PROTEUS project on university–school collaboration. With Marit Hoveid, he edited *Inquiry in Science Education and Science Teacher Education* (Akademika Forslag, 2013). He also evaluates science education projects for the European Commission and is a reviewer for *Teaching and Teacher Education* and *Journal of Education for Teaching*.

Dr Judith Harford is Associate Professor and Director of the Professional Master of Education at the School of Education, University College Dublin. She has published internationally in the areas of teacher education, history of women's education and education policy. She is Coordinator of the Teacher Education Policy in Europe Network and has recently served as a Convenor of the Teacher Education Research Network of the European Educational Research Association (EERA).

She has acted as external examiner to universities in Ireland, the United Kingdom and Australia, and as consultant to a number of European agencies.

Dr Brian Hudson is Professor of Education and until recently was Head of the School of Education and Social Work at the University of Sussex (2012–16). Currently he is the main organiser of the International Research Network on Didactics – Learning and Teaching of the World Education Research Association (WERA), a member of the WERA Council Outreach Committee, an Honorary Member of the Network on Didactics – Learning and Teaching of the European Education Research Association and Associate Editor of the *Journal of Curriculum Studies*. He was a founder member of the Teacher Education Policy in Europe (TEPE) network and previously served as Coordinator (2006–10) and as Chair (2010–14). He was awarded a National Teaching Fellowship in 2004 and most recently was Principal Investigator for the ESRC-funded research project 'Education and social outcomes for young people: Promoting success' (2013–15). He is also Honorary Professor at the University of Dundee, Adjunct Professor at the University of Ghana and Guest Professor at Karlstad University, Sweden.

Dr Marilyn Leask is a Visiting Professor of Education in the Institute for Education Futures at De Montfort University UK. Her career has involved teaching and leadership in various roles in primary and secondary schools, local authorities, and universities. She has been a Professor of Education in the UK at the University of Bedfordshire and Brunel University. For twenty-five years she has co-edited the major text book series used for secondary teacher training in the UK. She is an expert in the knowledge base required for teaching and in the use of digital technologies to make research based knowledge available to educators. She is a trustee of the international charity, the Education Futures Collaboration (EFC) set up to link researchers and teachers in developing and publishing the evidence base for education so it is freely accessible to teachers anywhere in the world. The EFC publishes summaries of research as concept maps called MESHGuides (www.mesh-guides.org).

Dr Joanna Madalińska-Michalak is Professor of Education at the Faculty of Education, University of Warsaw. She is President of the Polish Educational Research Association (PERA) (Polskie Towarzystwo Pedagogiczne), a member of the Council Board of the European

Educational Research Association (EERA) and a member of the Board of Teacher Educational Policy in Europe (TEPE). Currently she is serving as Chair of the Board of the TEPE network. She has long-standing research interests in comparative education, teacher education and educational leadership. She has published in the areas of teacher education, exemplary teachers and leaders, teachers' success and its conditions, teachers' and leaders' professional development and learning, and educational leadership.

Dr Hannele Niemi is Professor of Education (1998–) at the Faculty of Behavioural Sciences, University of Helsinki. She has also been Vice Rector (2003–9) and Dean (2001–3) at the University of Helsinki. She has had many memberships in scientific councils and editorial boards in Finland and Europe. Her main research interest areas are teachers' professional development, moral education and technology-based learning environments. She has published several articles and books on education in Finland and Finnish teacher education. She has been invited as Doctor or Professor of Honoris Causa in Universities in Finland (two universities), Romania and Singapore.

Dr Sarah Younie is the Co-Director of the Institute for Education Futures at De Montfort University UK, and has been involved in international research for over 25 years. She has contributed to the use of digital technologies in educational settings for UNESCO, EU and UK government agencies, including the BBC, HEA and JISC. As the UK Chair of the National Subject Association of IT in Teacher Education (ITTE) she conducted national research, including evidence for the Parliamentary Select Committee Inquiry into Education. Dr Younie is Editor-in-Chief for the Journal of Technology, Pedagogy and Education, and has published articles and books on teacher education. She is a trustee of the international charity the Education Futures Collaboration (EFC), which publishes summaries of research as concept maps called MESHGuides (www.meshguides.org).

Dr Pavel Zgaga is Professor of Philosophy of Education at the University of Ljubljana, Slovenia. His main research interests relate to philosophy and history of educational ideas, education policies and, in particular, higher-education studies. In the 1990s, he was State Secretary for Higher Education and Minister of Education and Sport of the Republic of Slovenia. After his return to academe, he served as a Dean of Education

Faculty. In 2001, he co-founded, and remains Director for, the Centre for Educational Policy Studies (CEPS).

Dr Björn Åstrand served as Dean for Umeå School of Education (2005–11) and is currently Senior Lecturer and Dean for Faculty Board for Teacher Education and Educational Science at Karlstad University, Sweden. His main research interests relate to early modern history, history of education and contemporary education (higher education, teacher education, history education, education systems). In 2016 he edited, together with Linda Darling-Hammond and Frank Adamson, the comparative volume *Global Education Reform: How Privatization and Public Investment Influence Education Outcomes* (Routledge). Currently he serves as Special Investigator for the Swedish government concerning the advancement of schools by making teaching more attractive and as member of the governmental School Commission.

1 History, context and overview: Implications for teacher education policy, practice and future research

Brian Hudson and Pavel Zgaga

History and context

This book is the result of over 20 years' collaboration through projects supported by the European Commission and especially from 10 years' collaboration within the Teacher Education Policy in Europe (TEPE) network. In particular, these chapters have their origins in contributions made at the network's eighth annual conference held at the University of Zagreb, Croatia, in 2014 on the theme of 'Overcoming Fragmentation in Teacher Education Policy and Practice'. The TEPE network was established in 2006 at Umeå University (Sweden) and the first TEPE conference was organised at the University of Tallinn (Estonia) in February 2007. Annual conferences have been organised every year since then and taken place in Ljubljana, Umeå, Tallinn, Vienna, Warsaw, Helsinki, Zagreb, Dundee and Malta.

The TEPE network itself built on earlier initiatives and in particular on the Thematic Network for Teacher Education in Europe (TNTEE) that is discussed in detail below, and which can be traced back over a period of more than 30 years overall. Prior to the 1990s, teacher education in Europe was rarely discussed as an issue of European or international cooperation in higher education. At a practical level, a new era was marked by the introduction of the European Union's Erasmus, Socrates and Leonardo programmes in the late 1980s and early 1990s. Direct collaboration between education institutions from EU countries increased substantially as a result. The 1990s were, at the same time, the beginning of a period of European Union enlargement. It was also very important for teacher education that special EU cooperation programmes were launched that supported broader cooperation in education among EU (Erasmus) and non-EU countries (Tempus; Erasmus Mundus).

The Socrates-Erasmus programme opened new perspectives for European cooperation in general education and made good progress in the early 1990s, particularly through the programme action on 'university cooperation projects on subjects of mutual interest'. Similarly, as in other areas of higher education, a thorough evaluation of teacher education was prepared in this context during the mid-1990s. In 1994, within a larger framework of investigating the Erasmus programme's effects, the European Commission funded a pilot project in this area: the Sigma–European Universities' Network. Within this network, 15 national reports[1] were produced for an Evaluation Conference that took place in June 1995, the proceedings of which were edited by Sander (1995) and published by Universität Osnabrück. These reports presented an extremely fragmented picture of the teacher education systems in the EU-15 of that time. Reports focused on initial teacher education as well as on in-service training in national contexts, but also reflected on new needs and perspectives in Europe.

In addition, a special report was included in a publication dealing with European cooperation in teacher education of that time, particularly regarding perspectives on the Erasmus programme in the area of teacher education (Delmartino & Beernaert, 1998). This publication was based on the lessons learned from the elaboration of the RIF (Réseau d'Institutions de Formation–Network of Teacher Training Institutions), which developed steadily from January 1990 onwards, following the organisation of the first European Summer University for teacher educators in October 1989 at the Hogeschool Gelderland, Nijmegen (NL), within the Erasmus programme. This publication is one of the most relevant information sources on European cooperation in teacher education for the period up until the mid-1990s. It may also be seen as part of a wider effort regarding research on teacher education in Europe, which began in Osnabrück in 1995, and as such represents the very first major transnational research programme in teacher education across Europe.

Subsequently, the European Commission supported 28 Thematic Networks in the 1996/97 academic year with the aim of enhancing the European dimension of university studies as part of the Socrates-Erasmus programme (Action 1). The Thematic Network on Teacher Education in Europe (TNTEE) was the only network devoted exclusively to teacher education. Its main objective was to establish a flexible multi-lingual transnational forum for the development of teacher education in Europe by linking together as many universities and other institutions as possible. The network was coordinated by the Board of Teacher Education and Research, Umeå University, Sweden. The sub-networks of the TNTEE focused on: (1) the culture and politics of professional formation; (2) the development of innovative strategies of cooperation between TE institutions, schools and education services; (3) promoting lifelong learning in and through teacher education: evolving models of professional development; (4) teacher education as a powerful learning environment – changing the learning culture of teacher education; (5) searching for a missing link – subject didactics as the sciences of a teaching profession; (6) developing a 'reflective practice' of teachers' work and teacher education by partnerships between researchers and practitioners; (7) intercultural education in teacher education; and (8) gender and teacher education.

The TNTEE had a close relationship with the European Educational Research Association (EERA) as well as national research associations across Europe from its inception. This close relationship has since been maintained through the TEPE network. In relation to the former, its work was launched in the EERA through a TNTEE-sponsored symposium within the Teacher Education Research Network at the European Conference on Educational Research (ECER) in September 1997 at the University of Frankfurt.[2] Another evaluation study of teacher education in EU countries was conducted within the TNTEE at the end of the 1990s (Sander, 1999). Further, the network organised a conference that was held at the Catholic University of Lisbon in May 1999.[3] However, the most significant output of the TNTEE was the *Green Paper on Teacher Education in Europe* (Buchberger et al., 2000), which was the first policy paper on teacher education in Europe produced in collaboration with experts from European teacher education institutions. The TNTEE formally ended in 1999, although it influenced further cooperation and networking and its website[4] is still active and well visited to this day.

One of the most direct outcomes of the TNTEE network at the level of institutional cooperation was an Erasmus Advanced Curriculum Development project, which aimed to develop joint European modules at doctoral level. The project was coordinated in the first phase by Umeå University (2000–2) as the Europeisk Doctorat en Lärarutbildning (EDIL) project, and in the second phase by the Pädagogische Akademie des Bundes in Upper Austria, Linz (2002–5) as the European Doctorate in Teaching and Teacher Education (EUDORA). The core group was based on a consortium of ten teacher education institutions from various European countries. Within this project, five intensive programmes and modules were developed and conducted, each on several occasions. These consisted of the following themes and, in most cases, provided opportunities for students to publish their research studies:

- educational policy analysis (EPAC)[5]
- innovative mother tongue didactics (IMUN)[6]
- active learning in higher education (ALHE)
- e-learning in higher education (eLEARN)[7]
- researching the teaching and learning of mathematics (MATHED)[8]
- researching social inclusion/exclusion & social justice in education (SI).

Summer schools were organised in various countries from 2002 onwards, the largest of which was held in Tolmin, Slovenia in 2005. This event involved about a hundred doctoral students and staff who worked in three parallel modules (EPAC, IMUN, MATHED).

It was against this backdrop that the Teacher Education Policy in Europe (TEPE) network was established as a self-supporting academic network at a meeting hosted by members of the Faculty of Teacher Education at Umeå University in 2006. As mentioned earlier, the first TEPE conference took place in Tallinn in 2007 while the second was hosted by the Faculty of Education at the University of Ljubljana in February 2008. The second conference led to the formulation of recommendations for teacher education policy at the local, national and European levels, which have helped steer the work of the network since. These conclusions and recommendations are published in Hudson and Zgaga (2008) and focus on the need to improve the image of teaching and the status of the teaching profession, and also on the importance of involving teacher education institutions as partners in the process of policy development. In particular, they highlight the need to advance research in and on teacher education, promote mobility and the European Dimension in Teacher Education, and to support the development of cultures for quality improvement in teacher education.

Publications aiming to present policy-related research in teacher education have continued to be produced following the conferences in Umeå, Tallinn, Vienna, Warsaw and Helsinki (Hudson et al., 2010;

Eisenschmidt & Löfström, 2011; Harford et al., 2012b; Michalak et al., 2013; Niemi et al., 2013). The relationship with the European Educational Research Association (EERA) has also continued, in particular through the financial support given by the EERA Council, to help fund a colloquium on quality assurance and teacher education at University College Dublin in 2010. This event resulted in a further publication by Harford et al. (2012a).

These developments led to further innovative projects in the context of European teacher education, including the Erasmus project EPTE (European Primary Teacher Education, 2009–11) that led to the creation of a one-year joint programme that links and integrates students and teachers from various schools and/or departments of teacher education from several European countries.[9] The programme was accredited in several countries and is carried out annually for groups of students at different locations. Credits acquired in this programme are fully recognised at home institutions under the Erasmus exchange principles.

OVERVIEW

Successful responses to the challenges of our time always depend, last but not least, on our understanding of historical processes and on taking account of the lessons we have learned from this. In reflecting not only on the history of the TEPE network but also on the history and context that immediately preceded its establishment, two trends become apparent. The first is an increasingly active process of internationalisation that goes beyond the 'Europeanisation' process referred to in the network's position paper from 2007. This process is apparent in some of the contributions to this book, and is reflected by the input of invited speakers at the conference in Zagreb. For example, Edem Adubra, Head of the Secretariat, International Task Force on Teachers for EFA at UNESCO, spoke on the theme of 'Fragmentation of Teacher Education: Responses from the Teacher Task Force Network' while Kwame Akyeampong, who is also a contributor to this book, spoke about 'Reconceptualising Teacher Education for a Post-2015 Education for All Agenda'. It was also reflected in the most recent TEPE conference at the University of Malta in May 2016 on the theme of 'Teacher Education from a Global Perspective'. The second trend that becomes apparent is the steady continuing growth of policy-related research in and on teacher education that was first initiated at the Sigma Network conference in 1995 (Hudson & Zgaga, 2008; Hudson et al., 2010; Eisenschmidt & Löfström, 2011; Harford et al., 2012; Harford et al., 2012b; Michalak et al., 2013; Niemi et al., 2013).

Specifically in relation to the theme of this book, the need for greater coherence between the different aspects of teacher education has been the focus of discussion in debates about teacher quality and teacher professionalism over a long period of time. Since the integration of teacher education within the university system (Zgaga, 2013), one of the most challenging issues has concerned the tension between subject studies and pedagogy – see Hudson et al. (1999). In addition, the 'universitisation' of initial teacher education is often perceived as a process that has widened the gap between the theoretical basis of the educational sciences and school-based teacher practice. Further, it has been observed that in the majority of countries there is no firm alignment between initial teacher education, induction and continuing professional development. The issue of what constitutes a 'European teacher' has been also raised at a broader European policy level since the mid-2000s (Schratz, 2005).

Accordingly, the following sub-themes were established prior to the Zagreb conference in order to explore this general theme of overcoming fragmentation by:

• linking educational sciences with subject methodologies

• addressing the relationship between university faculty and school-based teacher educators

• bridging the gaps between initial teacher education, induction and continuing professional learning, and

• embedding the 'European dimension' within national contexts.

In addition to these four sub-themes, participants were invited to interrogate other relevant aspects of fragmentation in teacher education. Important drivers within the European context have been the so-called Bologna Process and the EU strategies on education and research arising from the corresponding Lisbon Strategy (Zgaga, 2013). While these policy drivers are transnational in nature, those associated with teacher education are related to national systems and in many ways represent conflicting forces on teacher education institutions. Against this background, it can be seen that neoliberal policy initiatives have exerted influences that have resulted in even greater fragmentation in many ways, and we return to this discussion later.

The book as a whole is structured according to two organising principles from beginning to end. The *first* principle follows the logic of the teacher education continuum from initial teacher education through induction to continuing professional learning. The *second* organising principle reflects a focus from the local to the global. For example, the book begins with a consideration of the national contexts of Ireland, Finland, Poland, Sweden and Scotland before considering the European (Caena) and then the global (Younie, Leask and Akyeampong).

The contribution in Chapter 2 by Harford and Gray concentrates on the link between teachers' professional identity and how teachers perceive and carry out their roles. They draw attention to the impact of a student teacher's 'apprenticeship of observation' and the impact of initial teacher education on the construction, deconstruction and reconstruction of that experience, which has been widely researched in the field of teacher education. The main purpose of this chapter is to use the student-teacher voice as a basis for exploring the underlying fragmentation, or otherwise, of teacher education. They argue that fragmentation arises because teacher education has been challenged in making connections between the vast amount of in-depth research conducted at the level of the individual teacher, and the world of policy in which education is essentially seen as a systemic, industrial activity. In other words, a nuanced understanding of individual teacher characteristics and values does not translate into policies that acknowledge these characteristics and values. They argue further that student teachers do not enter the world of teaching via teacher education, but are always already within it as a result of their own schooling. In relation to student teachers, teacher education is, therefore, a 'phase change' between school-as-pupil and school-as-teacher, rather than 'entry into a profession'. In analysing their data, the tension is highlighted between teaching as an individually constructed set of beliefs, with 'care' as a central concept, versus teaching as an activity to be managed for optimum efficiency and competitive advantage, as in so-called new managerialism.

In Chapter 3, Niemi focuses on the training of mentors for new teachers in Finland. The chapter describes a pilot induction programme (2011–13) to support new teachers through mentoring. It summarises the needs of new teachers in Finland and how the pilot programme was developed using Finnish contextual knowledge and the experiences of the New Teacher Centre in California. The chapter also describes how the mentors who were developing the programme viewed their role in the induction. The mentors were interviewed in 2013. At the start of the chapter, the special features of the Finnish education system are described in order to provide a holistic picture of why new teachers need support in Finland, even though they have a high level of teacher education, including effective practicums, before they begin teaching. The pilot programme made visible the urgent need to create a teacher education continuum and support teachers through induction. Recommendations are made at the chapter's end on how to make induction a sustainable part of the education system.

The focus of Chapter 4 by Madalińska-Michalak is on the issue of the quality of teacher education in Poland. The contribution emphasises the importance of coherent, career-long development of teachers' learning in a changing context and of creating conditions for preparing teachers who are continuous learners themselves. It presents an overview of changes in teacher education in Poland from 1990 onwards in the setting of improving the quality of teaching and learning and, at the same time, the quality of higher education. This overview should be read as a description of the most important changes affecting teacher education and the teaching profession, and as an investigation into their aims and context in Poland. The chapter directs attention to future policy, research and practice related to a highly relevant need to develop a continuum of teacher education in Poland with a focus on teachers' career-long professional learning and their support in different phases of their professional career.

In Chapter 5, Åstrand discusses the issue of fragmentation in relation to teacher education in Sweden and the conditions for the struggle over academic rigour and professional relevance. He takes an historical perspective and outlines a series of reforms involving divergent strategies over the past century aimed at countering fragmentation. The analysis of improvement strategies addresses issues of cohesion, fragmentation and formation of teacher students. Teacher education has historically been described as primarily a training problem, a learning problem and as a policy problem and, accordingly, the ideas on what constitutes high-quality teacher education have shifted as well – and with that also strategies for countering fragmentation. Over a period of 100 years, several national as well as local strategies have been proposed in Sweden as unifying backbones of teacher education to overcome fragmentation. These fall into three classes according to their orientation towards, first, content; second, form of organisation and mode of execution; and, third, types of understanding. The first is considered in relation to subject-matter preparation as well as particular dimensions (for example the European dimension), preparation in foundations of education, scientific training and teaching practice. The second involves systemic models for teaching practice, formal models for collaborating schools and teachers, organisation of general studies and the organisation of institutions for teacher education. Third, the types of understanding involve a consideration of teachers as practitioners, professionals and civil servants, as well as one or several professions. Reforms for advancement of teacher education have also aimed at countering fragmentation and emphasised ideas that have complex roots in those classes of means but which have also suffered from 'historical amnesia' at times. This chapter draws upon historical records, contemporary records as well as research, and aims to reveal how different levels of fragmentation have not only survived but also increased despite various attempts to reduce fragmentation.

The approach taken in Scotland for supporting the development of teacher professionalism is the focus of Chapter 6 by Finn. The need for high standards for academic learning and professional education in the development of most modern professions is noted as being widely recognised. In Scotland, which has a fully independent professional regulatory body for teaching, these are key features of a new professionalism built around a consensus that teachers must accept responsibility for the development of their professional skills throughout their careers.

This is presented as an approach in which the need for trust is balanced with reasonable expectations of accountability. In summary, teachers are supported in keeping their skills and knowledge up to date, and they remain accountable for the quality of their work. The Scottish approach, while consistent with current international research, contrasts strongly with emerging trends in some countries and particularly in the neighbouring country of England, where a policy of increased deregulation and flexibility is leading to significant systemic change in schools. The chapter explores the advantages and risks arising from these different approaches to teacher education. In doing so, it reviews the key components of professionalism and of teacher professionalism; considers the perceived status of teaching as a profession; takes account of the reported views of teachers, researchers and parents; reports on a number of international perspectives; and, finally, offers a way forward that can enhance professionalism and protect high standards in the future.

The contribution by Caena in Chapter 7 looks at the background of the European policy drive to link initial teacher education, induction and CPD by building bridges across the worlds of higher education, schools, stakeholders and policy-makers, both within and beyond national contexts. Taking stock of the complexity and diversity of a 'messy' policy field, it views teacher education from a multi-level, socio-ecological perspective. Teacher education is seen as an activity system, the aims and outcomes of which are culturally shaped by its contexts, rules, roles and actors. Activity systems are characterised by ongoing contradictions and change, and are constantly interacting with neighbouring activity systems. The global dimension of teacher education – the pressure towards convergence, transparency, integration and consistency along the professional-learning continuum – could therefore be perceived as an external influence acting as a catalyst of change. The 'Europeanisation' of teacher education – traditionally characterised by cultural-historical peculiarities embedded in national contexts – is then bound to sharpen the existing contradictions, as well as boost innovative solutions to overcome issues and constraints. As a consequence, the teacher education continuum is viewed not only as related to underlying values of schooling and citizenship – which seem to mirror a global focus shift from knowledge input to competence outcomes, in a developmental and equitable perspective – but also in relation to its systemic relationships with other teacher policy areas. These might represent key variables locally, as hurdles or development factors: teacher status, career and motivation, selection and recruitment; quality control, assessment and evaluation for university providers, schools and teaching professionals, with the key role of effective teacher competence frameworks; and governance mechanisms balancing autonomy and control in relationships and roles of key stakeholders. This holistic, system perspective highlights the pivotal role of partnerships between universities and schools, as learning organisations for the development of individual teachers, teacher educators and professional communities. It also highlights the importance of reflective practice as a boundary object spanning different contexts, roles and cultures.

In Chapter 8, Younie and Leask address the issue of overcoming fragmentation between research and practice by managing and mobilising the professional knowledge base for teachers at a global level. They present a criterion for judging the quality and scope of such a professional knowledge base such that teachers can access, at the time of need, brief, up-to-date, quality-assured summaries of research and evidence, written with classroom application in mind to underpin their professional judgement in teaching specific subjects and specific threshold concepts to specific types and age groups of learners. They outline the way in which such a professional knowledge base requires an openly accessible database and forms of publication focused on impacts on practice. They also draw attention to the way in which, in the medical world, this type of research and publishing is known as 'translational research'. The chapter explores the practicalities of knowledge mobilisation and knowledge management that would provide a system to meet the above criterion. They make no claims for research to be applied undiluted in classrooms but instead present an understanding of evidence-informed practice (EPIC practice) as being derived from a combination of professional judgement, which includes the teachers' deep knowledge of the context, and the learners together with the research or evidence. They illustrate their thinking by referring to the development of the MESHGuides – 'Mapping Education Specialist knowHow' project. This initiative supports the translation of research knowledge into practical advice for teachers, thereby allowing them to become self-organised autonomous learners with respect to their own professional development.

Finally, in Chapter 9 Akyeampong widens the lens fully to take a global perspective on these issues, raising questions of equity on a transnational basis across countries of the world and also important aspects of equity in relation to practices within national contexts. This chapter draws attention to the international consensus that a Post-2015 Education for All (EFA) Agenda must include a strong focus on achieving equitable learning outcomes. Although teachers are recognised as central to achieving quality education outcomes, it is argued that many teacher education systems do not do enough to prepare teachers to meet the learning needs of diversified student populations. Questions are raised about ways in which teacher education can be organised and delivered to ensure that all teachers have the disposition, beliefs, commitment and capabilities to maximise every student's learning potential and also about what kind of teacher preparation has the potential to achieve this. The chapter argues that answers can be found in teacher education practice framed in terms of social justice and equity-based pedagogy. It interrogates the EFA narrative on teacher education for teacher quality and identifies gaps that have contributed to the widening gaps in learning outcomes. Further, it argues that fragmentation in teacher education practice has contributed to the situation where many teachers find it difficult working with disadvantaged groups or schools. It defines an agenda for learning to teach that focuses attention on developing every teacher's capacity to work relentlessly with students from all backgrounds, and asserts that this should be an uncompromising goal for a post-2015 EFA agenda for teacher education. In conclusion, the chapter explores the implications for teacher education policy and practice in both developing and developed countries.

IMPLICATIONS FOR POLICY, PRACTICE AND FUTURE RESEARCH

In this section of the chapter, we aim to highlight certain key integrative themes from these contributions and to identify the directions that have emerged for future research and development in relation to policy and practice. Of course, the main theme is presented by the very title of this book: fragmentation of teacher education, and why and how to overcome it. When reading individual chapters, it becomes clear that this topic is extremely broad and complex, and that it could be broken down into a vast number of aspects, already partly indicated in the introduction to this chapter. We will not duplicate here those aspects that are addressed in individual chapters as there is no need to do so. However, one can identify some transversal themes in the background of these contributions that cut across the majority of today's discussions on pre-university and university education in general – not only on initial teacher education. Accordingly, we are able to place our main theme into a broader focus.

Over the past two decades, research on teacher education – as a relatively new sub-field of educational research – has highlighted the deep and multiple fragmentations in this field. It appears that research findings have contributed to *some positive results*: making sure that all actors are informed of the potential harm brought about by fragmentation, helping to understand trends and problems in the field, as well as contributing to changing and improving policies and practices. It also appears that the distance between the educational sciences and subject studies in general has been shrinking (or at least it has begun to be perceived as a problem in need of a solution). Establishing a close relationship between university faculty and school-based teacher educators is gradually becoming recognised as a priority in many countries, and this also applies to bridging the gaps between the initial teacher education, induction and continuing professional learning of teachers. Some chapters in this book consider these aspects in greater detail.

A degree of progress has also been achieved in embedding the 'European dimension' within national contexts. In Europe, this is mainly due to the involvement of teacher education in the Erasmus programme, but the proportion of student teachers involved is still quite small when compared with other higher-education fields. On the other hand, the European Network on Teacher Education Policies (ENTEP),[10] a network of ministries of education from EU member states, was established as long ago as 2000, but unfortunately the cooperation between ENTEP and other teacher education research networks – e.g. Association for Teacher Education in Europe (ATEE);[11] the EERA Network: 10. Teacher Education Research;[12] and the TEPE network – has not been strengthened in over a decade and a half. On the contrary, not only does it appear that such cooperation does not exist, but a strange feeling exists that is not perceived as necessary despite the ENTEP network having been actively included at the outset of establishing the TEPE network, for example.

It is right here in the complex field marked by terms such as internationalisation, transnationalisation and globalisation that a series of new questions are arising that indicate the possibility of *emerging new forms of fragmentation*. Together with the remnants of the 'old forms', these 'new forms' are generating fresh problems for the further development of teacher education. Over the past three decades, education in general and teacher education in particular have entered the 'transnational world' (Bruno-Jofré & Johnston, 2014) and encountered 'growing national and global dilemmas' (Geo JaJa & Majhanovich, 2010). Briefly, in the past, teaching was predominantly a local and national issue but now educators and policy-makers must take the issue of teaching in a global world absolutely seriously as a major issue. Therefore, they need to 'understand global realities *much* better than they often do today' (Apple, 2011, 225) and researchers can be of a great help in this. The chapters in this book do not confront these issues directly, but several of them are clearly present in the background.

When it comes to policy consequences of educational research especially, one can find at the forefront of contemporary discussions a series of questions about the impact of the so-called *neoliberal agenda* on the development of (public) education. So far, this issue has been thoroughly discussed chiefly in the context of the 'Western' research paradigm; however, there is sufficient evidence that it must be regarded as a global issue. For example, if the European and North American debates are enriched with the perspectives from other world regions, this discussion would be much deeper and more comprehensive. It appears – for example, by impressions from the ECER 2015 or from the TEPE 2016 conferences – that in recent years the debate is gradually rising toward that level. We understand *neoliberalism* as much more than a set of economic policies, an ideology or a resetting of the relations between the state and the economy. Rather, we see it as described by Brown as:

> ... a normative order of reasoning developed over three decades into a widely and deeply disseminated governing rationality, neoliberalism transmogrifies every human domain and endeavour, along with humans themselves, according to a specific image of the economic. All conduct is economic; all spheres of existence are framed and measured by economic terms and metrics, even when those spheres are not directly monetized. In neoliberal reason and domains governed by it, we are only and everywhere homo oeconomicus ... as an intensely constructed and governed bit of human capital tasked with improving and leveraging its (monetary and nonmonetary) portfolio value across all of its endeavours and venues. (Brown, 2015, 9–10)

The impacts of such *neoliberalism*, in our case in particular managerialism, performativity and similar phenomena in schools, have been debated widely, and these issues are also reflected in this book. They not only affect education, but also *public services* more broadly. A general conclusion from current discussions is that contemporary societies envisage a trend that is profoundly changing the nature of education and thus the nature of the societies in which we live. From the age of the Enlightenment onwards, both academic and political debates on education have been framed within a broad humanistic paradigm; although this discussion developed in different directions and although arguments were sometimes not only different but opposing, there was a common and central aim regarding education: to empower individuals, cultivate the nation, modernise society, and the like. Now, however, learning has primarily become an 'investment in human capital'; its background is no longer the nation state and the national interest, but the global market and economic value. An exclusively economic paradigm penetrates all fields of educational theory and practice.

In higher education, universities as the traditional institutions of knowledge and scholarship are deeply challenged by requirements to focus on *producing 'useful' knowledge*; in the global market, traditional 'academic' knowledge no longer counts. Only that knowledge which makes a return on the investment is considered useful knowledge. This trend drives academic institutions to instrumentalise the knowledge production and, thus, to instrumentalise learning and teaching processes. Knowledge has been turned into *means*; it has lost its former purpose – one of its multiple purposes – of an *end*. This trend, of course, has a very profound impact on education theory and pedagogy.

The problem is even more difficult in schools and departments of teacher education when compared to other university departments and schools: it is not only about teaching and learning (as well as doing research) within an institution, but also about teaching and learning in schools across the country, for which these institutions are preparing future teachers. Schools and teachers – and, of course, the teachers of teachers – have been traditionally respected as institutions and as professions. Yet, more recently, schools and teachers – and the teachers of teachers – frequently find themselves the targets of public and political criticism (see e.g. Darling-Hammond, 2010, 36; Aubusson & Schuck, 2013, 331; Katz & Rose, 2013, 227). This phenomenon seems to be more pronounced the more a country is economically developed – in other words, the more a country is at the centre (and not on the periphery) of the *neoliberal* world.

In the recent past, education was considered a public-policy priority but it seems that today it has become a policy problem. Teachers are accused of being responsible for the poor performance of their students, and public schools have become too expensive for public budgets, for example. This shift raises questions about what led to this turnaround. Possible answers may be placed in a wide range of options that generally extends between two macro trends:

1. The first is the *universalisation of public education*: in the last century, education became universalised and in many countries compulsory education – or the 'expected' level of educational achievement in the population – extended well beyond primary education. This

is usually explained by the transition to a knowledge society and/ or economy. So-called universal education, of course, requires ever more teachers – and ever more public funds. It is no longer a challenge only for ministers of education but also for ministers of finance and their stakeholders such as taxpayers, banks and industry.

2. The second trend is the prevailing economic and political ideology of the recent decades in dealing with public services with an exclusive object of *austerity measures*. This turnaround has not only bitter financial but also fundamental *conceptual implications*. These consequences dramatically affect contemporary teacher education practices as well as teacher education research in a double sense.

One of them is that education is more and more often understood primarily as a private – and not a public – good. The idea has been expanding from its Anglo-Saxon birthplace into global dimensions. In Europe, it has had particularly destructive effects, for example, in some of the so-called countries in transition as well as recently in Greece, but it has also had an impact on the Nordic countries, which just ten years ago would have been hard to imagine (Lundahl et al., 2013). According to this understanding, education is – or at least should be – predominantly a concern of individuals and not of society. Education only brings 'costs' to society (and thus ultimately to us taxpayers), while it can be highly profitable for individuals, albeit only for certain individuals, perhaps.

We have heard from radical representatives of this new paradigm that *society doesn't exist*. What is out there, i.e. outside us as individuals, it is not *society* but *economy, labour market, employability* and so on. These categories must mainly be served by education systems, schools and teachers. However, the economy and its *invisible hand* also produce unemployment and impoverishment, not just wealth and abundance. They also create ignorance and passivity, not only educated and cultivated people. Yet, from the perspective of the *invisible hand*, this obviously cannot be seen. As a result, schools are accused of causing economic failure and other problems such as poor national results in the PISA studies and the low-ranking position of a school or a university. As a consequence, claims are made that there is something seriously wrong with teachers, teacher education and, last but not least, educational research, which is branded as irrelevant.

At this point, we encounter an issue that is not only a problem of contemporary teacher education research; it is a problem that arises from the cracks between social science research and public policies. The relationship between research and policy has been a sensitive and fragile issue since policy studies were established in the post-Second-World-War period. Today, it seems that the problem stems from the way in which the very concept of research is understood. *Research* is increasingly meant simply as an accumulation of data and facts (of course, by using sophisticated modern methods) while a researcher must abstain from making critical insights and conclusions. In this paradigm, the researcher is no longer a public actor, but an individual who – by signing the project agreement – agrees to behave objectively and neutrally. A researcher shall provide systematically elaborated facts and figures and leave any critical remark arising from them to those who pay. Such a concept of research directly contradicts the traditional concept of academic research as an independent, argumentative and critical treatment of all issues at stake (i.e. the 'search for truth').

This is one of the most serious problems that research in the social sciences and the humanities in particular – and educational research as part of it – must deal with today. The more education is treated as a policy problem, the more we have to deal with this issue and with the relationship between research, policy development and politics: national and moreover transnational politics. Research should not only provide data – i.e. rough material for policy decision-makers – but must provide critical analyses that point 'to contradictions and to spaces of possible action' (Apple 2011, 229). All of this also applies strongly to research on teacher education and, in consequence, to teacher education in the broadest sense.

However, there are also signs of cracks at the heart of the neoliberal world itself following the IMF Research Department's recent publication entitled 'Neoliberalism: Oversold?' (Ostry, Loungani & Furceri, 2016). Not only do the authors acknowledge the term *neoliberal agenda*, which they refer to as a label used more widely by critics than by actual architects of the policies, but they also raise fundamental questions about aspects of the neoliberal agenda that have not delivered as expected. The authors pose questions about the effectiveness of two aspects of the neoliberal agenda in particular. First, they consider the movement of capital across a country's borders (so-called capital account liberalisation) and second 'fiscal consolidation', better known as 'austerity measures' and related to policies to reduce fiscal deficits and debt levels. In so doing, they reach the following 'three disquieting conclusions':

- The benefits in terms of increased growth seem fairly difficult to establish when looking at a broad group of countries.

- The costs in terms of increased inequality are prominent. Such costs epitomise the trade-off between the growth and equity effects of some aspects of the neoliberal agenda.

- Increased inequality in turn hurts the level and sustainability of growth. Even if growth is the sole or main purpose of the neoliberal agenda, advocates of that agenda still need to pay attention to the distributional effects (Ostry, Loungani & Furceri, 2016, 40).

It is not just the recognition of increased inequality that results from austerity policies but also the impact of this on the level and sustainability of economic growth that is most significant for our field. The authors describe this as 'the very thing that the neoliberal agenda is intent on boosting' (ibid., 41) and highlight the need for a 'more nuanced view of what the neoliberal agenda is likely to be able to achieve'. They argue that the evidence of the economic damage due to inequality requires policy-makers to be more open to redistribution than they currently are. Moreover, they highlight the need to design policies that mitigate some of the impacts in advance as 'so called pre-distribution policies' (ibid.). They especially call for increased spending on education and training as a means to expand equality of opportunity.

It is at this point in particular that we can see convergence with the Post-2015 Education for All Agenda and the arguments made by Akyeampong in Chapter 9 of this book concerning the need to focus strongly on achieving equitable learning outcomes at a global level. The consideration of teacher education from a global perspective foregrounds this inequality as a core challenge for the world as a whole but also highlights challenges for contemporary societies and education systems at the national level at the same time. Education's crucial role relative to this challenge is also highlighted in the UNICEF/ UNESCO report on the Global Thematic Consultation in the Post-2015 Development Agenda (Sayed, 2013), which stresses education as a 'fundamental human right'. The report calls for two main education-specific goals to be addressed as part of the future development framework: *equitable access* and *equitable quality education*. This perspective was reinforced by the General Assembly of the United Nations in September 2015 which ratified 17 Sustainable Development Goals (SDGs) that are intended to shape international development through to 2030. In particular SDG No. 4 focuses on education and sets the goal of ensuring inclusive and equitable quality education and promoting lifelong learning opportunities for all. This development framework highlights the need for associated research and evaluation and also provides a powerful signal in terms of the direction for future research in and on teacher education that is related to the goal of ensuring inclusive and equitable quality education and promoting lifelong learning opportunities for all.

CONCLUSIONS

A few years ago, Linda Darling-Hammond wrote that, for teacher education, this is perhaps the best of times and the worst of times (Darling-Hammond, 2010). Although she associated this position only with the USA, we believe that her description is still valid today – in the broadest sense. There are many actors across countries with a strong commitment to improving teaching but there are also many forces in the environment that conspire to undermine these efforts, as she articulated it.

If we consider yet another renowned author, Burton Clark, the doyen of studies in higher education, he wrote that 'schools of education' cannot and should not have 'one purpose' (e.g. in the present circumstances a purpose of serving the economy and the world market, i.e. instrumentalisation and vocationalisation of the idea of education at large). He supported his position by analysing three horizons: 'the peculiar constraints placed upon schools of education in their university locations; a new conception of modern forms of knowledge that we may apply to the production and dissemination of knowledge in teacher education; and finally practical networks of organisation within and outside of schools of education that are context specific and point to multiple lines of reform' (Clark, 1999, 352). In conclusion, he argued that teacher education is not an area in which a single organisational pattern can be developed and used. Patterns rather 'come out of year-by-year trial and error, incremental adjustments that both test what is possible here and now and what routes lead best to long-term desirable change' (357). We would add that there is a need to monitor these experiments, adjustments and changes through research and ongoing reflection, evaluation and discussion.

Upon reading the recommendations made almost 20 years ago and practically exclusively intended for the discussion in the USA, it is possible to refresh the theoretical position for understanding teacher education today and in the global context. Earlier, we mentioned that in recent times teacher education has begun to overcome some forms of fragmentation, but new forms have also started to appear. Attention should be paid to both the former and the latter. Critical analysis of the existing organisational frameworks and processes in the field of teacher education is no longer just a matter for narrowly specialised researchers and policy-makers; it has become a matter of economic analysis, general politics and, ultimately, public opinion at large. This shift is part of the trend due to which we are living in the best of times and the worst of times. Times, however, that are simultaneously the best and worst require a lot of hard work – in our case, both experimentation in the teacher education field and research in and on teacher education. With this book, we aim to offer a modest contribution to this goal.

POST SCRIPTUM

A major challenge for scholars, and in particular the authors' of the chapters in this book, is to ensure that they are up to date in their papers and not to circumvent the issues and concerns raised by the passing of time and especially by recent events. As Hegel once remarked the owl, which is the traditional symbol of wisdom, spreads its wings only at the end of the day, in twilight. Scholarship faces this dilemma and is therefore a risky business: a risk to miss the latest events, a risk to publish too soon and for outputs to arrive too late. The preparation of this monograph was impacted by this risk as all chapters were completed in late spring 2016 just prior to some momentous world events in Europe that we therefore, try to respond it briefly in this Postscript.

In particular we are referring to "Brexit", the event of 23 June 2016 following the referendum on European Union membership in the UK that not only marks British and European *political* horizons, but which affects and will affect *all other dimensions of social life*, not least education and teacher education. Fragmentation, which is discussed from several perspectives by the authors of the chapters in this book, received new – and worrying – impulses at the beginning of the summer of 2016.

European education systems have common conceptual roots and have been influenced by the ideas of the Enlightenment as well as the even older cultural, philosophical and scientific tradition. These ideas and traditions have contributed significantly to the development of education in the modern globalized world. However in over two centuries of development (i.e., in the process of implementation of these ideas which was challenged by diverse national traditions) some essential conceptual elements of the European educational systems were lost leading to the mutual incomparability and incompatibility of these systems. These issues were put at the forefront of the agenda of the meetings of Ministers of Education nearly four decades ago, in the early stages of the European integration process. Some of the major obstacles first encountered in aiming to develop greater economic, political, cultural and all-round cooperation and integration between European nations were the fundamental differences in educational systems – and their associated fragmentation. Against these differences, the EU has gradually set out to facilitate and promote a strong "European identity" through the medium of education: thus Euro-centrism challenged national curricula (Sultana, 1995).

As illustrated by the authors of the chapters in this book, teacher education has been a particularly vulnerable area in this regard. Strategies and instruments which should contribute to greater cohesion – whilst maintaining cultural specificities – of the European educational space such as Socrates/Erasmus programme, have been taken up in almost all areas of higher education earlier and more strongly than in the specific area of teacher education. This area has more often than not been a victim of academic neglect in higher education. In a broader European context, a few notable progressive movements in this area were observed in the last decade. European and national policies should be built on these positive developments further; the authors of the chapters in this book present several considerations and constructive proposals in this direction.

Unfortunately however, at this moment it is not possible to make optimistic forecasts. Whatever Brexit really means, it will tend to extend fragmentation by isolating the UK from shared events, research and developments across the EU. Anthony Finn's chapter in this book focuses, however, on areas in which educational developments in parts of the UK are already closer to those within the European Union than to the prevailing priorities in the UK's largest country. As a result of

Brexit, there is now an increasing perception that Scotland can better protect its distinctive educational and sociological integrity and traditions by remaining within the European Union than by continuing to share an ideologically less attractive identity within the UK. While Scotland and England will always be close, not just in Geography, Brexit could therefore offer the contradiction that the end of a membership in one political union (the EU) could lead to pressure for the end of one of much longer standing (Anglo Scottish Treaty of Union, 1707), in order that Scotland can maintain and strengthen the very links which the referendum sought to break.

However, it is not an issue that is just about Brexit and the withdrawal of one of the largest EU member states from the common European efforts, The overall effects of this event and especially its impact on the deepening of Euro-scepticism and growing Nation-Centrism (Chalaby, 2007) across Europe also needs to be considered. Teacher education was traditionally excluded (and, last but not least, jealously guarded) from the list of the national priorities of international cooperation and integration. The arguments were various ranging from claims that this is an area considered "too weak" in the academic sense and in comparison with other higher education and research areas to be included on the priority list. The argument was also made that teacher education is too imbued with the peculiarities of the national curriculum, language, school interpretations of local and European history, the impact of cultural and religious traditions, etc. However, all these arguments are associated with what we expose in this book as the *fragmentation problem*, which at the same time highlights the necessity to overcome this problem. More intense all-European cooperation in the field of education, assisted by the authorities in member states, could significantly contribute to this aim.

Finally it seems that even this "front" of European integration is now in the process of withdrawing and we can only hope that this is a "strategic" and not "headless" withdrawal. We believe that the current trends need to be answered in a proactive way by educators and especially educational researchers making a significant contribution to the restructuring of the "front" and supporting a new "advance". The optimistic note of this postscript is based on the fact that over the past two decades a strong and fairly homogenous European community of educators and educational researchers (as well as other similar communities) have emerged, which can be no longer stopped either by Brexit or by Nation-Centrism.

NOTES

1   Reports from Austria, Belgium, Denmark, Finland, France, Germany, Greece, Ireland, Italy, Luxemburg, the Netherlands, Portugal, Spain, Sweden and the United Kingdom.
2   http://tntee.umu.se/archive/symposium970924.html#keypaper.
3   http://tntee.umu.se/lisboa/call-for-papers.html.
4   http://tntee.umu.se.
5   https://tepe.wordpress.com/epac-2004/.
6   https://tepe.wordpress.com/imun-2004/.
7   https://tepe.wordpress.com/elearn-2004/.
8   https://tepe.wordpress.com/mathed-2003/ and https://tepe.wordpress.com/mathed-2005/.
9   See e.g. www.epte.info/ and www.pef.uni-lj.si/758.html.
10 http://entep.unibuc.eu/.
11 www.atee1.org/.
12 www.eera-ecer.de/networks/network10/.

REFERENCES

Apple, M. W. (2011). Global crises, social justice, and teacher education. *Journal of Teacher Education*, 62(2), 222–234, doi: 10.1177/0022487110385428.

Aubusson, P. and Schuck, S. (2013). Teacher education futures: Today's trends, tomorrow's expectations. *Teacher Development: An International Journal of Teachers' Professional Development*, doi: 10.1080/13664530.2013.813768.

Brown, W. (2015). *Undoing the Demos: Neoliberalism's Stealth Revolution*. New York: Zone Books.

Bruno-Jofré, R. and Johnston, J. S. (eds) (2014). *Teacher education in a transnational world*. Toronto: University of Toronto Press.

Buchberger, F., Campos, B. P., Kallós, D. and Stephenson, J. (eds) (2000). *Green Paper on teacher education in Europe: High quality teacher education for high quality education and training*. Thematic Network on Teacher Education in Europe. Umeå: University of Umeå. Retrieved from http://tntee.umu.se/publications/greenpaper.html.

Chalaby, J. (2007). Beyond Nation-Centrism: Thinking International Communication from a Cosmopolitan Perspective. *Studies in Communication Sciences: Journal of the Swiss Association of Communication and Media Research*, 7(1), pp. 61–83.

Clark, B. R. (1999). Constraint and opportunity in teacher education: Reflections on John Goodlad's 'Whither schools of education?' *Journal of Teacher Education*, 50(5), 352–357, doi: 10.1177/002248719905000505.

Darling-Hammond, L. (2010). Teacher education and the American future. *Journal of Teacher Education*, 61(1–2), 35–47, doi: 10.1177/0022487109348024.

Delmartino, M. and Beernaert, Y. (1998). Teacher education and the ERASMUS Program. Role, achievements, problems and perspectives of teacher education program in ERASMUS. *Journal of European Education*, doi: 10.2753/ EUE1056-4934300356.

Eisenschmidt, E. and Löfström, E. (eds) (2011). *Developing quality cultures in teacher education: Expanding horizons in relation to quality assurance*. Tallinn: Tallinn University.

Geo JaJa, M. A. and Majhanovich, S. (eds) (2010). *Education, language, and economics: Growing national and global dilemmas*. Rotterdam, Boston, Taipei: Sense.

Harford, J., Hudson, B. and Niemi, H. (eds) (2012a). *Quality assurance and teacher education: International challenges and expectations*. Oxford: Peter Lang.

Harford, J., Sacilotto-Vasylenko, M. and Vizek Vidović, V. (eds) (2012b). Research-based teacher education reform: Making teacher education work. Special issue of *Reflecting Education*, 8(2), pp. 1–5.

Hudson, B., Zgaga, P. and Åstrand, B. (eds) (2010). *Advancing quality cultures for teacher education in Europe: Tensions and opportunities*. Umeå: University of Umeå.

Hudson, B. and Zgaga, P. (eds) (2008). *Teacher education policy in Europe: A voice of higher education institutions*. Umeå: University of Umeå. Retrieved from www.pef. uni-lj.si/tepe2008/documents/a-voice-from.pdf.

Hudson, B., Buchberger, F., Kansanen, P. and Seel, H. (eds) (1999). *Didaktik/ fachdidaktik as the science(-s) of the teaching profession? Thematic Network for Teacher Education in Europe*, vol. 2(1). TNTEE Publications. Retrieved from http://tntee. umu.se.

Katz, M. B. and Rose, M. (2013). *Public education under siege*. Philadelphia: University of Pennsylvania.

Lundahl, L., Erixon Arreman, I., Holm, A.-S. and Lundström, U. (2013). Educational marketisation the Swedish way. *Education Inquiry*, 4(3), doi: 10.3402/edui. v4i3.22620.

Michalak, J., Niemi, H. and Chong, S. (eds) (2013). *Research, policy, and practice in teacher education in Europe*. Łódź: University of Łódź.

Niemi, H., Multisilta, J. and Löfström, E. (eds) (2013). *crossing boundaries for learning – through technology and human efforts*. Helsinki: Cicero Learning Network, University of Helsinki.

Ostry, D. O., Loungani, P. and Furceri, D. (2016). Neoliberalism: Oversold? *Finance and Development*, 38–41.

Sander, T. (1999). (ed.) *Teacher education in Europe in the late 1990s. Evaluation and quality*, vol. 2(2). TNTEE Publications. Retrieved from http://tntee.umu.se/ publications/publication1_2.html.

Sander, T. (ed.) (1995). European conference: Teacher education in Europe: Evaluation and perspectives. Universität Osnabrück, 23–24 June.

Schratz, M. (2005). What is a '*European teacher*'? A discussion paper. European Network on Teacher Education Policies (ENTEP). Retrieved from www.sdcentras.lt/ pla/res/Schratz.pdf.

Sayed, Y. (2013). Envisioning Education in the Post-2015 Development Agenda: Report of the Global Thematic Consultation on Education in the Post-2015 Development Agenda, UNICEF/UNESCO.

Sultana, R. G. (1995). A uniting Europe, a dividing education? Euro-centrism and the curriculum. *International Studies in Sociology of Education*, 5:2, 115-144, DOI: 10.1080/0962021950050201

United Nations (2015). *Transforming our World: The 2030 Agenda for Sustainable Development*, https://sustainabledevelopment.un.org/?menu=1300

Zgaga, P. (2013). The future of European teacher education in the heavy seas of higher education. *Teacher Development: An International Journal of Teachers' Professional Development*, doi: 10.1080/13664530.2013.813750.

2 Emerging from somewhere: Student teachers, professional identity and the future of teacher education research

Judith Harford and Peter Gray

> *Teaching is really quite a strange profession. It is probably the only career someone can choose where they already have extensive experience of what they at least believe is involved.* (Martin)

INTRODUCTION

The link between teachers' professional identity and how teachers perceive and carry out their role is widely acknowledged, at least within the teacher education community. The impact of a student teacher's 'apprenticeship of observation' and the impact of initial teacher education on the construction, deconstruction and reconstruction of that fertile experience has been widely researched, albeit using a diverse range of terminologies. Submissions for ECER (European Conference on Educational Research) in 2015, for example, included at least 20 papers (around 10% of total submissions) exploring student-teacher identities from a variety of autobiographical perspectives. The research presented here is our own interpretation of student-teacher identity based on autobiographical essays ('credos') from one particular cohort of student teachers.

However, the purpose of this chapter, in line with the overall theme of the book, is to use the student-teacher voice as a basis for exploring the underlying fragmentation, or otherwise, of teacher education. We argue that fragmentation arises because teacher education has been unable or unwilling to make connections between the vast amount of in-depth research conducted at the level of the individual teacher, and the world of policy in which education is essentially seen as a systemic, industrial activity. In other words, a nuanced understanding of individual teacher characteristics and values does not translate into policies that acknowledge these characteristics and values. In this chapter, we argue that student teachers do not enter the world of teaching via teacher education, but are always already within it as a result of their own schooling. In relation to student teachers, teacher education is, therefore, a 'phase change' between school-as-pupil and school-as-teacher, rather than 'entry into a profession'. This tension will emerge as we explore the autobiographies of the student teachers that form our data.

TEACHER EDUCATION RESEARCH

The relationship between teacher education and the state is, in most countries, characterised by a high level of regulation. Teaching is seen as an area of vocational education where state intervention in supply is necessary to ensure that enough qualified teachers enter the profession. Now, however, teacher education has moved into the university sector, driven partly by national policies and partly by the pan-European Bologna Process.

With university status comes pressure for research and the need to develop research communities, leading teacher educators to self-awareness as researchers. Teacher education research has only recently begun to develop community self-awareness, for example by forming networks such as the Teacher Education Policy in Europe Network (TEPE), Teacher Education Quality through Integrating Learning and Research (TEQUILA) and the International Network for Teacher Education (INFO-TED). This is partly as a result of the historical roots and vocational basis of 'teacher training' as opposed to the more reflective stance implied by 'teacher education'. Teacher education, as a community, has been under increasing pressure to produce research and publications. The demand for research in teacher education is not generally driven by detailed analysis of the related 'problem space', with some exceptions, such as the Teaching and Learning Research Programme (TLRP) in the UK. This problem space is dominated by a number of concepts such as 'the theory–practice gap', 'practice shock' and 'professional identity', none of which can be rigorously defined or quantified. Nor is the pressure to publish driven by meaningful analysis of the impact of what is published, although this situation is (slowly) changing due to demands for 'responsible research and innovation' (Owen et al., 2013) and related changes in research governance (e.g. the Research Excellence Framework in the UK). Teacher educators, however, have limited possibilities for large-scale research projects. Teacher education research therefore typically involves small but powerful qualitative studies, generally concerning factors influencing teaching and teacher behaviours. Our research in this chapter follows this pattern. Teacher educators do the best they can with the opportunities available to them, and have become skilled in exploiting a range of methodologies such as ethnography, phenomenography and case-study research, as Flyvbjerg (2001) recommends in order to re-establish the moral authority of social science. We position ourselves here as ethnographers in relation to the teacher-research community, in which both of us have been immersed for some time, and believers in the power of narrative, in its various forms, to shape identity.

One consequence of the extensive use of narrative in teacher education research is, however, that there is a huge amount of research on teacher and student-teacher identities (Beijaard et al., 2004). This research is informed by many different perspectives, but often starts from the premise that teacher-identity formation, and the development of teacher professionalism, involves changing beliefs (von Wright, 1997). We use professionalism here in a positive sense, indicating that the professional teacher can use academic and experiential or experimental knowledge to improve practice. Sugrue (1997, 172) argues that

> ... the general social milieu, as well as apprenticeships of observation, tend to reinforce the myth of the 'natural teacher' (Britzman, 1986) and initial teacher education and school cultures frequently reinforce the isolation of the teacher by privileging the capacity to control and deliver the curriculum over more collegial approaches which are vital to subsequent school-based attempts to promote and sustain renewal and professional growth ...

This illustrates an overall tension apparent in the material used in our study, which is based on analysis of the teaching credos (reflective essays) of 100 student teachers undertaking a one-year diploma programme in a university in the Republic of Ireland. This tension is generated by individual student teachers' desire for agency on one hand and the normative demands of the system on the other. Before we start to explore this, however, we need to examine current thinking on teacher professional identity.

Teacher professional identity

Teacher professional identity has been extensively researched and has generated a tapestry of complex definitions and interpretations. According to Beijaard, Verloop and Vermunt (2000), it relates to how teachers perceive expertise in terms of subject matter, didactic and pedagogical expertise. It is contextual, multiply relational/emotional, storied and central to teachers' in-class practices and beliefs (Day et al., 2006). A strong professional identity contributes to teachers' self-efficacy, motivation commitment and job satisfaction and is hence a critical factor in becoming an effective teacher (Flores & Day, 2006). Lasky (2005) sees it as how teachers define themselves to themselves and to others, with Beijaard et al. (2004) suggesting that it reflects the understanding an individual has of himself/herself as a teacher. We will return to this point below. A number of scholars have discussed how professional identity evolves over time and across different phases of the teacher lifecycle (Ball & Goodson, 1985; Huberman, 1993; Sikes, Measor & Woods, 1985), while more recently there has been a focus on how teacher professional identity is influenced by school reform agendas and a wider policy arena (Sachs, 2000; MacRuairc & Harford, 2008). As will be seen when we explore our data, the tension here is between teaching as an individually constructed set of beliefs, with 'care' as a central concept, versus teaching as an activity to be managed for optimum efficiency and competitive advantage, as in so-called 'new managerialism' (Lynch, Grummell & Devine, 2012). This tension is not insurmountable, but it is helpful to think about how teacher education can contribute to the formation of identities capable of dealing with it constructively.

In the literature, there is recognition of the significance of teachers' own experience of schooling in the formation of their professional identity as teachers, an acknowledgement that the 'core of the personal' will inevitably contribute to 'the core of the professional' (Loughran 2006, 112). Feiman-Nemser (2001, 1029) notes that teachers negotiate their professional identity by 'combining parts of their past, including their own experience in school, and in teacher preparation, with pieces of their present'. Bullough (1997, 95) concurs, noting

> ... midst the diversity of tales of becoming a teacher and studies of the content and form of the story, two conclusions of paramount importance to teacher educators emerge: prior experience and beliefs are central to shaping the story line, as is the context of becoming a teacher.

Childhood experiences of schooling, teacher role models, family and significant others also impact on identity formation (Knowles, 1992; Sugrue, 1997; Lamote & Engels, 2010). Notwithstanding this extensive body of research in the area of teacher professional identity, we argue that insufficient attention has been paid, by initial teacher education, to the impact of a student teacher's 'apprenticeship of observation' and the impact of teacher education on the construction, deconstruction and reconstruction of that fertile experience. However, our interest here is threefold. Firstly, we want to establish self-understanding as a meta-concept, a means of gathering the disparate strands of teacher education research. Secondly, we will use the evidence from the credos to suggest how this self-understanding might be enhanced by the use of autobiographical techniques in teacher education. Thirdly, we want to argue for a stronger central narrative in research-based teacher education, capable of resisting the 'new managerialism' and arriving at a form of professionalism that incorporates the emotional and relational aspects of teaching as well as its achievement of results.

Conceptual framework

Student teachers bring with them a range of pre-existing beliefs or lay theories of teaching to their teacher education programmes. Lay theories are essentially beliefs that have developed organically over time. Student teachers do not consciously learn them; rather, they represent tacit knowledge, which is neither examined nor critiqued (Holt-Reynolds, 1992). Korsgaard (2014) argues that there is an underlying 'layer' of rationality in the mind that enables perceptions and experiences to be assembled into a unified whole, in this case the 'experience of schooling', also known as the 'apprenticeship of observation'. The experience of initial teacher education is often transmissive, although teacher education, over the past 20 or 30 years, has been moving towards a more active form of teacher education in which reflection and even research are prioritised. Nevertheless, we are still reliant on student teachers to make a unified whole out of this 'heap of unrelated ideas', as Korsgaard (2014) puts it. The fragmentation of teacher education research, and of educational research in general, works against this construction of a whole because the idea of research is itself seen both as an extension of the natural scientific method and an attempt to construct meaning from discourse and the life-world. These two world-views are often wrongly conflated in education (Flobakk, 2015), leading to false conclusions being drawn about causality.

Holt-Reynolds (1992) argues that 'communicating the abstracted principles of professional practice to students of teaching is qualitatively unlike communicating the abstracted principles of any other profession'. Lortie (1975) introduced the concept of the pupil as a type of apprentice in *Schoolteacher: A Sociological Study* and, while often contested and debated, it has remained an enduring metaphor in teacher education research for over four decades. Essentially his argument is that student teachers, unlike apprentices in any other profession, come to teacher education programmes having spent many years observing and implicitly evaluating their teachers' practices. This experience by its very nature, Lortie argues, results in student teachers' preconceptions of what it is to be a teacher and, while 'intuitive and imitative rather than explicit and analytical' (Lortie, 1975), these implicit beliefs are nonetheless highly significant in the development of a student teacher's emerging identity.

The crucial point here is that there is evaluation as well as observation. Evaluation implies a rational thought process, linking what is observed (actions) with intended consequences. One of the most common observations from the credos was the difference in effectiveness between 'passionate' and 'boring' teachers, something that surfaced in around 85% of the credos. These evaluative judgements go largely unchallenged by external evidence and are therefore still in place when student teachers begin their initial teacher education. Furthermore, pupil judgements are themselves, by some accounts, the most valid form of evidence about teacher effectiveness (Gray & Corbin, 2010), formed as they are by collective observation over extended periods. Without incentives to engage in critical reflection, pupil opinion becomes entrenched as 'student teacher opinion'.

Some scholars contend that these implicit beliefs are highly resistant to change within teacher education programmes unless they are 'seriously challenged and problematized' (von Wright, 1997, 257). Feiman-Nemser (2001, 1016) notes:

> The images and beliefs that pre-service teachers bring to their pre-service preparation serve as filters for making sense of the knowledge and experiences they encounter. They may also function as barriers to change by limiting the ideas that teacher education students are able and willing to entertain.

She continues:

> Unless teacher educators engage prospective teachers in a critical examination of their entering beliefs in light of compelling alternatives and help them develop powerful images of good teaching and strong professional commitments, these entering beliefs will continue to shape their ideas and practices. (Ibid. 1017)

Korthagen, Loughran and Russell (2006, 1026) concur:

> A student teacher's learning (how powerful, useful, and meaningful it is to them) and its relationship to the teaching that created (or inhibited) that learning need to be specifically linked to the learning of their students when they are in the role of teacher.

Tapping into the content of those beliefs should, therefore, be a fundamental goal of teacher education programmes.

CONTEXT

Teacher education programmes in the Republic of Ireland are high-status, over-subscribed programmes that typically attract a very high calibre of entrant (Harford & MacRuairc, 2008; Harford, 2010). Programmes operate at undergraduate and postgraduate level for the training of both primary and post-primary teachers. Teacher education as a 'discipline' is centrally vested in the higher-education arena, with education departments nationally located in universities or colleges of education. This means that the foundation disciplines (history of education, philosophy of education, sociology of education and psychology of education) are central to the formation of teachers, with an expectation that students will engage at a high level with the relevant theoretical literature. Initial-teacher-education (ITE) programmes for primary and post-primary teachers are facilitated through a range of concurrent (undergraduate) and consecutive (postgraduate) programmes. All programmes that lead to registration must be professionally accredited by the Teaching Council, whose functions are to promote teaching as a profession, promote continuing professional development, maintain a register of teachers, establish Codes of Professional Conduct and generally to regulate the profession. It has thus has been central to advocating new directions for ITE (Hyland, 2012; Sahlberg, Furlong & Munn, 2012) including the issuing of guidelines around entry criteria and school placement. Recently, both undergraduate and postgraduate programmes have been extended in order to deepen the experience student teachers have of their practicum placement, as well as to augment their research skills and further develop their pedagogical content knowledge. From September 2012, in order to retain their professional accreditation from the Teaching Council all concurrent (undergraduate) ITE programmes must have a duration of four years (240 ECTS credits), and from September 2014 all consecutive (postgraduate) programmes must last for two years (120 ECTS credits).

The particular programme from which the data sample was selected is a one-year postgraduate programme for the preparation of post-primary schoolteachers. This is a consecutive programme, wherein students are already graduates in their own subject areas. Students also choose two specialist subjects, with weekly lectures, teaching practice, supervision and evaluation on both.

Research questions

- The central question in this research is: how do student teachers recall, interpret and negotiate their prior experiences and beliefs about schooling and how does this experience impact on their professional identity?

- A related question is: how can teacher education programmes provide opportunities for student teachers to develop, interrogate and make sense of their emerging professional identity?

Emerging themes also include the impact of the sociocultural and institutional context (Kerby, 1991) on identity formation, and the tension involved in identity formation as student teachers resist or embrace different perspectives, particularly in the practicum.

Data collection

Cultivating a habit of reflection in student teachers has become the cornerstone of all teacher education programmes. Several approaches have been tested, including autobiographical writing, portfolios, reflective discussion groups and video analysis. In this particular study, student teachers were asked to write a teaching credo that linked their apprenticeship of observation with their teaching practice.

The data for this analysis were derived from the teaching credos of student teachers (n=100) undertaking a consecutive ITE programme, as described above, in the Republic of Ireland. The credos were written while the students were in their second and final semester of the programme. Inductive coding was used to identify the broad themes and common points of reference. We then focused on a smaller number of selected credos for the analysis.

ANALYSIS: DOMINANT THEMES IN THE STUDENT TEACHERS' CREDOS

Analysis of the credos yielded five key themes, listed below (the figure in parentheses relates to percentages of the total number (n=100) of credos in which the particular theme was clearly visible).

1. Teaching the way you were taught yourself (92%)

2. Vivid memories of 'good' and 'bad' teachers and what characterised them (86%)

3. Complexity of the teaching process (78%)

4. Becoming a teacher of a particular subject due to positive experience in school (67%)

5. Influence of choice of school for teaching practice (34%).

We provide examples of all these below, with quotations from the credos.

Teaching the way you were taught yourself

The power, and almost the lure, of their own schooling was apparent across 100% of the credos although, of course, the credo provided an opportunity for student teachers to express their feelings in a way rarely available to pupils at the time. Students recalled vivid and intricate memories of their own teachers and their approach to teaching. In their teaching, the majority (over 80%) relied initially on approaches they themselves had experienced as pupils. This created a sense of security, a sense of control:

> When I was in school, I was used to the 'chalk and talk method' – that worked for me, so I guess when I started teaching, I used the same approach. Very quickly I realised that while this method may have worked for me, it was not working for many of my pupils. I literally had to wean myself off this method I had grown up with and felt comfortable with. In doing that, I exposed myself, having to try new methodologies, especially ICT, which I was innately uncomfortable with. The temptation of reverting to what I knew, what I was secure in, stayed with me for at least three or four months. (*Fionn*)

> When I was in secondary school, all of my classes were streamed according to ability so I only experienced a particular teaching style which was aimed at the highest achieving students. When I began teaching, I realised I too was teaching to the top of the class, aiming my teaching at the highest achievers. It wasn't too long before I realised that more than half of the class just weren't following what I was doing and I had to rethink my whole approach. (*Oisin*)

Complexity of the teaching process

Many respondents (78%) homed in on the complexity of teaching, a complexity they were singularly unaware of when sitting in front of teachers as pupils. Student teachers' experience of the practicum had clearly and quite dramatically demonstrated the scale of preparation and planning that is inherent in any well-executed class. They were also keenly aware of the fact that as pupils they were witnessing 'front-stage' behaviours, which were only possible because of advance preparation and planning:

> When I was in school, I never once thought of the kind of preparation that teachers had to actually put into lessons. Yes, I noticed which

teachers gave homework and which teachers marked it well and in a timely manner, but I don't think I ever once reflected on preparation time. I suppose I just thought that the teacher 'knew' the subject and so was able to 'do it'. It was only when I started teaching myself that I realised there was a huge amount of work involved in actually delivering a lesson, and that moving from one part of a lesson to another required planning and a certain knowhow. (*Maureen*)

I thought that teaching was really about your subject and that if you knew your subject well, then it was easy enough. When I started to teach myself, I realised that there was so much more going on that just subject mastery. I almost felt like I had a list of integrated 'bits' I needed to master – a series of parts – planning, communication, organisation, differentiation – as well as subject mastery. It took me a long time to get them all in sync. (*Sean*)

Vivid memories of 'good' and 'bad' teachers and what characterised them

The great majority (around 86%) of students recalled in vivid detail their experiences of 'good' and 'bad' teaching. Words or phrases associated with good teaching included: professional; passionate; fair; consistent; providing detailed feedback on homework in a timely manner; human; helping pupils achieve goals; organised; creative; inspiring; challenging; having firm control and sound knowledge of their subject:

My most inspiring teacher embodied what teaching as a vocation means – a genuine love of her subject and a care for the pupils. She was always organised and prepared, she looked like a teacher, was clearly passionate about her subject and treated all pupils with care and respect. We in turn treated her with respect, doing our best to learn, doing our homework and working well together in class. I remember being happy and stimulated in all of her classes. (*Fiona*)

Students recalled 'bad' teachers as those who were: unprepared; lacking in organisation; not interested in their subject area; incapable of controlling classes; often late or absent; having no obvious interest in the pupils, emotionally or academically. They recalled these teachers as: relying heavily on the textbook; using traditional teaching and learning methodologies, often including rote-learning; being either poor in classroom management or using fear in order to control the class; appearing uncomfortable in their subject area. Around 55% used the technique of contrasting examples of 'good' and 'bad' teachers.

> I remember as if it was yesterday my maths teacher. I was weak at maths and struggled to understand, and was actually quite tense going into maths. My teacher was hopeless. He always arrived late, frequently had to leave the class 'to deal with an issue', never knew where we had left off the previous day, rarely if ever took up our copies, and made it clear to everyone he didn't want to be there. (*Colm*)

Another student recalled her Irish teacher displaying similar characteristics:

> She was always late. My abiding memory of her is always walking to the room after the bell, carrying a cup of coffee and eating a biscuit. We would file into the class, and she would take out a book of notes on a play or novel we were supposed to have read. Instead of ever reading the play or novel with the class, she took out a small book of notes which you could buy in the shop, and she wrote the notes out verbatim on the board. We then all wrote down the notes and were supposed to memorise the material, never once having read the novel or play. At the time I thought it was strange. Now, having sat through lectures on methodologies and best practice, I know it was shocking. (*Charlotte*)

Here, the qualities of good and bad teachers are described in everyday language that students, at least in post-primary education, would recognise. This in turn leads to questions as to why student opinion is so undervalued by educational researchers (INSTEM, 2015). Nevertheless, self-understanding here is based on hindsight rather than foresight (as is the case in the following section).

Becoming a teacher of a particular subject due to a positive experience in school

Sixty-seven percent of the group chose to become teachers of subjects they themselves had experienced positively in school.

> I had a wonderful teacher of English and history throughout most of my secondary education – I was really very lucky in this. It was a small school so I had the experience of this teacher in first, second and third year and again in fifth and sixth. It was because of

his inspiring teaching that I grew to love these subjects and knew when I was about 15 and thinking of university that I would study them. While I didn't really think at the time about being a teacher, that idea kind of crept in when I thought of a career, towards the end of college. In many ways, it felt like the most natural thing in the world. I couldn't believe that someone was going to pay me to talk about [Emily] Dickinson or [W. B.] Yeats! I have no doubt but that Mr [deleted]'s brilliant teaching was fundamental to my various decisions. (*Emily*)

Another student reflected:

I had great experiences with my English and Geography teachers – both were young, enthusiastic and dynamic teachers, who really engaged us. It was clear they also cared about us – not just about our academic study. I respected them both hugely. It is interesting that they were themselves quite tight – I would often see them together – and it struck me they were similar in many ways – committed, hard-working, bright and caring. I developed a love for both of their subjects and I think it is no coincidence I decided to become a teacher of English and Geography. I had loved history all through primary school and would always comment it was my favourite subject if anyone asked me. But my experience of history teaching was very disappointing and, even though I tried to stay interested and work on my own, this was hard to maintain and I slowly lost my passion for it. (*Mark*)

Here, the element of self-understanding consists in envisioning a future self, modelled on significant others, even when that self is not wholly in line with one's personal preferences. The self is thus seen as an external object that can be adapted to have the characteristics of others, through foresight. This object can be placed on a trajectory in which its characteristics remain constant over time, and one interesting absence from the student teachers' accounts is changes in personality over time. Pupil perceptions, it seems, are for life.

Influence of choice of school for teaching practice

Some of the students (34%) who did their teaching practice in the same school they attended as pupils were even more influenced in their emerging practice by their apprenticeship of observation:

I teach in the very rooms where I spent six years as a pupil observing some very talented and brilliant teachers and some not so talented or brilliant. In many ways my apprenticeship of observation is ongoing. I slotted very quickly into the role of teacher, as I was so familiar with the environment and felt very in touch with the pupils, having sat behind the same desks for many happy years. The majority of the teachers who taught me were still there. I felt very fortunate when I compared myself to my fellow student teachers, many of whom were teaching in a different school to the one they had attended, and many of whom as student teachers were inhabiting a completely different world to what they had experienced in school. It was only as I noticed my fellow student teachers grow in confidence and in their ability to reflect on their teaching that I realised the first few months of my own teaching were almost stymied because I was fitting back into a very safe, familiar environment, in many ways simply replicating the practice of teachers I had observed some five or six years earlier. (*Kieran*)

This is a situation that is likely to be relatively rare in the experience of student teachers, but nevertheless provides a significant insight into the power of the past and of place in structuring the self. The environmental or spatial aspects of teaching are often undervalued (McNally & Blake, 2010) and this passage draws our attention to the need for teacher educators to understand that the self is formed in and by spaces.

IMPLICATIONS FOR TEACHER EDUCATORS

Initial teacher education, in too many instances, seeks to supplant unarticulated tacit images of teaching by privileging what are regarded as more scientific, and more adequately grounded research-based versions. (Sugrue, 1997, 222)

As Sugrue observes, entrants to teacher education programmes, unlike entrants to any other profession, already have insight into what the profession entails. They are 'insiders' (Pajares, 1992) who are already in tune with what it means to be a teacher, and are in the Irish context, unlike many of the pupils they will encounter, high achievers who have already championed an education system in which they will now work. Our argument here is that the current state of research in teacher education is such that it is very difficult for student teachers to separate their experience of school from the 'rational', and supposedly research-based, perspective on teacher education. Teacher education research, in other words, does not provide a sufficiently strong or clear narrative to overcome past experience. Equally, the performativity currently expected of teachers creates tensions between the emotional commitment to make things better for children and young people, and the imposed professional commitment to quantitative performance. This tension is not fully addressed by teacher education, simply because it is not until student teachers enter the profession that they experience it. The lack of continuity between initial teacher education and subsequent professional development, even in cases where some induction support is provided, leads teachers to reproduce this tension in their teaching. It has been problematic to introduce reforms in teaching, such as the Curriculum for Excellence in Scotland (Reeves, 2008), or Inquiry-based Science Teaching in EU projects (INSTEM, 2015), precisely because teachers are forced to choose between care, in a wide sense, and performance, at least as currently measured. Making this explicit using autobiographical reflection may be an effective way of helping new teachers to deal with the problem.

CONCLUSIONS

What emerges from this research is that the strongest and most deep-rooted part of student teachers' identity rests with their own experience as pupils. This should be recognised within initial teacher education, which should empower student teachers to identify, chart and problematise their apprenticeship of observation. Indeed, some teacher educators (including, but not limited to, one of the authors) are already doing this and have been for some time. Other authors, notably Bullock (2011), have problematised the 'apprenticeship of observation', markedly in its relation to pedagogical content knowledge. Bullock (2011, 152) observes that pedagogical content knowledge 'is more a convenient way for researchers to name new teachers' expertise than a productive line of reasoning for thinking about the development of teachers' professional knowledge'. He thus draws attention to the same point we are making here, which is that teacher education research is about naming and meaning-making rather than about 'propositional knowledge'.

By setting out their own pedagogical baseline, based on their experiences as pupils, student teachers can build new knowledge on a firmer foundation, based on an understanding of that experience and new learning about what good teaching is and should be. Student teachers should thus be encouraged to:

- uncover their lay beliefs
- share them in a peer-learning environment
- critically analyse them, based on the pedagogical and reflective skills they have been honing
- identify where there is dissonance and consonance between their autobiographies as learners and the teaching and learning climate they wish to foster in their classrooms.

They should not be overly confessional in their probing of this experience. Equally, they should link this past experience of practice with new learning and new knowledge from their teacher education programmes and, crucially, from the research base. This personal and professional journey should not be confined to initial teacher education but should form a key pillar of lifelong professional development.

Teacher educators must not only assist student teachers in recognising what constitutes effective teaching, but should also empower them to analyse the evidence on which they make such judgements. This will give student teachers the foundations on which to build good practice, instead of reverting to their experience as pupils. However, teacher educators, as researchers, should also be more active and collaborative in opening research towards the domain of teaching and learning, as distinct from the world of academic publishing. Part of this process, as we have suggested in this chapter, is to recognise that practitioner narratives are as powerful as statistical evidence if properly used to stimulate thinking about the 'whys' and 'hows' of teaching and learning.

Student teachers should also be supported in a developmental way by symbiotic partnerships between schools and universities. This means that student teachers must be supported in critically analysing the learning that is taking place in the practicum, while cooperating (mentor) teachers must themselves engage in a similar analysis of their own apprenticeships of observation and their own professional identities. Recent moves in Norway, for instance, have seen the creation of 'university-schools' as a model, along the lines of teaching hospitals. These schools bring research into schools and school staff into the university, breaking down the so-called theory–practice gap in a new way.

We argued in our introduction that teacher education research is dominated by a number of these overarching concepts such as the 'theory–practice gap' and 'professional identity'. Based on our work with the credos, we suggest that 'self-understanding' provides a meta-concept that links many of the sub-themes emerging from many years of teacher education research (Hofbauer & Planer, 2015). For example, in the 2015 round of proposals for the teacher education research network of the European Conference on Educational Research (ECER), over 50% of 225 proposals had a recognisable connection to some form of self-understanding.

This illustrates a major problem in teacher education research, and in educational research more generally. Differences in terminology, arising from the diverse theoretical bases of teacher education, have created a multiverse. Subtle semantic and methodological distinctions separate the universe of 'self-efficacy' from the universe of 'self-construction through narrative'. The analysis of the credos presented here suggests that student teachers themselves are able and willing to negotiate their own 'professional selves', without extensive references to research, provided they are given the opportunity to voice their own experiences and to relate them to practice (see e.g. Fielding, 2011). This is unfortunate since an appreciation of the wide range of teacher education research on self-understanding would undoubtedly be useful for student teachers at this formative stage, providing it can be gained without struggling through hundreds of densely written research papers. We take the point made by Åstrand (Chapter 5 in this volume) that 'fragmentation' can be seen as a positive thing, forcing students to engage with complexity. On the other hand, the teacher education community has a much smaller voice in research policy, in our opinion, than its size warrants, simply because it has been unable to articulate a clear narrative about what it already knows and about what needs to be researched in future.

The opportunity for teacher education research is thus to bring together the whole spectrum of research on the teacher self in an integrative way. By this, we mean that different research strands need to spend some time on considering their commonalities rather than arguing for their differences. There will of course be considerable resistance to an integrative approach, which might appear to ignore these methodological differences. It relates to research cultures in teacher education where small-scale projects using interviews or other narrative methods are the norm, and where researchers are rarely able to participate in large-scale studies. This does not negate the value of existing research, but means that there needs to be a new way of bringing research together. Conventional meta-studies are not appropriate as there is no robust statistical method of comparing 'effect sizes' as, for example, in John Hattie's well-known meta-study of meta-studies (Hattie, 2009).

We should not, however, see this as a homogenising approach but as a process of unification in the interests of responsibility. We use 're-sponsibility' here in the sense that it is used in the phrase 'responsible research and innovation' (Owen et al., 2013). This means that responsibility in research is broadened out, from an intradisciplinary responsibility to established norms and traditions ('making better things'), to a societal responsibility to 'make things better'. The credos analysed here point to just such an attitude of responsibility in the student teachers. The credos contribute to our knowledge of the value systems of student teachers, but it would be useful to be able to compare an international sample of credos across a wide range of national systems.

How would this play out in teacher education research? Broadly speaking, teacher education does not do 'blue-sky' research, but carries out research within a constrained system. A range of structural factors and social attitudes combine to make certain topics 'researchable' while others are not. This is not just a question of ethics, where we might argue that research on, for example, the benefits of corporal punishment for learning would be completely unacceptable, at least in the UK. It is a wider question concerning the governance of teacher education research, including sub-questions around ethics, impact, access to results and the purposes of education. As we have argued here, teacher education research is often characterised by struggles over terminology and meaning that need to be at least partly resolved if student teachers are to regard themselves as part of a research-based profession, rather than as apprentices of their former teachers, or as human resources within a management system. Teachers' self-understanding, for example, seems to be a concept sufficiently broad to accommodate much of the existing research in teacher education, and sufficiently clear in its meaning to avoid lengthy debate about definitions. What is lacking is a way of not merely measuring 'self-understanding' in a psychometric sense, but of assessing self-understanding in a formative way so as to continue moving the concept forward and, more importantly, to make it useful to teachers, student teachers, and thus pupils and their learning.

Currently, the discourses of 'performativity' and the so-called 'new managerialism' impose a specific kind of identity regime on teachers. Lynch, Grummell and Devine (2012) argue that this is characterised by a reduction in the role of 'care' as an element of teacher identity. In particular, demands for increasing performance, whether in Ireland or elsewhere in Europe, result in tension between the desire to care for pupils and the desire to care about overall results. The credos indicate that care is a central concept for student teachers and that the continuum between caring and not caring is where teacher quality is measured.

Recommendations for policy and practice

The implications for policy reach beyond the processes of teacher education. One of the most frustrating aspects of studying student-teacher autobiographies is that they generate a desire to go back in time and just tell those teachers how they were doing from a pupil perspective, whether they were doing really well or really badly. An increased appreciation of pupil voice would be valuable, not just as part of school decision-making but as part of the teaching and learning process. This needs to be taken up by researchers as much as policy-makers since one of the authors, in a synthesis report on EU science education projects (INSTEM, 2015), and in subsequent project evaluations, has been surprised by the reluctance of otherwise rigorous researchers to ask pupils what they think about new teaching methods.

Policy in relation to teacher education research in the European Union has been strong on rhetoric but weak on funding, partly because responsibility for education lies with the member states. As we have discussed, the powerful messages picked up by student teachers in the course of their school education are drowning out the more confused and yet more subtle messages emanating from the research community. Policy-makers would gain much from engaging with teacher education research at European or international level, but researchers need to make that engagement easier and more directed. If we could tell stories as powerful as those in the student credos studied here, they might listen harder.

REFERENCES

Ball, S. J. and Goodson, I. F. (1985). Understanding teachers: Concepts and contexts. In S. J. Ball and I. F. Goodson, (eds), *Teachers' lives and careers*. London: Falmer Press.

Beijaard, D., Meijer, P. C. and Verloop, N. (2004). Reconsidering research on teachers' professional identity. *Teaching and Teacher Education*, 20, 107–128.

Beijaard, D., Verloop, N. and Vermunt, J. D. (2000). Teachers' perceptions of professional identity: An exploratory study from a personal knowledge perspective. *Teaching and Teacher Education*, 16, 749–764.

Bullock, S. M. (2011). *Inside teacher education*. Rotterdam: Sense Publishers.

Bullough, R. V. (1997). Practicing theory and theorizing practice in teacher education. In J. Loughran and T. Russell, (eds), *Purpose, passion and pedagogy in teacher education*. London/Washington, DC: Falmer Press.

Britzman, D. P. (1986). Cultural myths in the making of a teacher: Biography and social structure in teacher education. *Harvard Educational Review*, 56(4), 442–456.

Day, C., Kingtona, A., Stobart, G. and Sammons, P. (2006). The personal and professional selves of teachers: Stable and unstable identities. *British Educational Research Journal*, 32(4), 601–616.

Doyle, W. (1990). Classroom knowledge as a foundation for teaching. *Teachers College Record*, 91, 347–360.

Feiman-Nemser, S. (2001). From preparation to practice: Designing a continuum to strengthen and sustain teaching. *Teachers College Record*, 103(6), 1013–1055.

Fielding, M. (2011). Patterns of partnership: Student voice, intergenerational learning and democratic fellowship. In N. Mockler and J. Sachs, (eds), *Rethinking educational practice through reflexive research: Essays in honour of Susan Groundwater-Smith*. Dordrecht: Springer.

Flobakk, F. (2015) *The development and impact of educational neuroscience – A critical discourse analysis*. PhD Thesis. Trondheim: Norwegian University of Science and Technology. Retrieved from www.ntnu.edu/svt/research/theses/2015/.

Flores, M. A. and Day, C. (2006). Contexts which shape and reshape new teachers' identities: A multi-perspective study. *Teaching and Teacher Education*, 22(2), 219–232.

Flyvbjerg, B. (2001). *Making social science matter*. Cambridge: Cambridge University Press.

Gray, P. and Corbin, B. (2010). Towards a theory of fun. In J. McNally and A. Blake, (eds), *Improving the professional learning of teachers*. London: Routledge.

Harford, J. (2010). Teacher education policy in Ireland and the challenges of the 21st century. *European Journal of Teacher Education*, 33(4), 349–360.

Harford, J. and MacRuairc, G. (2008). Engaging student teachers in meaningful reflective practice. *Teaching and Teacher Education*, 24(7), 1884–1892.

Hattie, J. (2009). *Visible learning: a synthesis of over 800 meta-analyses relating to achievement*. London: Routledge.

Hofbauer, S. and Planer, J. (2015). Teacher education research – a reference to a European research space? A historical and comparative view on ECER Proposals

(2008–2012). Paper presented at the European Educational Research Conference, Budapest, 8–11 September.

Holt-Reynolds, D. (1992). Personal history-based beliefs as relevant prior knowledge in course work. *American Educational Research Journal*, 29(2), 325–349.

Huberman, M. A. (1993). *The lives of teachers*. New York: Teachers' College Press.

Hyland, Á. (2012). *A review of the structure of initial teacher education provision in Ireland*. Dublin: Higher Education Authority Ireland.

INSTEM (Innovative Networks in Science, Technology, Engineering and Mathematics). (2015). *WP2 structured synthesis report on project knowledge*. Innsbruck: INSTEM. Retrieved from www.instem.tibs.at.

Kelchtermans, G. (1996). Teacher vulnerability: Understanding its moral and political roots. *Cambridge Journal of Education*, 26(3), 307–324.

Kerby, A. (1991). *Narrative and the self*. Bloomington: Indiana University Press.

Knowles, G. J. (1992). Models for understanding pre-services and beginning teachers' biographies: Illustrations from case studies. In I. F. Goodson, (ed.), *Studying teachers' lives*. London: Routledge.

Korsgaard, C. M. (2014). The normative constitution of agency. Retrieved from www.people.fas.harvard.edu/~korsgaar/Essays.htm.

Korthagen, F., Loughran, J. and Russell, T. (2006). Developing fundamental principles for teacher education programs and practices. *Teaching and Teacher Education*, 22, 1020–1041.

Lamote, C. and Engels, N. (2010). The development of student teachers' professional identity. *European Journal of Teacher Education*, 33(1), 3–18.

Lasky, S. (2005). A sociocultural approach to understanding teacher identity, agency and professional vulnerability in a context of secondary school reform. *Teaching & Teacher Education*, 21, 899–916.

Lortie, D. (1975). *School-teacher: A sociological study*. Chicago: University of Chicago Press.

Loughran, J. (2006). *Developing a pedagogy of teacher education. Understanding teaching and learning about teaching*. New York: Routledge.

Lynch, K., Grummell, B., and Devine D. (2012). *New managerialism in education: Commercialization, carelessness and gender*. London: Palgrave Macmillan.

MacRuairc, G. and Harford, J. (2008). The role of reflective practice in a growing culture of new managerialism and performativity in schools: Views from the Republic of Ireland. European Conference on Educational Research, Gothenburg, 10–12 September.

McNally, J. and Blake, A. (2010). *Improving the professional learning of teachers*. London: Routledge.

Owen, R., Bessant, J. and Heintz, M. (eds) (2013). *Responsible innovation: Managing the responsible emergence of science and innovation in society*. London: John Wiley & Sons.

Pajares, F. (1992). Teachers' beliefs and educational research: Cleaning up a messy construct. *Review of Educational Research*, 62, 307–332.

Reeves, J. (2008). Between a rock and hard place: Curriculum for excellence and the quality initiative in Scottish schools. *Scottish Educational Review*, 40(2), 6–16.

Sachs, J. (2000). The activist professional. *Journal of Educational Change*, 1, 77–95.

Sahlberg, P., Furlong, J. and Munn, P. (2012). *Report of the International Review Panel on the Structure of Initial Teacher Education Provision in Ireland*. Dublin: Department of Education and Skills, Republic of Ireland.

Sikes, P., Measor, L. and Woods, P. (1985). *Teacher careers: Crises and continuities*. Lewes: Falmer Press.

Sugrue, C. (1997). Student teachers' lay theories and teaching identities: The implications for professional development. *European Journal of Teacher Education*, 20(3), 213–25.

Swain, S. S. (1998). Studying teachers' transformations: Reflections as methodology. *The Clearing House*, 72(1), 23–35.

von Wright, M. (1997). Student teachers' beliefs and a changing teacher role. *European Journal of Teacher Education*, 20(3), 257–266.

3   Towards induction: Training mentors for new teachers in Finland

Hannele Niemi

INTRODUCTION

This chapter describes a pilot induction programme (2011–2013) to support new teachers through mentoring. It summarises the needs of new teachers in Finland and how the pilot programme was developed using Finnish contextual knowledge and the experiences of the New Teacher Centre in California. The chapter also describes how the mentors who were developing the programme viewed their role in the induction. The mentors were interviewed in 2013. At the beginning of the chapter, the special features of the Finnish education system are described in order to provide a holistic picture of why new teachers need support in Finland, even though they have a high level of teacher education, including effective practicums, before they begin teaching. The pilot programme made visible the urgent need to create a teacher education continuum and support teachers through induction. Recommendations are made at the end of the chapter on how to make induction a sustainable part of the education system.

INDUCTION AS PART OF THE CONTINUUM OF TEACHER EDUCATION

The induction of new teachers has become one of the key priorities in developing teacher education in the European Union. By reviewing the latest research evidence and comparing policies from several member states, the European Commission produced a *Handbook for Policymakers* in an attempt to introduce induction programmes in all member countries (European Commission, 2010). It proposes that all new teachers should have an induction phase in their early careers. Newly qualified teachers often experience a 'praxis-shock' when they confront the daily reality of school. They may feel stressed, especially in schools where they are expected to cope with complex new situations on their own.

The European Commission proposes that teachers' professional development should be supported through a three-phase model: initial teacher education, induction (for new teachers, 3–5 years after graduation) and in-service teacher education. This continuum is needed for teachers' career-long development. The aim is that member states will develop coherent and system-wide induction programmes for beginning teachers (European Commission, 2010, 3):

> This professional development of teachers is a lifelong process that starts at initial teacher education and ends at retirement. Generally this lifelong process is divided in specific stages. The first stage concerns the preparation of teachers during initial teacher education, where those who want to become a teacher master the basic knowledge and skills. The second stage is the first independent steps as teachers, the first years of confrontation with the reality of being a teacher in school. This phase is generally called the induction phase. The third phase is the continuing professional development of those teachers who have overcome the initial challenges of becoming a teacher.

The importance of the teacher education continuum is based on many studies that have investigated teachers' professional learning and growth. Kay Livingston (2012a,b) and Livingstone and Shiach (2010) argue that a teacher learning continuum is required because teachers must learn throughout their careers; preservice time is only a starting phase of career-long professional development. Many processes, such as identifying and exploring teachers' own assumptions and personal experiences about learning and teaching through dialogue with peers and teacher educators in preservice time, as well as the development of questioning and critical enquiry, are important (Livingston & Shiach, 2010), and these processes should also be supported later in teachers' careers.

Career-long professional learning requires that professional-development programmes are organised for teachers. Optimally, they should take into account the entire spectrum of teacher learning (Schwille, Dembélé & Schubert, 2007). However, the provision of induction programmes does not seem to be common or well-organised. According to member states' own data (www.eurydice.org), only 18 member states offer new teachers systematic support (induction) in their first years of teaching. Even though there are some forms of support for new teachers (Scheerens, 2010, 16), the arrangements are not systematic:

> Member States undertake little systematic co-ordination of the different elements of teacher education. This results in a lack of coherence and continuity, especially between a teacher's initial professional education and subsequent induction, in-service training and professional development. Often, these processes are not linked to school development and school improvement or to educational research.

New teachers' problems are recognised worldwide (Conway, Murphy, Rath & Hall, 2009). OECD reports provide an overview of the many ways of organising induction. There is enormous variation among countries. The forms of support can be mandatory national programmes, support processes provided by local schools or more or less project-based arrangements. Typically, even if there are formal induction programmes or formal induction at the school level, not all teachers have the opportunity to participate. Thus, the need to support new teachers is well-recognised, but many countries are still trying to organise the provision of support successfully.

Finland has a reputation for being a successful country educationally (OECD, 2003, 2010, 2013). However, Finland does not have any mandatory national or local programmes for new teachers. Local schools usually provide new teachers with a short introduction. This is more technical and administrative, providing an overview of the locations and daily practices in the school. Otherwise, new teachers participate in in-service training that is designed for all teachers.

The need for induction has been recognised in Finland. Schools are becoming very complicated workplaces. The Finnish education system places a strong emphasis on equity and inclusion (OECD, 2006; Niemi, 2014). It demands that teachers work with very heterogeneous student groups and identify students' learning problems as early as possible. New teachers, after graduation, must meet all professional demands immediately.

The Advisory Board for Professional Development of Education Personnel, which was set up by the Ministry of Education and Culture, proposes that an entity for continuing professional development between initial and continuing education should be created. Newly qualified teachers need support in the process of transitioning from study to work. This support should be provided to all new teachers (Hämäläinen, Hämäläinen & Kangasniemi, 2015, 7).

This chapter describes a pilot project that was started in 2011 to support new teachers through mentoring. The chapter summarises new teachers' needs in Finland and how mentors themselves see their role as part of the induction. At the beginning of the chapter, the special features of the Finnish education system will be described in order to provide a holistic picture of why new teachers need support in Finland, even though they have a high level of teacher education, including effective practicums, before coming to school (Niemi & Jakku-Sihvonen, 2006; Niemi, 2012b).

THE FINNISH EDUCATION SYSTEM SETS HIGH LEVELS OF RESPONSIBILITY FOR NEW TEACHERS

A purposeful policy aimed at equity, a high level of education for all, and excellent teachers has been identified as the main reason for Finnish educational success (Laukkanen, 2007; Niemi, 2012b; Sahlberg, 2011). The Finnish education system allows teachers a great deal of professional freedom, but it also makes the profession very demanding. From 2014 to 2016, in the Finnish education system there were large national core-curriculum reforms for both basic education and high schools. Both reforms aimed at strengthening students' twenty-first-century skills. Local schools and their teachers are in the middle of these change processes and are designing their local curricula, which should be ready in August 2016. These reforms should be integrated with the leading principles of the education system, which will be summarised below.

Equity and lifelong learning as basic values

Niemi and Isopahkala-Bouret (2012) summarised the major features of the Finnish education system that influence teachers' work. Their analysis reveals that Finnish education policy has three main principles that guide all activities throughout the education system. These principles are *equity*, which means providing equal opportunities to every learner regardless of their social, ethnic and economic background (OECD, 2006); *flexible educational structures*, which allow continuing one's education, even in the case of a failure; and a *high level of education* for the entire population. Lifelong learning is integrated with all levels of the system from early education to adult education. Teachers are responsible for much more than simply providing teaching contents. Students must be ready to continue studying at the next level of education and learn new skills, and schools must support their personal growth (Niemi & Isopahkala-Bouret, 2012). In basic education (Grades 1–9), there is no streaming or tracking. Teaching happens in mixed-ability groups. Teachers must take care of different learners and also identify which kinds of special support students need. Teachers must make a huge number of pedagogical decisions every day, and must communicate about students' learning problems with parents, special-needs teachers, social workers and nurses. Teachers must also act as partners in multi-professional groups for students' well-being.

Professional autonomy

Teachers have a great deal of freedom in their teaching. The national core curriculum provides the basic values and frames (Halinen & Holappa, 2013). Schools are responsible for the local curriculum, which is designed by teachers and principals. Local partners, such as parents and other stakeholders, are invited to contribute. Teachers have the freedom to choose what kind teaching and learning materials they use and which kinds of teaching and assessment methods they apply. The leading principle is that they make choices and decisions that support various learners' growth in the best possible way (Halinen & Järvinen, 2008).

Enhancement-led evaluation system

Finnish education's evaluation system has been described as enhancement/improvement-led evaluation (Kumpulainen & Lankinen, 2016; Niemi & Lavonen, 2012). Evaluation is performed for the sake of improvement, not ranking. Teachers' work is not determined by high-stakes testing or outside control. In Finland, there is no standardised testing. The evaluation system aims to determine which kinds of improvements are needed for better learning outcomes. Local education providers (municipalities) are responsible for the quality of educational services and assessment methods. Teachers also use enhancement-led evaluation in student learning. This means that formative evaluation methods are used to decide how to support various learners. Toom and Husu (2012) write:

> Added to this, the task of assessment is to help pupils form a realistic image of their learning and development. It is also stated, that pupil assessment forms a whole, in which on-going feedback from the teacher plays an important part. With the help of assessment, the teacher guides the pupils in becoming aware of their thinking and actions and helps them understand what they are learning.

In Finland, there is neither an inspectorate nor probation time. New teachers are fully licensed when they start their work in schools after they graduate from teacher education programmes. New teachers must fill a professional role from the very beginning of their careers. They are expected to be capable of meeting all national and local educational aims in schools. They have five years of high-quality academic preservice education in universities, integrating theory and practice and emphasising teacher autonomy. In spite of preservice experiences, the transition to a school community can be surprising. New teachers must meet all professional demands immediately when they start their work, and they have hundreds of interactions every day in school. These demands burden all teachers but, more specifically, new teachers do not necessarily have the strategies or models needed to cope with all these professional tasks. Finland is also becoming a multicultural society, and teachers face an increasing amount of student heterogeneity in classrooms.

NEW TEACHERS' NEEDS IN THE FINNISH EDUCATION SYSTEM

To obtain more evidence about new teachers' needs, three surveys were implemented in 2010, 2013 and 2015. The first one collected data (n=445) from student teachers at two large universities to illustrate what kind of competencies teacher education had provided them with (Niemi, 2011, 2012a,c). The questionnaire consisted of 40 items regarding a broad range of teachers' work in classrooms, in the school community and in cooperation with various education partners. The results suggested that the student teachers were satisfied with the skills and competencies they had achieved regarding classroom teaching. They assessed that they had good basic skills in designing teaching, had good content knowledge and managed classroom pedagogy well. They had internalised ethical commitments regarding teaching and also saw teaching as a lifelong learning career in which they would be responsible for their own professional development. They reported that they had the lowest competencies in cooperating with the school community and with partners outside the school, particularly with parents. The second challenging area was teaching a diversity of pupils and preparing them for the future.

The same questionnaire was also distributed to newly qualified teachers (Niemi & Siljander, 2013). The questions were changed to determine the biggest needs among newly qualified teachers (NQTs). This survey was conducted among a group of new teachers ($n=40$) who had participated in Teacher Union courses for newly qualified teachers. They responded to the same questions as the student teachers but described areas in which they would need the most support in their work. They were representatives of different geographical areas in Finland. The third survey was organised in 2015 ($n=102$) and also distributed to newly qualified teachers who had participated in Teacher Union courses in the previous two years.

We found a great deal of consistency among the student teachers' and newly qualified teachers' experiences. Those competencies that were weakest during teacher education were on the top-ten list in terms of requests for support and mentoring. Student teachers assessed that they had good basic skills in terms of classroom work including content knowledge and pedagogy, and NQTs also felt that they would not need support in this regard during their first-year work. Instead, they felt they needed support in guiding and helping students with learning difficulties and differentiating teaching for them. Students' needs and preparing students for their future are key areas in which new teachers are struggling. In addition, cooperating with parents was among the top-ten priorities in 2013. Teachers still required support regarding those competencies with which they had struggled during teacher education. The needs of NQTs were very similar in both surveys. Among the top-ten areas of need, there were six professional tasks that were the very same, and almost in the same order. The most urgent task is to find solutions for how to act in a conflict situation, such as mobbing. All tasks were related to students' learning and well-being, especially for differentiating and helping different kinds of learners. Even administrative tasks were related to arrangements for students' transfer to have extra support in their learning. All Finnish schools must also have a students' welfare group. It is multi-professional support group with special-needs teachers and health and social professionals to help students when they have troubles in their life. This cooperative work is often very challenging for a new teacher.

An interesting difference between the 2013 and 2015 data for NQTs is that the newest survey's top-ten list includes curriculum planning and students' ICT skills. This can be seen as a direct consequence of the new national core-curriculum reform in 2014–2016. Schools must have their own school-based curricula designed and ready for implementation in August 2016. Schools had two years to develop their own local curricula. The reform emphasises learning and learning environments in the framework of twenty-first-century skills also consisting of digital learning solutions. From these studies, we learn that the areas in which teachers need support are not stable. They are connected with the actual situation and ongoing reforms in schools. However, in the Finnish case, major needs are related to student welfare and how to make learning meaningful for students.

**Table 3.1 Newly qualified teachers' self-assessments:
'I need support or mentoring in the following tasks'**

1=Not at all or very little, 2=A little, 3=Somewhat, 4=Much, 5=Very much

Professional tasks in which support is needed	2013 n=40		Professional tasks in which support is needed	2015 n= 102	
	M	SD		M	SD
Acting in conflict situations (such as mobbing)	3.63	.98	Acting in conflict situations (such as mobbing)	3.56	1.04
Working with a student welfare group	3.45	1.26	Differentiating of teaching	3.51	1.05
Differentiating of teaching	3.23	1.14	Working with a student welfare group	3.27	.98
Administrative tasks (information letters, reports, student transfers to other groups or schools, work diaries)	3.15	1.23	Revising students' learning environments	3.26	1.08

Evaluating and grading of students	3.15	.84	Evaluating and grading of students	3.25	1.11
Evaluating students' learning capacity	3.05	1.24	Evaluating students' learning capacity	3.24	.10
Cooperation with parents	3.05	1.19	Developing of school curriculum	3.20	.92
Preparing students ready for daily life	3.03	1.21	Developing applications of modern information technology	3.18	1.13
Supporting a learner's individual growth	3.03	.97	Administrative tasks (information letters, reports, student transfers to other groups or schools, work diaries)	3.16	1.03
Development of own educational philosophy	2.93	1.23	Self-regulated learning	3.04	1.03

In interviews with 20 NQTs in 2013 in the capital-city area, we also identified the following categories:

Needs related to discussing and asking for support

New teachers explained that they had managed daily work fairly well, but there were many situations in which they needed to discuss their experiences with someone else. Many had peer teachers who acted as important partners. Some mentioned having special-needs teachers as supporters when experiencing difficulties with pupils. However, the main message was that new teachers would need someone with whom they can share experiences and reflect. They also mentioned that it was important to clarify their own aims and that, in this process, confidentiality would be very important.

Cooperation with parents

Parents were mentioned in almost every new teacher's interview. Some mentioned difficulties with parents but, even when there were no special difficulties, new teachers regarded cooperation with parents as demanding. They wanted to have more support in this area. They also mentioned that in preservice teacher education they did not have experience of working with parents.

Differentiating teaching

New teachers described how, even though they were confident regarding content knowledge and had the competencies needed to use different kinds of teaching methods, they were uncertain how to differentiate teaching for different learners. During lessons, it became too hectic to find such solutions. New teachers would like to discuss this with someone who could help them design and implement teaching in such a way that all learners can learn.

Difficult students – behavioural problems

New teachers describe how they usually manage classroom situations fairly well. However, there are also students who have behavioural problems. These students can behave aggressively or cause many kinds of trouble in the classroom. Such situations can create emotional burdens and trigger high levels of stress among new teachers. They would like to discuss these difficult situations and find ways to handle them.

THE NEW TEACHER CENTRE AS A REFERENCE FOR A FINNISH INDUCTION PROGRAMME

Finland does not have any mandatory programme for mentoring or supporting NQTs. There have been pilots in which peer-mentoring provided extra help at the school level for new teachers and, at the same time, for all teachers (Jokinen et al., 2008). However, support for new teachers is still developing. The Finnish National Board of Education funded a pilot project (2011–2013) to determine how new teachers could be supported. The first author of this chapter led that project. The initial step in the project was to determine what is most important when supporting new teachers.

There are many models of new-teacher induction in different countries. However, in most cases it consists of mentoring. In the TALIS survey (Scheerens, 2010, 157), a mentor is defined as a person who is assigned to a new teacher to help and advise him or her. The quality of mentors has been seen as a key factor in successful and effective induction programmes (Moir & Gless, 2001; Moir, Barlin, Gless & Miles, 2009). Feiman-Nemser

(2001, 2008) and her colleagues (Feiman-Nemser, Carver, Schwille & Yusko, 2000; Feiman-Nemser & Norman, 2001; Katz & Feiman-Nemser, 2004) emphasise that continuity in teachers' professional development is important, as is the quality of mentors.

As a frame of reference, the Finnish mentoring project selected the mentoring model of the New Teacher Centre (NTC) in California. It has an over-20-year history of training mentors for new teachers in the United States. Representatives of the NTC (Moir & Gless, 2001, 112) stress:

> Supporting new teachers is complex and demanding work, and it involves learning skills other than those that most classroom teachers possess. It is critical, therefore, that we think not only about what a new teacher needs to be successful but also what a mentor teacher needs to know and be able to do in order to support a new teacher.

The ultimate aim of NTC mentoring is for students in the classroom to experience high-quality teaching and increased learning outcomes. Induction programmes aim to accelerate new teachers' effectiveness, making them more aware of how to help different students learn successfully. Other aims are to strengthen new teachers' leadership capacity and improve teacher retention (Figure 3.1).

Figure 3.1 The main principles of the NTC model for mentoring (Adapted from the original, The New Teacher Center 2011)

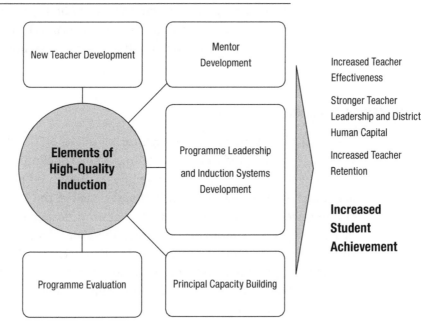

According to the NTC model, a key factor in supporting new teachers is the quality of mentors. Therefore, selecting and training mentors is a high priority.

In the NTC mentor programme, the following criteria are important when working with novice teachers:

- Mentors intimately know the communities, school sites and classroom contexts of their novice partners.

- Mentors provide support that is responsive to the assessed individual needs of their beginning teachers.

- Mentors facilitate new teachers, guiding them to use observation, collaborative lesson design, model teaching, veteran-teacher observation, reflection, the analysis of student work, goal-setting and assessment against professional standards.

- Mentors model the importance of designing classroom instruction based on assessed student needs.

Mentors may have many functions: on the one hand, they are supporters of new teachers. On the other, they are also the brokers of policy-makers, tasked with promoting student learning via their influence on new teachers (Moir & Gless, 2001). Not every outstanding classroom teacher is necessarily a talented mentor. Moir and Gless emphasise the following selection criteria: strong interpersonal skills, credibility with peers and administrators, a demonstrated curiosity and eagerness to learn, respect for multiple perspectives, and outstanding instructional practice.

THE FINNISH PILOT PROGRAMME STARTS

The principles of induction and mentoring in the NTC induction programme were adopted as core guidelines when the Finnish model was being developed. The selected group of 13 experienced Finnish teachers, along with the author of this chapter, visited the NTC and had a training week in November 2011 to obtain a deeper understanding of how to train high-quality mentors. The group had a special task: to learn how the Finnish system could utilise the NTC's experiences and develop a Finnish model for induction. Most participants also had a mentee during the project and had to simultaneously learn what it means to be a mentor.

The pilot group began their mentoring and creating the model for induction simultaneously. This would not have been possible without these teachers' earlier multifaceted professional experiences. Many had experience of supervising and mentoring student teachers, and some had been academic counsellors. Some teachers also had supervisor training for work counselling. However, they did not have experience being a mentor during induction. Over 1.5 years (2011–2013), the group was trained based on the core ideas of NTC mentoring, and the teachers reflected on their own growth as mentors and shared their experiences. During that time, they drafted a handbook for the Finnish model of induction and mentoring (Niemi & Siljander, 2013).

The Finnish context is different in many respects to the NTC, which is in the United States. In Finland, all teachers have five years of high-quality teacher education via obtaining academic MA degrees (Niemi & Jakku-Sihvonen, 2006; Niemi, 2012a). Schools can only hire qualified teachers who fulfil both content knowledge and pedagogical requirements. Teacher retention is high, and teachers are satisfied with their profession (TALIS, 2013). In the United States, mentors face much greater heterogeneity among teachers and their competencies, and schools can be very different depending on the area. In Finland, the equity principle means that all schools should be good schools and that parents do not need to be afraid regarding what their local school is like. There are no private schools, and school sizes are usually smaller than in the USA. Geographically, Finnish schools can also be very remote.

In the NTC model, mentors were mainly full-time. Mentoring was organised systematically in local schools and had a clear position in the school regions that participated in the induction programme. In the Finnish context, we could not plan for exclusively full-time mentoring. Only the biggest cities can hire full-time mentors. We had to find a model that can be used for both part-time and full-time mentoring during induction.

In June 2013, the pilot group published *New teachers' mentoring. Towards students' and teachers' wellbeing through mentoring* (Niemi & Siljander and the group for developing mentoring, 2013), in which mentor training, relevant structures and the administrative practices of induction were described. The focus of the Finnish model is students' and teachers' well-being. The mentors' task is to help new teachers promote student learning and holistic growth, especially for students with special needs. They should also help new teachers find their role in the school community and work with parents and other interest groups. Mentors can support new teachers in pedagogical issues but, based on earlier studies, the major focus should be on different learners' needs and interaction with other partners, particularly with parents. Mentors should also support new teachers in viewing students' cultural background as a resource.

Aims of mentoring

The handbook sets six important aims for the Finnish model of induction (Niemi & Siljander, 2013):

- Supporting and advancing new teachers' professional growth and development after preservice teacher education.

- Promoting new teachers' ability to manage their own work, retention and well-being.

- Taking care of and promoting student well-being in schools.

- Fulfilling quality standards in basic education and ensuring that all students can have a high-quality education.

- Supporting mentors' professional growth and development.

- Enhancing school culture and the school community in an attempt to provide a professional-learning community.

Mentors' training

In the handbook, it was recommended that mentor training be organised by universities' continuing education centres for teachers, together with teacher-training departments and teacher educators. Trainers should be university teachers and teacher educators with high-quality experience as teachers in schools. The programme should be at least five ECTS (European credit transfer system) points, which means at least 140 hours of learning on the mentor's part, including five intensive days over 1–1.5 years, depending how those intensive days are arranged. Between the intensive days, there is individual work with one's own mentees and ongoing reflections about the mentors' joint electronic platform. The following topics should be covered in the training programme:

- Mentors' professional growth, identity and roles

- New teachers' needs and support for their professional development

- The ethics of mentoring and guidance, especially confidentiality in mentors' work

- Communication, principles of dialogue, active listening dialogue and the language of mentoring

- Tools for e-mentoring and documentation.

During the mentor training, each mentor should have a mentee with whom the mentor meets at least once or twice a week. The mentor will visit the new teacher's school and classroom. Together, the mentor and mentee plan how often they meet, how often the mentor visits the new teacher's classroom, how student learning will be observed in classrooms and which kinds of tools the new teacher will use for documenting his or her own learning and his or her students' learning. The important aim is that the new teacher finds the tools and practices with which to manage his or her work all year round and to determine how the new teacher can meet the needs of various learners and ensure a high-quality education for all students. The trained mentor can be in the mentee's own school or come from outside, depending on the local circumstances.

What are the criteria to become a mentor?

Because the number of new teachers can vary in different years and in different regions, there can be full-time or part-time mentors. However, all mentors must have training in mentoring. The selection criteria to participate in mentor training are that mentor teachers must have least five years of teaching experience; high emotional intelligence and excellent interaction skills; to show evidence of constructive family–school cooperation, the latest knowledge about the school curriculum; experiences working as an adult educator; respect among teachers; and they must be committed to lifelong learning.

BECOMING A MENTOR IS A PROCESS

Becoming a mentor to a new teacher is a long process. The work is different from teaching students in classrooms. The teachers who developed the pilot programme for mentoring and were also mentors to new teachers were interviewed. In the following descriptions, their experiences are summarised. In the analysis, the same categories were used as were found in earlier studies of mentoring (Lieberman, Hanson & Gless, 2012). In the Finnish study, the following thematic content could be found:

Building a new identity

Becoming a mentor means adopting a new identity: it is becoming a facilitator and building a scaffold for a mentee. It is a long process of learning to ask questions rather than giving answers. Mentors describe it as a process of learning to listen and finally seeing mentoring as a mutual learning process. A large part of their growth was to learn to ask questions and lead the discussion in such a way as to support the new teacher.

> Indeed, it has been quite a path for myself and a change ... and then I see it as important ... when you put your own job into words.
> (*Mentor 2*)

> So you are listening and then, in a way, you have to grasp that it is not just that you, as a more experienced worker, are giving something but that both parties have given something and taken something away.
> (*Mentor 4*)

> I learned, maybe, to guide that discussion in such a way that it no longer wandered here and there, but I did not impose some specific direction on it. (*Mentor 2*)

Mentors also described their role as different from the role of a teacher in a school. They had to face a young professional's growth process, and support was needed when a new teacher was tired. They had to keep in mind two levels of learning processes. The first was related to new teachers. Mentors facilitated new teachers in reflecting on their own growth. The second concerns how new teachers could understand students' growth and learning processes. They guided new teachers to understand situations from students' perspectives and viewpoints. They also helped new teachers to keep their problems in perspective and overcome difficult situations.

Facing challenging contexts with mentees

The mentors reported that they needed to help new teachers in challenging situations involving difficult students or parents. Mentors described how it was necessary to discuss difficult topics and even crises with their mentees. Sometimes, they had to be available 24 hours a day via emails and online. They also learned that they had to start from the mentees' situation and viewpoint. Every difficult situation is unique, and discussions about various solutions are important. Mentors also found situations related to new teachers' personalities or behavioural styles to be challenging.

> It was difficult to maintain the relationship in such a way that you could find the tools that would suit a given mentee. (*Mentor 9*)

> Sometimes, it is difficult if the issue is a mentee's personality or style. Often, he or she cannot see this, though it may influence a child. (*Mentor 5*)

> When there was a difficult group or student ... helping to find out what kinds of solutions there could be was challenging. (Mentor 3)

Mentors described how facing mentees' crises was emotionally burdening. They emphasised their need for support as mentors and opportunities to share these experiences.

Developing trusting relationships

Some mentors felt they had a great deal of mutual interaction in their relationships with their mentees. It was more like a peer relationship, although the mentor's role was to provide encouraging feedback. Some mentors wanted to keep the relationship very work-related. However, the most important aspect of the relationship was confidentiality.

> Well, with my mentee, we had a very easy collegial relationship and, in fact, a very positive relationship. There were no problems; it was just fine. She was always happy to have encouragement. (*Mentor 6*)

> We had a very work-related relationship. We did not share any other issues ... We spoke only about work-related issues and did so confidentially. (*Mentor 2*)

The confidential relationship also included the mentor acting as a supporter of the new teacher, and no evaluation or other mentee-related information was given to the principal or other teachers.

Accelerating teacher development

Encouragement and positive feedback were the most important ways to support mentee development. Mentors also learned that their task is not to set objectives for the mentee. That is the mentee's own duty and process. Mentors can only be supporters and facilitators.

> ... and I certainly give a lot of positive feedback. I always did so when it went fine and a mentee succeeded – just a normal interaction – but I always aimed to avoid criticising and being a know-it-all. (*Mentor 5*)

> We decided that she (a mentee) would choose where her professional development would start and the target we would aim at. (*Mentor 7*)

Some mentors also spoke about networks they had recommended that mentees use to find new tools and inspiration.

Learning leadership

Mentors became aware of how much experience and competence they had with teaching and school life. When mentoring, they also began to understand that they were leaders.

> A hero leader – that has fallen off. As a mentor, you must have a much lower profile and use you own knowhow and your attitudes as a background. I think that my thoughts about leadership have changed, particularly because of this mentor training. (*Mentor 7*)

> If you compare being a mentor to a more traditional boss position, the major difference is that you do not say how to do something. You merely say that the mentee will see that it is a process. Thus, interaction is fairly important in this role. (*Mentor 6*)

We can conclude that becoming a mentor is a long process. Even though all mentors in the pilot group had lengthy teaching experience, the process of creating a new professional identity took time. We discovered that mentor training is needed for conceptual change and finding new and relevant ways to support the professional development of mentees.

The mentors' biggest problem was how to find time for mentoring and visiting new teachers' classrooms. So far, there is no official system in Finland and all mentoring practices are designed on a case-by-case basis. The leadership role required mentors to build new concepts. Leadership is based on interaction and support, not giving direct answers or commands.

LESSONS LEARNED

In trying to find new solutions in terms of organising support for new teachers, there have been pilot projects regarding mentoring for new teachers in Finland. One has focused on how to ensure that the professional community supports all teachers' work and uses group mentoring to facilitate new teachers' development (Jokinen et al., 2008). The pilot described in this chapter, the latest project, aimed to create a programme to support new teachers through the use of a senior colleague as a personal mentor (Niemi & Siljander, 2013).

The first training cycle of mentors was conducted in 2013–14 after the special group of 13 teachers was organised. A group of 22 experienced teachers participated in the mentoring course. The training was organised according to the handbook's principles. All teachers had mentees, and they started to adopt new identities as mentors. The feedback from mentors and mentees was excellent. Both mentors and mentees also expressed their delight because they had learned so much from one another. Both groups also had a unanimous message: induction and support for new teachers are greatly needed.

Even though the programme was successful, we still have concerns about the future.

Integration with the education system

Projects and pilots are important for opening up new mentoring scenarios and creating new knowledge for the sake of providing new teachers with support. Yet, projects cannot solve the real problem in a larger sense. Induction requires national and local structures. In the Finnish case, induction should be negotiated and accepted nationally by the Ministry of Education and Culture, the Finnish National Board of Education, municipal authorities, the teacher trade union and universities' teacher education departments. There is an urgent need to integrate the induction of new teachers into the structure of the education system.

School leaders' support

The pilots strongly confirm the NTC's view that principals' support is a key factor. Mentors do not work for principals, but school leaders play an important role in organising mentoring at a local level. Each new teacher should have an induction plan in which mentoring plays an essential role. Mentors could also be a huge resource for principals and school communities in school development.

Time and space for mentors and mentees

Mentors should have an agreement to serve as facilitators for new teachers. The basic requirement is that they have training for that job. They also need a contract that defines their rights and responsibilities, as well as a salary and rewards resulting from mentoring, irrespective of whether they are full-time or part-time mentors. Further, mentees need an agreement that allows them to participate in an induction programme and define how it is integrated into their work. Without time allocation and practical arrangements, induction is not sustainable. Teachers' and mentors' professional development requires continuity, and this should be taken into account when organising induction.

Coordination between preservice, induction and in-service training

In the Finnish education system, teachers are educated in universities' teacher education departments. Universities also have further education centres for graduated teachers. Coordination between preservice, induction and in-service training is necessary to provide relevant support for new teachers.

Listen to new teachers' needs

In induction and mentor training, we must know what the national objectives for teachers' work and school outcomes are. We must also know which aspects of education teachers need help with. In addition to these system-level issues, mentors must see that every new teacher is unique and must be met individually.

The focus on student learning

Induction is provided to new teachers, but the ultimate aim is for students to be exposed to high-quality teaching. Induction is not a separate part of the education system. It targets the provision of high-quality education to all students. Competent mentors can improve teacher performance and well-being, which increases student well-being and learning outcomes.

Every country has its own educational objectives and challenges. Education in Finland has enjoyed a strong international reputation because of the high learning outcomes among 15-year-old students in terms of PISA measurements.

The weakest link in Finnish teacher education is induction, which is practically missing. New teachers face so many complicated school conditions and demands in the Finnish education system that, in spite of their high-quality preservice education, they need support when starting their teaching careers.

REFERENCES

Conway, P. F., Murphy, R., Rath, A. and Hall, K. (2009). *Learning to teach and its implications for the continuum of teacher education: A nine-country cross-national study.* Report commissioned by the Teaching Council, Ireland.

European Commission. (2010). *Developing coherent and system-wide induction programmes for beginning teachers: A handbook for policymakers.* Staff Working Document SEC (2010) 538 final. Brussels: Directorate-General for Education and Culture.

Feiman-Nemser, S. (2001). From preparation to practice: Designing a continuum to strengthen and sustain teaching. *Teachers College Record*, 103(6), 1013–1055.

Feiman-Nemser, S. (2008). Teacher learning. How do teachers learn to teach? In M. Cochran-Smith, S. D. Feiman-Nemser and D. McIntyre, (eds), *Handbook of research on teacher education. Enduring questions in changing contexts.* New York/Abingdon: Routledge/Taylor & Francis.

Feiman-Nemser, S., Carver, C., Schwille, S. and Yusko, B. (2000). Beyond support: Taking teachers seriously as learners. In M. Scherer, (ed.), *A better beginning: Supporting and mentoring new teachers.* Alexandria, VA: Association for Supervision and Curriculum Development.

Feiman-Nemser, S. and Norman P. (2001). From initial preparation to continuing professional development. In R. Moon, S. Brown and M. Ben-Peretz, (eds), *International companion to education*. London: Routledge.

Halinen, I. and Holappa, M. S. (2013). Curricular balance based on dialogue, cooperation and trust – the case of Finland. In W. Kuiper and J. Berkvens, (eds), *Balancing curriculum regulation and freedom across Europe*. CIDREE Yearbook. Enschede: SLO Netherlands Institute for Curriculum Development CIDREE.

Halinen, I. and Järvinen, R. (2008). Towards inclusive education: The case of Finland. *Prospects*, 38(1), 77–97.

Hämäläinen, K., Hämäläinen, K. and Kangasniemi, J. (eds) (2015). Paths to continuing professional development. The challenges and future of state-funded professional development of education personnel. The memorandum of the advisory board for professional development of education (in Finnish, abstract in English). *Publications of the Ministry of Education and Culture*, 2015(10).

Jokinen, H., Morberg, Å., Poom-Valickis, K. and Rohtma, V. (2008). Mentoring newly qualified teachers in Estonia, Finland and Sweden. In G. Fransson and C. Gustafsson, (eds), *Newly qualified teachers in Northern Europe. Comparative perspectives on promoting professional development*. Gävle: University of Gävle.

Katz, D. and Feiman-Nemser, S. (2004). New teacher induction in a culture of professional development. In J. Goodlad, (ed.), *The teaching career*. San Francisco: Jossey-Bass.

Kersaint, G., Lewis J., Potter R. and Meisels, G. (2007). Why teachers leave: Factors that influence retention and resignation. *Teaching and Teacher Education*, 23(6), 775–794.

Kumpulainen, K. and Lankinen T. (2016). Striving for educational equity and excellence: Evaluation and assessment in Finnish basic education. In H. Niemi, A. Toom and A. Kallioniemi, (eds), *Miracle of education: The principles and practices of teaching and learning in Finnish schools* (second revised edition). Rotterdam: Sense Publishers.

Laukkanen, R. (2007). Finnish strategy for high-level education for all. In N. C. Sognel and P. Jaccard, (eds), *Governance and performance of education systems*. Dordrecht: Springer.

Lieberman, A., Hanson, S. and Gless, J. (2012). *Mentoring teachers. Navigating the real-world tensions*. Santa Cruz and San Francisco: New Teacher Center and Jossey-Bass.

Livingston, K. (2012a). Approaches to professional development of teachers in Scotland: Pedagogical innovation or financial necessity? *Educational Research*, 54(2), 161–172, doi:10.1080/00131881.2012.680041.

Livingston, K. (2012b). Quality in teachers' professional career-long development. In J. Harford, B. Hudson and H. Niemi, (eds), *Quality assurance and teacher education: International challenges and expectations*. Bern: Peter Lang.

Livingston, K. and Shiach. L. (2010). A new model of teacher education. In A. Campbell and S. Groundwater-Smith, (eds), *Connecting inquiry and professional learning*. London: Routledge.

Moir, E. and Gless, J. (2001). Quality induction: An investment in teachers. *Teacher Education Quarterly*, 28(1), 109–114.

Moir, E., Barlin, D., Gless, J. and Miles, J. (2009). *New teacher mentoring. Hopes and promise for improving teacher effectiveness.* Cambridge, MA: Harvard Education Press.

Niemi, H. (2011). Educating student teachers to become high quality professionals – a Finnish case. *CEPS Journal, 1*(1), 43–66.

Niemi, H. (2012a). Relationships of teachers' professional competences, active learning and research studies in teacher education in Finland. *Reflecting Education, 8*(2), 23–44.

Niemi, H. (2012b). The societal factors contributing to education and schooling in Finland. In H. Niemi, A. Toom and A. Kallioniemi, (eds.), *Miracle of Education: The principles and practices of teaching and learning in Finnish schools.* Rotterdam: Sense Publishers.

Niemi, H. (2012c). Teacher education for high quality professionals. An analysis from the Finnish perspective. In O-S. Tan, (ed.), *Teacher education frontiers. International perspectives on policy and practice for building new teacher competences.* Singapore: CENSAGE Learning.

Niemi, H. (2014). Purposeful policy and practice for equity and quality – a Finnish case. In S. K. Lee, W. On Lee and E. L. Low, (eds), *Education policy innovations: Levelling up and sustaining educational achievement.* Singapore: Springer.

Niemi, H., and Isopahkala-Bouret, U. (2012). Lifelong learning in Finnish society – Empowering different age groups through learning. *International Journal of Continuing Education and Lifelong Learning, 5*(1).

Niemi, H., and Jakku-Sihvonen, R. (2006). Research-based teacher education. In R. Jakku-Sihvonen and H. Niemi, (eds), *Research-based teacher education in Finland. Reflections by Finnish teacher educators.* Turku: Finnish Educational Research Association.

Niemi, H. and Lavonen, J. (2012). Evaluation for improvements in Finnish teacher education. In J. Harford, B. Hudson and H. Niemi, (eds), *Quality assurance and teacher education: International challenges and expectations.* Oxford: Peter Lang.

Niemi, H, Siljander, A. M. and the group for developing mentoring (2013). Uuden opettajan mentorointi. Mentoroinnilla oppilaan ja opettajan hyvinvointiin. (New teachers' mentoring. Towards students' and teachers' well-being through mentoring). Helsinki: Palmenia Centre for Continuing Education, University of Helsinki.

OECD. (2003). *First results from PISA 2003. Executive summary.* Retrieved from www.oecd.org/education/preschoolandschool/ programmeforinternationalstudentassessmentpisa/34002454.pdf.

OECD. (2006). *Equity in education. Thematic review. Finland country note.* Retrieved from www.oecd.org/document/3/0,2340,en_2649_34531_36296195_1_1_1_1,00.html.

OECD. (2010). *PISA 2009 results: What students know and can do: Student performance in reading, mathematics and science* (volume I). Paris: OECD.

OECD. (2013). *PISA 2012. Results in focus. What 15-year-olds know and what they can do with what they know.* Paris: OECD.

Sahlberg, P. (2011). *Finnish lessons: What can the world learn from educational change in Finland?* New York: Teacher College Press.

Scheerens, J. (ed.) (2010). *Teachers' professional development. Europe in international comparison. An analysis of teachers' professional development based on the OECD's Teaching and Learning International Survey (TALIS).* Luxembourg: Office for Official Publications of the European Union.

Schwille, J., Dembélé, M. and Schubert, J. (2007). *Global perspectives on teacher learning: Improving policy and practice.* Paris: International Institute for Educational Planning; UNESCO.

TALIS (2013). Results. An International Perspective on Teaching and Learning. DOI:10.1787/9789264196261-en. Paris: OECD.

Toom. A. and Husu. J. (2012). Finnish Teachers as 'makers of the many': Balancing between broad pedagogical freedom and responsibility. In H. Niemi, A. Toom and A. Kallioniemi, (eds), *Miracle of education: The principles and practices of teaching and learning in Finnish schools.* Rotterdam: Sense Publishers.

4   Teacher education in Poland: Towards teachers' career-long professional learning

Joanna Madalińska-Michalak

INTRODUCTION

This chapter focuses on the issue of the quality of teacher education, one of the key subjects in the current debate on the directions of educational policy in the EU. The contribution emphasises the importance of coherent, career-long development of teachers' learning in a changing context and creating conditions for preparing teachers who are continuous learners themselves. It presents an overview of changes in teacher education in Poland from 1990 onwards in the setting of improving the quality of teaching and learning and at the same time the quality of higher education. This overview should be read as a description of the most important changes affecting teacher education and the teaching profession, and as an investigation into their aims and context in Poland. The chapter directs attention to future policy, research and practice related to a highly relevant need to obtain a continuum of teacher education in Poland with a focus on teachers' career-long professional learning and their support in different phases of their professional career.

Extensive research on schools across the globe leads to the conclusion that student achievement is directly related to the quality of teachers. In discussions on education, teachers' work is recognised as the most important factor influencing the quality of education at school (Abbott, 1988; Darling-Hammond, 1999; Hattie, 2003; Michalak, 2010; OECD, 2005). At the same time, it is stressed that the quality of teachers, the quality of their professionalism and the degree of professionalisation among them depend on the quality of their teacher education, and this is reflected in European policy documents published by both the European Commission (2005, 2007) and European Council (2007).

The attention devoted to the quality of teachers' work and the quality of education is reflected in research priorities concerning teaching, learning, teachers' professional development and school leadership. The issue of improving the quality of teachers' education is a key subject in the current debate on the directions of educational policy in the European Union. It is one of the main goals of the process of reforming education systems in European countries.

This chapter examines recent changes in teacher education at the system and school levels in Poland and indicates its role in creating and sustaining integrated professional-learning cultures to support teacher education in the initial and induction phases of the continuum. Teacher education is perceived in connection with higher education and its changes and challenges.

The changing context of the education system in Poland

The current setting for teacher education in Poland is partly shaped by shifting social, economic and political circumstances, whether local, national or global in nature. The rapidly changing context of the education system in Poland over the past 25 years has brought about significant changes in the legislation, which has become the basis for introducing important reforms in education.

The new basic principles of the Polish school system were established by the School Education Act of 7 September 1991 (with further amendments). The 1999 Education Reform Act on Implementation of the Education System Reform (with further amendments) introduced a new structure for the Polish school system. In light of the existing law, higher education in Poland forms a separate system and is based on the Higher Education Act of 12 September 1990 (uniform text published in the *Journal of Laws of the Republic of Poland* of 1990, No. 65 pos. 385). Higher education is a dynamic and expanding area in Poland, which has seen an almost fivefold increase in the number of students since 1990. The education system in Poland is centrally managed by two institutions – the Ministry of National Education (general and vocational education) and the Ministry of Science and Higher Education (higher education). It is only the national educational policy that is developed and carried out centrally, while the administration of education and the running of schools are decentralised.

THE EDUCATION SYSTEM

Considering the reforms of education and their results, one can state that the Polish education system has moved from the emphasis on the transmission of information and on vocational education and training that prevailed under communism to an education system that aims to equip its citizens with a more rounded education focused on knowledge construction, and the development of skills and competencies.

The education system has been constructed so that it has to enable learners to adapt to a rapidly changing world, especially the pace and scope of economic, social and cultural change. It was adapted to the provisions of the Constitution and the system reform of the state. The Constitution of the Republic of Poland refers to fundamental freedoms and citizens' rights. It states that every person has the right to education and that education is compulsory until the age of 18. Education in public schools is free of charge. Parents are free to choose schools other than public ones for their children. Citizens and institutions have the right to establish primary, lower-secondary, upper-secondary and post-secondary schools and higher-education institutions as well as child-care centres.

Children's participation in preschool has significantly improved in recent years but is still below the EU average. Poland has achieved one of the best results in Europe in terms of the participation of young people aged 15–24 in education at ISCED 1–6 levels (from primary education to doctorate programmes) and the number of young people holding upper-secondary qualifications. Poland is one of the EU's top performers in reducing early school leaving and raising the level of basic skills tested by the PISA survey, including the average level as well as the levels of low-performing and top-performing students. Between 2000 and 2012, Poland made the most rapid progress in the EU with regard to increasing the number of young adults holding higher-education qualifications in the 30–34 age group.

International education surveys show outstanding progress in learning outcomes at the end of compulsory education: Polish pupils' achievements at this education level are currently classified in PISA above or at least at the average level among the most developed countries cooperating within the framework of the EU and OECD. It is worth stressing that Poland's PISA results in 2000 were one of the factors impelling reform in schools and teacher education there over the past two decades. In the 2000 PISA examination, Poland's average student score was 479, well below the OECD average of 500 points (OECD, 2001). More than 21% of students reached only Level 1 or below. The PISA 2000 results also showed a real disparity between the educational competencies of students in the general education system and the basic vocational schools. Nearly 70% of basic vocational school students tested at the lowest literacy level. However, thanks to a series of school reforms that began in the late 1990s, Poland has dramatically reduced the number of poorly performing students in the past ten years and, in the 2009 and 2012 PISA tests, ranked among the top 15 OECD countries (OECD, 2009, 2010, 2014). Since its first participation in PISA, Poland has been able to increase the share of top performers and simultaneously reduce its share of low performers in mathematics, reading and science. The average difference in results, between the top 20% and bottom 20%, is 97 points, slightly lower than the OECD average of 99 points.

The above-mentioned achievements of Polish education co-exist with the deep decentralisation of management of the education system and new policies on improving the quality of teaching staff. Repressed before the transformation of the political system, the organisational and financial potential was unlocked after 1989. Most educational tasks at preschool- to upper-secondary-school levels are currently managed by a local authority. The organisational and financial responsibility of local authorities for developing education stimulated local educational ambitions and helped lift the burden of debt regularly incurred to finance educational tasks when these fell within the remit of the governmental administration.

At the level of post-secondary education, especially in higher education, the potential of non-public education was unlocked, supported by the considerable private expenditure of learners and their families. Decentralisation of the management of education has recently been reinforced by the steadily growing autonomy of schools and higher-education institutions (HEIs). A policy based on learning outcomes has been introduced in school and higher education in line with the European Qualifications Framework to provide schools, HEIs and teachers with greater autonomy in organisation of the educational process.

TEACHER EDUCATION IN POLAND IN THE CONTEXT OF IMPROVING QUALITY IN HIGHER EDUCATION

In the central point of the discussion in this section, I place the challenges that the education of teachers is nowadays facing in the context of improving the quality of education at the higher-education level.

This section explores characteristic aspects of the higher-education system and teacher education in Poland. It describes certain main features of teacher education and the major assumptions concerning the work of teacher educators in Poland and its conditions.

The higher-education system

Higher education is among the most rapidly developing areas of social life in Poland. Over the past 25 years (1990–2014), it has undergone in-depth sudden quantitative and institutional transformation. The socio-economic and political changes have allowed HEIs to return to the tradition of academic autonomy. The biggest academic centre in Poland is Warsaw, followed by Cracow, Wroclaw, Poznan, Łódź, Lublin, Gdansk and Katowice. In total, 43.4% of students study in these centres, wherein the students of daily studies comprise 53.3% of the total number of students in these academic centres. In the 2013/14 academic year, there were 1 550 000 students and 98 735 academic teachers in 439 higher-education institutions.

Since the beginning of the change in the Polish political system (under the new legislation: Higher Education Act of 12 September 1990, uniform text published in the *Journal of Laws of the Republic of Poland* of 1990, No. 65 pos. 385 and the Education System Act introduced on 7 September 1991), the number of HEIs in Poland has gradually increased (see Table 4.1).

Table 4.1 Number of higher-education institutions in Poland between 1992 and 2014

Academic year / Type of HEIs	Public HEIs	Non-public HEIs	Total
1992/1993	106	18	124
1995/1996	99	80	179
2000/2001	115	195	310
2005/2006	130	315	445
2008/2009	132	326	458
2013/2014	133	306	439

Source: Based on: www.nauka.gov.pl/szkolnictwo-wyzsze/dane-statystyczne-o-szkolnictwie-wyzszym/

The number of students has risen almost fivefold and more than one third of this growth consists of students from non-public HEIs. In 2005, the biggest number of students in Poland so far was recorded – in total, there were 1 953 832 students (1 333 032 of whom were students of public HEIs). The gross enrolment ratio for tertiary education, representing the ratio of all people learning at a particular educational level to the whole population of people at the age formally ascribed to this educational level (in the case of tertiary education: 19–24 years old), was 48.9%. On the other hand, the net enrolment ratio, showing the proportion of the number of actual students at the age formally ascribed to a particular level among the whole population of people formally ascribed to that educational level, amounted to 30.0% for tertiary education. Since 2006, we have been able to observe the tendency for the number of students to decrease and, in 2013, there were 1 549 877 students, of whom 1 151 315 were enrolled at state HEIs (see Figure 4.1). The gross enrolment ratio equalled 50.4%, while the net enrolment ratio amounted to 39.3%. In 2005–2013, the population of students generally decreased by 20.7% – including 13.6% in state HEIs. The number of graduates is growing steadily. Demographic changes causing the number of candidates for higher education to decrease are the reason for these phenomena. On the other hand, those born in the baby-boom period are now finishing their studies. This situation is presented in Figure 4.1 below.

It is worth mentioning that Poland holds fourth place in Europe (after the United Kingdom, Germany and France) in terms of the number of people enrolled in HE. Each year, almost half a million young people begin their education at universities and colleges. Polish universities offer more than 200 high-quality study programmes as an integral part of the EHEA. Most schools also offer their courses in foreign languages. Poland conforms to the Bologna Process guidelines in European higher education. A degree system based on the three-cycle structure has been successfully implemented together with the European Credit Transfer and Accumulation System (ECTS). The European standard in HE makes it easier for students to obtain recognition of their qualifications in other countries.

Figure 4.1 The general number of students in HEIs and number of students in public HEIs in 2004–2013

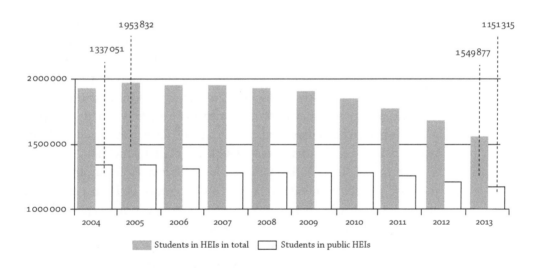

Source: Based on data published by GUS (Central Statistical Office) under the theme 'Szkoły wyższe i ich finanse' [Higher Education Institutions and Their Finances]. The data are published at www.stat.gov.pl*

* Data collected on 30 November for each year in the period 2004–2013

External quality assurance of higher education is carried out by an independent agency for tertiary education called the Polish Accreditation Committee (PKA). This committee was established under the name State Accreditation Committee on 1 January 2002 in compliance with the Act on Higher Education of 12 September 1990, and its tasks and working procedures were redefined and expanded by the currently effective Law on Higher Education of 27 July 2005. The PKA is the first independent institution, established by a legal act of the highest importance, working within the higher-education system in Poland to improve the quality of education in all public and non-public HEIs forming the system, authorised to conduct assessments of compliance with the requirements to provide education and to evaluate its quality in first-, second- and third-cycle studies, postgraduate programmes, and to evaluate the activities of basic organisational units of HEIs. On 15 April 2009, the State Accreditation Committee was officially accepted in the European Quality Assurance Register for Higher Education (EQAR), founded to enhance transparency and trust in quality assurance. The EQAR publishes and manages a register of quality-assurance agencies that substantially comply with the European Standards and Guidelines for Quality Assurance (ESG) to provide the public with clear and reliable information on quality-assurance agencies operating in Europe.

The PKA is an organisation of experts diagnosing the condition of higher education and conducting systematic activities in order to enhance the quality of education. Evaluations conducted by the PKA are obligatory and a negative assessment of the committee may lead to the suspension or withdrawal of authorisation to provide a degree programme in a given field of study and at a given level of study on the basis of a decision of the minister responsible for higher education.

Currently, Polish HE is facing various challenges. Poland is implementing the recommendations of the Conference of Ministers of the country-signatories to the Bologna Declaration. Moreover, work has been undertaken to bring degree-programme requirements closer to the European Qualifications Framework (EQF). Regarding the European Central Policy on HE, in its educational policy the Ministry of Science and Higher Education in Poland underlines the importance of developing human capital as Poland's and Europe's main asset and as a crucial element of the Lisbon Strategy. The ministry called for the implementation of lifelong learning as a *sine qua non* to achieve the Lisbon objectives. Polish universities need to improve their performance, to modernise themselves, to become more accessible and competitive and to play their part in the creation of the knowledge-based society envisaged by the Lisbon Strategy. This crucial sector of both the economy and society needs in-depth restructuring and modernisation if Poland is not to lose out in competition through shortcomings in education, research and innovation.

In view of the unquestionable huge quantitative success emphasised in many international reports, improving the quality of programmes and the efficiency of the HE system has become a priority. Since 2007, increasing the quality of studies and the efficiency of the higher-education system in Poland has emerged as a priority. Amendments to the Higher Education Act were officially introduced on 1 October 2011, concentrating on three areas:

- an efficient model of managing higher education

- a dynamic academic career model, and

- an effective educational model.

The new legislative changes were inspired by the need to adjust the higher-education system to the unprecedented growth of requirements faced by Polish higher education, and the need to harmonise the domestic system with the solutions implemented within the European Higher Education Area. New financing mechanisms for higher education based on the outcomes of research and teaching work have been introduced in order to achieve the reform's goals. The financing system has been altered so that an ever greater share of funds is distributed through competitions and tenders, and the scale of state financing depends on the quality of results in both teaching and research. The second key means of achieving these goals is to integrate curricula with the European Higher Education Area and thus increase students' and university and college teachers' mobility through: i) deregulation of teaching standardisation and increasing the autonomy of HEIs in terms of creating specialisations and curricula in accordance with the National Qualifications Framework within the Bologna Declaration; ii) closer links between HEIs, the external sector and the economy by including practitioners in the work on university and college curricula and teaching; iii) greater internationalisation of HEIs through involving foreign university and college teachers and Polish ones working abroad in national education, and opening HEIs more widely to foreign students; and iv) shortening the career paths of researchers and teachers by simplifying the habilitation procedure for Polish scientists and researchers and equating the status of independent scientists and researchers working in Poland and abroad.

The established systemic solutions were designed to provide, on the one hand, better quality for Polish students, thus better preparation for the changing economy, and, on the other, the opportunity for Polish scientists and researchers to participate in the greatest world research projects and the prospects for the steady development of Polish HEIs, as well as a continual increase in their teaching and research potential. The reform paid attention to the need for modern management and effective competition as regards scientific research, but also to the need to strengthen academic ethics and the constant concern over the master–student relationship.

It is worth mentioning that the Polish government's latest proposals concerning improving the quality of higher education show that the strategy of higher-education development in Poland – as contained in documents devoted to changes in higher education – is expressed in the language of economics, theory of organisation and theory of effectiveness. The reforms are presented as giving HEIs greater freedom in operational decisions and removing unnecessary constraints in financial and human-resource management. However, it is crucial to see these reform processes as processes of re-regulation: not the abandonment by the state of its controls but the establishment of a new form of control. In this way, the state also provides a new general mode of less visible regulation, a much more 'hands-off', self-regulating regulation (Ball, 2003, 217). Recognising the degree of 'competitiveness' in higher education as the most important indicator of 'quality' shows beyond any doubt that the quality of higher education will be achieved by promoting competition instead of cooperation in this area and will be directed at assessing the effects of education.

Teacher education – the overall characteristic

Teacher education is part of the education system and reflects the characteristics of that system. The rapidly changing context of education has pushed for a radical reform process of the education system driven by repeated state interventions. This process has entailed reforms of teaching and teacher education in Poland. Teacher education has been adjusted to the principles of a pluralist democracy and a market economy. Initial-teacher-education institutions have become autono-mous, centrally prescribed curricula were abandoned and changes in both the methodology and content of study have occurred. All teacher education institutions operate in both the public and non-public educa-tion sectors.

Teacher education and training standards were formulated in the Regulation of the Minister of Science and Higher Education on initial teacher-training standards (2012). This legislation regulates initial teacher education for school-education teachers, thus defining train-ing models or paths that lead to qualifications required to practise the teaching profession. The minimum qualification for teaching at (i) pre-primary level, (ii) primary level, and (iii) lower-secondary level is a ter-tiary education degree at Bachelor level, which lasts three years. For those intending to work at upper-secondary level, the final qualification is a Master's degree. At present, teachers who hold a higher-education diploma (a Bachelor's or Master's degree) represent 98% of all teachers working in the school-education sector. Master's degree studies seem to be the most popular route for the training of teachers in school educa-tion of all levels. In Poland, the high quality of preschool education is guaranteed by the very well-prepared teaching staff at nursery schools. Mostly they are university graduates holding a Master's degree (84.0% of teaching staff), and less often holding a Bachelor's degree (11.8%) (Smoczynska, 2014, 84).

In 2000, a four-stage teacher career-progression structure was imple-mented in Poland. It distinguishes the following:

- trainee teacher (nauczyciel stażysta)
- contract teacher (nauczyciel kontraktowy)
- appointed teacher (nauczyciel mianowany)
- chartered teacher (nauczyciel dyplomowany).

Chartered teachers who have outstanding professional achievements may be awarded the honorary title of education professor.

In Poland, in the 2013/14 school year among the whole group of teachers, 49% were chartered teachers, 27% appointed teachers, 16.4% contract teachers and 7.6% trainee teachers (see Table 4.2).

Table 4.2 School teachers by professional grade, 2013/2014

	Trainee teachers	Contract teachers	Appointed teachers	Chartered teachers	Total
Number of teachers	50 211	108 773	178 738	324 697	662 420
Full-time teachers	22 177	75 919	140 609	292 960	531 665
Part-time teachers	28 035	32 854	38 129	31 737	130 755

Source: A. Smoczynska (ed.), *System of Education in Poland*, 92

In order to be promoted to a higher grade, a teacher should:

• hold the required qualifications

• complete a 'probation period' (the period preceding an application for promotion) and receive a positive assessment of their professional achievements during this period (the teacher follows an individual professional-development plan during the probation period), and

• have their application for promotion approved by a so-called qualifying board or, in the case of a contract teacher, pass an examination before an examination board.

In Poland, since 2009 there has been a decline in graduates in the field of education (see Figure 4.2), and between 2009 and 2013 the population of students of initial teacher education generally decreased by 37.4% – including 26.8% in state institutions of teacher education HEIs. However, there are no measures in place to monitor teacher supply. Effective observation of such factors could therefore be an important first step for Poland, as for other countries, towards preventing possible shortfalls or surpluses in the number of teachers.

Figure 4.2 The general number of students of preservice TE in total and the number of students of preservice education in public HEIs in Poland, 2004–2013

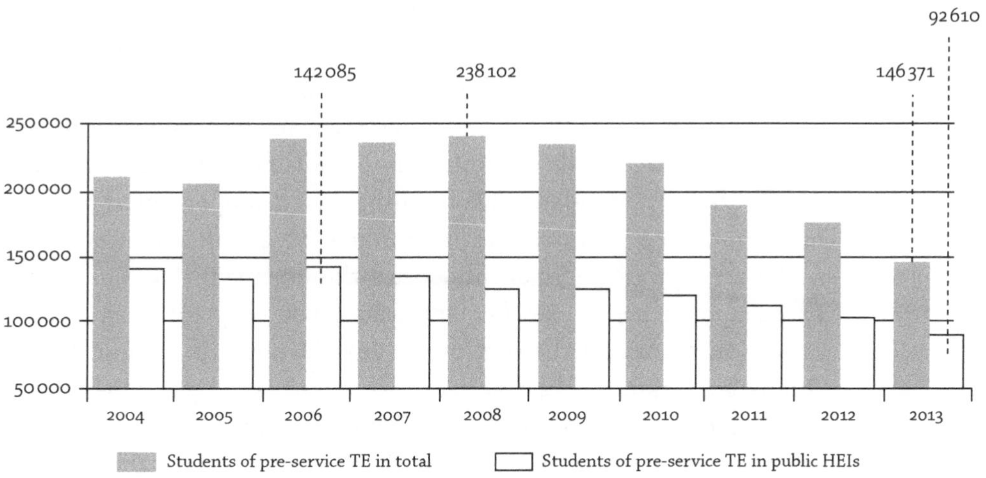

Source: Based on data published by GUS (Central Statistical Office) under the theme 'Szkoły wyższe i ich finanse' [Higher Education Institutions and Their Finances]. The data are published at www.stat.gov.pl*

* Data collected on 30 November for each year in the period 2004–2013

Initial teacher education

Initial teacher education is provided within two sectors of the education system: the higher-education sector and the school-education sector (until 2015). The degree programmes, including first-, second- and long-cycle programmes, are offered within university-type HEIs, namely in universities, technical universities, polytechnics and academies. Non-degree postgraduate programmes are offered in non-university HEIs (without rights to confer the academic degree of doctor). In the school-education sector, college programmes are offered (although are now being phased out), including teacher-training colleges and foreign-language teacher-training colleges.

Admission to initial teacher education is governed by the general entrance requirements for entry to tertiary education rather than by specific selection criteria for teacher education. The main prerequisite is to hold the final upper-secondary examination certificate. For access to Master's programmes, the performance at Bachelor level is taken into account. Alternative pathways to a teaching qualification are rare in Poland and are only available for future foreign-language teachers. They were introduced because of the shortage of qualified foreign-language teachers and the urgent need for their recruitment. In order to become a language teacher in this way, it is necessary to obtain a certificate confirming language skills at 'proficient' or 'advanced' levels as well as a certificate in foreign-language teaching awarded upon the completion of a non-degree, postgraduate programme or a qualification course.

Reflecting international influences, the emergence of competence-based approaches to teacher education, not only to initial teacher education but across the continuum, may be noted in Poland. Teacher competence frameworks have been introduced recently and they specify what candidates for teachers should know, understand and be able to do in the form of 'learning outcomes'. They contain a description of the skills and competencies a teacher should have.

Initial teacher education is organised according to two models, i.e. a concurrent model and a consecutive one. The *concurrent* model of initial teacher education dominates in Poland. Teachers for ISCED 0 and Grades 1–3 of ISCED 1 are trained exclusively according to the concurrent model.

The minimum requirement for professional training for future pre-primary teachers (ISCED 0), primary teachers (ISCED 1) and lower-secondary teachers (ISCED 2) amounts to 13.8% of the whole programme (European Commission/EACEA/Eurydice, 2013, 26). The part of professional training within initial teacher education for lower-secondary teachers amounts to less than 10% of the whole programme (around 8.3%). This proportion of professional training for upper-secondary teachers in Poland is quite low compared with the average amount of around 20% in the majority of EU countries. Only in Belgium (Flemish community) can we find the same very limited time being spent on professional training during initial teacher education. The amount of professional training provided for secondary teachers is more closely linked to the level prospective teachers are intending to teach at (lower or upper secondary) than to the level of the programme and final qualification (Bachelor's or Master's).

In Poland – as in other countries in Europe – practical training in a real working environment is a compulsory part of professional training in initial-teacher-education programmes. Such placements in schools are unremunerated and typically last no more than a few weeks. The minimum length of in-school placement during the initial education of pre-primary, primary and general (lower and upper) secondary teachers is below 200 hours, as in countries such as Belgium (French community for ISCED 3), Bulgaria, the Czech Republic (except for ISCED 0), Germany, Cyprus (for ISCED 2 and 3), Romania, Slovakia, Croatia and Turkey (ibid., 29). Practical training is organised at different points in the programme, but is normally supervised by a mentor (usually a teacher in the school), with periodic assessment by educators at the initial-teacher-education institution.

Even though in Poland there are no central guidelines for providers of initial-teacher-education programmes relating to training in educational research, in fact the knowledge and practice of educational research for prospective teachers is included in initial-teacher-education programmes and recognised as an important aspect of teacher preparation, which should help teachers incorporate classroom and academic research results into their teaching (European Commission, 2007).

External quality assurance of initial teacher education for pre-primary, primary and general (lower and upper) secondary education (ISCED 0, 1, 2 and 3) is carried out by the Polish Accreditation Committee (Polska Komisja Akredydacyjna, PKA) in order to enhance the quality of teacher education. Evaluations conducted by the PKA are obligatory. External review aims to achieve an independent judgement concerning the quality of education provided within a particular setting. Such evaluations may affect teacher education programmes in various ways, for example, by giving rise to plans for improvement, or impacting on funding.

The qualification profile of teacher educators

In Poland, as in other EU countries, teacher educators are a highly heterogeneous group. This is linked to the fact that the organisation of teacher education is diversified. Initial teacher education is provided in several different types of HEIs (for example, at universities, polytechnics, pedagogical academies, physical education academies, agricultural academies, professional institutions of higher education and colleges) and comprises several different stages involving various bodies or individuals. Due to the variety of continuing-professional-development providers, there is also heterogeneity among teacher educators in this area. According to the different teacher education institutions, we can identify teacher educators who are:

- Academic teachers (faculty members in such HEIs as, for example, universities and pedagogical academies; academies of physical education; technical universities; academies of fine arts and academies of music; teacher-training colleges; foreign-language teacher-training colleges) for student teachers, who are responsible for teacher preparation and provide course work and conduct research as professional studies, some of whom are student teachers' supervisors.

- School teachers who empower and support student teachers in their practices of classroom teaching and other aspects of their professional work. They provide instruction or supervision of clinical experiences of prospective teachers. They are student teachers' advisers.

- Staff from different agencies who design, implement and evaluate professional studies for teachers and provide in-service teacher training (e.g. staff from regional centres of teachers' professional development).

In terms of academic qualification requirements, teacher educators in HEIs must have at least an advanced degree (Master's or doctorate) in the areas they teach (Law on Higher Education of 27 July 2005). Teacher educators are not necessarily required to have practical teaching experience or to hold schoolteaching qualifications. However, according to the Higher Education Act of 27 July 2005, all teacher educators who are academic teachers are obliged to upgrade their professional qualifications. This means that they have to take care of their professional development and can expect support from experienced academic teachers holding the academic title of professor or an academic degree of *doktor habilitowany* (habilitated doctor) as these teachers are obliged to participate in development and training of research staff.

Teaching in teacher education is seen as a complex task, involving a wide range of pedagogical knowledge, skills and understanding. Teacher educators' work on preservice courses generally includes: teaching students in HEIs, supervising students on school placements, engaging in research, service to the school sector and service to HEIs. In addition to teacher educators' teaching and service roles, teacher educators, especially those working at universities, are required to be active in their research pursuits and publish their work in accepted academic formats.

So, in many ways, teacher educators' work is similar to that of other academic staff in that they teach and research, including publishing papers and books and presenting papers at conferences. As the above account shows, in Poland the understanding teacher educators' work is closer to the conventional academic model of teaching, research and service to the university. Most Polish teacher educators' centre their work on their teaching and researching roles.

The general expectations are that most teacher educators will facilitate the learning of student teachers through reflective practice as a model of the good practitioner. Discourses of reflective practice are central to the ways in which teacher education and working in schools are understood.

Induction programme

A new national induction scheme was introduced in 2000, designed to support newly qualified teachers during their first three years of teaching. The scheme is extensive and school-based. Its introduction marks a shift in awareness of the continuing need of the newly qualified teacher for professional development and support, and a greater emphasis on the professional responsibility of established teachers towards newcomers to the profession.

Since 2000, each newly qualified teacher in Poland is employed as a trainee teacher for the first nine months, and is supervised and mentored during this time by a mentor, an experienced teacher employed in the school at Appointed or Chartered Teacher level. A mentor is appointed, providing personal, social and professional individualised support to beginning teachers to help them overcome the difficulties they may experience as newcomers to the profession, and thus help reduce the likelihood that they will leave the profession early. Support measures include regular discussions of progress and problems, assistance with the planning and assessment of lessons, participation in other teachers' class activities and/or classroom observations, special compulsory training and visits to other schools/resource centres. The next phase (contract teacher, lasting two years and nine months) is again supervised and supported. This means that newly qualified teachers receive support throughout the first three and a half years of teaching.

The induction phase is seen as a support programme for beginning teachers. During the induction, newly qualified teachers carry out all the tasks incumbent on experienced teachers, and are remunerated for their work. The induction has important formative and supportive components for beginning teachers as they receive additional training, personalised help and advice on school premises. The function of this induction process is to help beginning teachers construct their professional identity and develop professional practices suited to the realities of school and integrated into their conceptions of good teaching. The induction period encourages and motivates beginning teachers to be active agents instead of passively applying ideas or practices suggested by other people. Within schools, the most important elements of this induction procedure include peer coaching, quality evaluation, appraisal, portfolio evaluation and collaboration on practical tasks.

Continuing professional development

Continuing professional development refers to formal and non-formal training activities that may, for example, include subject-based and pedagogical training. Staff training is provided by HEIs within postgraduate studies and teacher-training colleges that offer relevant courses, but the main providers of this type of in-service training are in-service teacher-training establishments. HEIs provide complementary education and staff development courses independently within their autonomy. The National In-Service Teacher Training Centre, called the Centre of Education Development (*Ośrodek Rozwoju Edukacji*), functioning within the school-education sector, supports reforms in teacher professional development and provides special conferences, meetings and staff-development courses for the whole country, often together with foreign institutions or within the framework of international educational programmes. The Regional Centres of Teaching Methodology, run by respective regional self-government authorities, provide staff-development courses and, though on a limited scale, complementary educational courses within specialisations that are in short supply in a given region.

In-service training is provided along two paths: as complementary education that enables teachers to obtain higher or additional qualifications, and as staff development that enables teachers to update or upgrade their skills. Complementary education covers the courses of study that lead to a higher level of education or additional qualifications, and staff development covers the forms of refreshment that enrich the working techniques of teachers within the qualifications they already have. The financing of complementary education and staff development is guaranteed in the Teachers' Charter, which provides that the state budget allocates for this purpose an amount equal to 2.5% of the planned expenditure on teachers' salaries. These amounts can be increased through additional allocations by local authorities, donations and sponsoring.

Continuing professional development (CPD) has gained considerable importance over the years in Poland. Although teachers' engagement in CPD is not stated in terms of a professional duty, CPD in Poland, as in Denmark, Ireland, Greece, France, the Netherlands, Sweden, Iceland and Norway, is clearly linked to career progression (see European Commission/EACEA/Eurydice, 2013, 58). Therefore, even if CPD is not explicitly required for promotion, it remains an important advantage. Participation in CPD activities is viewed positively in teacher evaluation.

QUALITY TEACHER EDUCATION AND A CONTINUUM OF TEACHER CAREER-LONG PROFESSIONAL LEARNING

The issue of improving the quality of teachers' education and the quality of teaching and learning is a priority and one of the main goals of the process of reforming educational systems not only in European countries. In many countries across the globe, attention is devoted to the quality of teachers' work and the quality of their education, and is reflected in research priorities concerning teaching, teaching as a profession, learning, teachers' professional development and school leadership. Regarding the contemporary challenges of transforming and improving educational outcomes that teachers and school leaders have to face up to, all teachers, not just some, have to be equipped for effective learning in the twenty-first century. This requires a rethinking of many aspects, including, among others:

- developing teaching as a profession
- improving the societal view of teaching as a profession
- recruiting top candidates into the profession
- retaining and recognising effective teachers, and
- the path for growth and supporting teachers in continuing professional development. (OECD, 2011)

There is growing recognition that the complex, diverse and changing contexts in which teachers work means they need to revise, add to and enhance their knowledge and skills continually throughout their careers and engage in different forms of professional development according to their own and their pupils' needs. However, for many teachers, their development paths remain disjointed, with no sense of teacher education as a progressive journey of professional learning. Realising the vision of a continuum of teacher career-long professional learning that meets teachers' individual learning needs and is balanced with school, local, national and international needs means reconceptualising both teacher education and the role of teacher educator.

The complexity of teachers' diverse professional-learning needs requires collaborative approaches to teacher education that provide access to blended professional learning; different knowledge, skills and expertise in practice and research; and a rich mix of teacher educators. This calls for stronger partnerships that help connect teachers with their peers in their own school and in other schools and enable greater interaction and interdependence between different teacher education providers and stakeholders. The Council of the European Union in its conclusions of 20 May 2014 on effective teacher education (2014/C 183/05) recognised the potential of enhanced cooperation, partnership and networking with a broad range of stakeholders. The council's conclusions acknowledged that teacher education programmes 'should draw on teachers' own experience and seek to foster cross-disciplinary and collaborative approaches, so that education institutions and teachers regard it as part of their task to work in cooperation with relevant stakeholders such as colleagues, parents and employers'. The development of effective and sustainable collaborative approaches to teacher education requires shifts in systems, cultures and practice and ongoing professional development for teachers and teacher educators.

A portrayal of Polish education in the context of the country's educational reality and the government's proposed changes to higher education indicates that the notion of *quality* is one of the key ideas for debating teachers' education in Poland (Michalak, 2010). The debate about what constitutes quality teacher education in Poland is a live issue, and new expectations for teacher education have emerged out of national exigencies, yet are influenced by shared European policies. These expectations have led to attempts to create new policies for accelerating the quality of teacher education. Special attention is paid to ensuring high-quality initial teacher education, the process of induction and continuing teacher professional development. Teachers not only have a central role to play in improving educational outcomes, but are also at the centre of the improvement efforts themselves. In the education system in Poland, it is not that top-down reforms are ordering teachers to change, but that teachers are embracing and leading reform, taking responsibility as professionals (OECD, 2011).

The comparative study on teacher education between Poland and Ireland, which centred on the opportunities to learn to teach (Conway, Murphy, Rath & Hall, 2009) during initial teacher education, with a focus on the school–university relationship and parameters of engagement with pedagogy in teaching practice schools, showed that the concept of integrated professional-learning cultures in the professional preparation of teachers is central to understanding the review and reforms of teacher education in Poland (Conway, Murphy & Madalińska-Michalak, 2012). In the study, special attention was paid to the teacher education at system and school levels and its role in creating and sustaining integrated professional-learning cultures to support teacher education in the initial and induction phases of the continuum. Regarding an integrated professional culture, learning to teach is seen as a task for all in the school. All teachers are encouraged to improve teaching and learning, to collaborate and share practice, and to continue to grow in their profession. The findings showed that opportunities to learn are influenced by the values held in this area by the chief stakeholders: the regulatory bodies for teacher education that lay down the minimum requirements in terms of pedagogical preparation and school-based experience, the university-based teacher educators, the cooperating schools, their principals and teachers and, not least, the student teachers themselves. One of the core conditions for learning to teach might be an assisted performance (Tharp & Gallimore, 1988; Conway & Artiles, 2005). It situates the person learning to teach in a sea of relationships and cultural symbols that shape, and are shaped by, the learner. From this perspective, while learning to teach, student teachers draw not only on the knowledge, beliefs and skills they have acquired, but also on the cultural and historical legacy of previous generations of teachers – that is, the knowledge embedded in their respective society's cultural tools and signs. Assisted performance can come in many guises in teacher education. It can include co-planning and/or co-teaching with a mentor teacher or student-teacher peer, and may also include various forms of observation, feedback and support that can be broadly seen as forms of mentoring. The study findings also showed that the quality of learning for prospective and beginning teachers during the practicum is intrinsically connected to the type of learning culture that prevails in the school, as well as the partnership arrangements existing between the placement school and the university or teacher-training college. Schools that have an integrated professional culture offer the optimum conditions for learning to teach, but there can be considerable variation in the experience of students (Moore-Johnson, 2004; Conway et al., 2011; Hobson et al., 2009) and this reflects the professional-learning culture of the individual schools as well as differences at the institution and system level.

Focusing attention on the process of building up the culture directed at achieving the desirable quality of teachers' education shows that any cultural change requires engagement and ownership by all levels of staff within teacher education institutions. When the student perspective is made central to the definition of quality, it makes sense to use frontline staff – teacher educators – to be the architects of a quality culture. Teacher educators have the most frequent contact with students. They engage on a personal level and obtain information that cannot be gained from impersonal surveys about the quality. They have intimate knowledge of what is required to meet and exceed students' expectations. Improving quality should be perceived as a way of teaching prospective teachers and teachers.

It is interesting that so little space in educational literature and documents concerning educational policy (Snoek & Žogla, 2009; Snoek, Swennen & van der Klink, 2010) is devoted to conditions conducive to becoming a university teacher/teacher educator. This situation seems disturbing, especially in relation to the role ascribed to academic teachers in shaping desirable practices in the higher-education area that translate themselves into creating high-quality education in lower-level schooling. In view of the inadequate number of research projects on inclusion in the teacher-educator profession and on their constant professional development, there is an urgent need to pay adequate attention to the profession of teacher educator and teacher educators themselves. Therefore, it is necessary to undertake research on the quality of teachers' education and the professional development of teacher educators. Given the challenges that higher education is facing nowadays, questions arise about how much teacher educators are engaged in their own professional development and in what way their process of becoming teacher educators is shaped. What is speeding up and what is slowing down the course of this process? How do teacher educators cope with everyday university life, which forces them to constantly strike a balance between the traditional academic *sacred* and the contemporary *profane*, posing a series of economic challenges. How do they cope with the antinomy between the mass reach of education (mass, anonymous audience) and the sense of the need to notice and take into account a personal, individual entity of a student/future teacher?

CONCLUSIONS

The presented considerations on the issue of the quality of teacher education in Poland – an issue that is a key subject in the current debate on the directions of educational policy in the EU – pointed our attention to future policy, research and practice related to a highly relevant need to obtain a continuum of teacher education in Poland with a focus on teachers' career-long professional learning and teachers' support in different phases of their professional career.

The chapter presented the most important changes in teacher education and the teaching profession in Poland from 1990 onwards in the context of improving the quality of teaching and learning and, at the same time, the quality of higher education. Nowadays, as a result of different reforms, the Polish system has a framework that supports professional progression and formally recognises the skills and knowledge of expert teachers through its career-progression structure. The changes introduced in the Polish Teachers' Charter and its amendments have reinforced the role of the school and of experienced teachers in providing more incremental and graduated support for those learning to teach during ITE and induction. The induction process is directed to helping beginning teachers construct their professional identity and develop professional practices suited to the realities of school and integrated into their conceptions of good teaching. The induction period encourages and motivates beginning teachers to be active agents instead of passively applying ideas or practices suggested by other people. The career structure that has been introduced in Poland has helped to reward continuing professional development and support experienced teachers who act as mentors. One can observe many positive changes in teacher education and teachers' work in Poland. However, the process of enhancing the quality of teacher education and, in consequence, the quality of teachers, the quality of their professionalism and the students' educational achievements is – by definition – an ongoing process.

The research on teacher education and some of the documents of the current Teacher Education Policy in Europe (as mentioned in this chapter) showed that teacher education is best viewed as a continuum. The concept of integrated professional-learning cultures in the professional preparation of teachers, as was pointed out in this chapter, can serve as a central concept for understanding the review and reforms of teacher education in Poland nowadays and in the near future. It is worth stressing that an important element in the creation and sustaining of integrated learning cultures is the provision of support at the system level in different phases of teachers' professional career in terms of, for example, training for mentors, reduced classroom hours for newly qualified teachers, time allocated for professional-development opportunities, and recognition of professional development across one's career and others'.

Introducing major reforms in order to make quality education and quality teacher education is never unproblematic, and there has been considerable debate within Poland on some aspects, not least the new demands being made on higher education, teacher educators, school teachers and school principals. School cultures can differ widely, and the role of the principal is crucial in setting the tone, creating the conditions for learning at school and allocating responsibilities. It seems likely that the attitudes of principals and experienced teachers, as reflected in the learning culture of the school, will continue to have a major influence on the 'learning to teach' experience of novice teachers. Sharing the professional experience and expertise of experienced teachers with newcomers is an important part of their role and it enriches initial teacher education.

The changes proposed by the Polish government are to contribute to creating better conditions for the functioning of HEIs by improving the effectiveness of public expenditure on higher education in Poland. These changes are primarily – as assumed by educational policy-makers and the creators of these changes – pro-qualitative in nature. Thus, the financing of higher education is to be first of all connected with promoting the best organisational units within HEIs and the best students and doctoral students in such a way as to stimulate competition among them concerning the level of scientific research, methodology and study. Many of the government-proposed reforms aimed at reinforcing educational quality seem justified in view of the present reality and can lead to positive changes approved of by society.

The analysis of teachers' education in Poland contrasted with other European solutions shows that it is worthwhile to consider – in addition to the benefits brought about by changes introduced by educational authorities – a few solutions that have not been used in Poland yet.

1. Limiting the number of students/candidates for teachers in HEIs depending on the demand for teachers and a simultaneous significant increase in funds for education (introducing an independent financing line). The Ministry of Education would sign contracts with HEIs offering particular teachers' education curricula (a kind of licence for educating teachers). Universities and colleges would declare their annual recruitment limits. A non-government agency would probably be better, but these do not yet exist in Poland and their introduction would certainly require new significant legal regulation. Both of these solutions require a prospective policy of employing teachers, constant monitoring of needs, and flexible responding to the threat of a teacher deficit.

2. Selection within a higher-education institution not only at the level of entrance exams, but also in relation to a choice of teachers' education. Universities and colleges should take a student's academic achievements into account prior to the recruitment process so that only the best can have a chance to become teachers. A smaller number of students should be provided with very good preparation for work at school by expanding the educational offer with content that is currently lacking.

3. Increasing the level of qualification requirements. Following the example of most European countries, requirements should be introduced for teachers to obtain a Master's degree to be able to teach at the lower-secondary level and higher. This requirement should be gradually expanded among primary-school teachers.

Much of the education policy in Poland focuses on improving teacher quality, but most policies lack strong research support. The management of teacher quality is an important pathway through which principals affect school quality. The fact that less effective teachers are more likely to leave schools run by highly effective principals validates our measure of principal quality. In Poland, experimental programmes for ensuring teacher quality are developing. The key to the future is to validate and replicate those that prove successful and to eliminate those that do not. Doing this requires strong research and evaluation activity to match the policy experimentation.

REFERENCES

Abbott, A. (1988). *The system of professions: An essay on the division of expert labour.* Chicago/London: University of Chicago Press.

Ball, S. J. (2003). The teacher's soul and the terrors of performativity. *Journal of Education Policy*, 18(2), 215–28.

Conway, P. F. and Artiles, A. A. (2005). A socio-cultural perspective on teacher performance assessment. In F. P. Peterman, (ed.), *Designing performance assessment systems for urban teacher preparation*. Mohawk, NJ: Lawrence Erlbaum.

Conway, P. F., Murphy, R., Delargey, M., Hall, K., Kitching, K., Long, F., McKeon, J., Murphy, B., O'Brien, S. and O'Sullivan, D. (2010). *Learning to Teach Study (LETS): Developing curricular and cross-curricular competences in becoming a 'good' secondary teacher*. Department of Education and Skills-funded study, Cork: School of Education, University College Cork.

Conway, P. F., Murphy, R., and Madalińska-Michalak, J. (2012). Integrated learning cultures and learning to teach: Norms, values and the next generation of teachers in two cultures. In Boufoy-Bastick, B., (ed.), *The international handbook of cultures of professional development for teachers. Collaboration, reflection, management and policy.* Strasbourg: Analytrics.

Conway, P. F., Murphy, R., Rath, A. and Hall, K. (2009). *Learning to teach and its implications for the continuum of teacher education: A nine-country cross-national study*. Report commissioned by the Teaching Council, Ireland. Retrieved from www.teachingcouncil.ie.

Darling-Hammond, L. (1999). *Teacher quality and student achievement: A review of state policy evidence*. Seattle, WA: Center for the Study of Teaching and Policy, University of Washington.

European Commission. (2005). *Common European principles for teacher competences and qualifications*. Retrieved from http://ec.europa.eu/education/policies/2010/doc/principles_en.pdf.

European Commission. (2007). *Improving the quality of teacher education*. Retrieved from http://ec.europa.eu/education/com392_en.pdf.

European Commission/EACEA/Eurydice. (2013). *Key data on teachers and school leaders in Europe. 2013 ed. Eurydice report*. Luxembourg: Publications Office of the European Union.

European Council. (2007). Conclusions of the council and of the representatives of the governments of the member states. Meeting within the council of 15 November, 2007, on improving the quality of teacher education. *Official Journal of the European*

Union, C300, 6–9. Retrieved from http://eurlex.europa.eu/LexUriServ/LexUriServ. do?uri=OJ:C:2007:300:0006:0009:en:PDF.

Hattie, J. (2003). *Teachers make a difference. What is the research evidence?* Australian Council for Educational Research. Retrieved from www.det.nsw.edu.au/proflearn/ docs/pdf/qt_hattie.pdf.

Hobson, A. J., Malderez, A., Tracey, L., Homer, M., Ashby, P. Mitchell, N., McIntyre, J., Cooper, D., Roper, T., Chambers, G. and Tomlinson, P. D. (2009). *Becoming a teacher. Teachers' experiences of initial teacher training, induction and early professional development.* Final Report. Research Report No DCSF-RR115. University of Nottingham.

Karta Nauczyciela [Teacher's Charter], Act of 26 January 1982, *Journal of Law*, 1997, 56, item 357 with further amendments.

Michalak, J. M. (2010). Teacher education in the context of improving quality in higher education in Poland. Paper presented at TEPE 2010 conference, Tallinn. Retrieved from http://eduko.archimedes.ee/files/tepe2010_submission_29.pdf.

Moore-Johnson, S. (2004). *Finders and keepers: Helping new teachers survive and thrive in our schools.* San Francisco: Jossey-Bass.

Mullis, I. V. S., Martin, M. O., Minnich, C. A., Stanco, G. M., Arora, A., Centurino, V. A. S. and Castle, C. E. (eds) (2012). *TIMSS 2011 Encyclopedia: Education policy and curriculum in mathematics and science, volumes 1 and 2.* Chestnut Hill, MA: TIMSS & PIRLS International Study Center, Boston College.

OECD. (2001). *Knowledge and skills for life – first results from PISA 2000.* Paris: OECD.

OECD. (2005). *Teachers matter: Attracting, retaining and developing teachers.* Paris: OECD.

OECD. (2009). *What students know and can do. Student performance in reading, mathematics and science. Comparing countries' and economies' performance.* Paris: OECD. Retrieved from www.oecd.org/dataoecd/54/12/46643496.pdf.

OECD. (2010). *PISA 2009 results: What students know and can do: Student performance in reading, mathematics and science.* Paris: OECD Publishing.

OECD. (2011). *Building a high-quality teaching profession. Lessons from around the world.* Paris: OECD Publishing.

OECD. (2014). *PISA 2012 results in focus: What 15-year-olds know and what they can do with what they know.* Paris: OECD Publishing.

Rozporządzenie Ministra Edukacji Narodowej i Sportu z 3 sierpnia 2000 r. w sprawie uzyskiwania awansu zawodowego przez nauczycieli, Dz.U. 2000, Nr 70, poz. 825 [Regulation of the Ministry of National Education and Sport of 3 August 2000 concerning the acquisition of teachers' professional titles. *Journal of Law*, 70, item 825].

Rozporządzenie Ministra Nauki i Szkolnictwa Wyższego z dnia 17 stycznia 2012 roku w sprawie standardów kształcenia przygotowującego do wykonywania zawodu nauczyciela, Dz.U. 2012 poz. 131 [Regulation of the Minister of Science and Higher Education of 17 January 2012 on initial teacher-training standards, *Journal of Law*, item 131].

Smoczynska, A. (ed.) (2014). *The system of education in Poland.* Warsaw: Foundation for the Development of the Education System, Polish Eurydice Unit.

Snoek, M., Swennen, A. and van der Klink, M. (2010). The teacher educator: A neglected factor in the contemporary debate on teacher education. In B. Hudson, P. Zgaga and B. Åstrand, (eds), *Advancing quality cultures for teacher education in Europe: Tensions and opportunities*. Umeå: Umeå School of Education, Umeå University.

Snoek, M. and Žogla, I. (2009). Teacher education in Europe: Main characteristics and developments. In A. Swennen and M. van der Klink, (eds), *Becoming a teacher educator. Theory and practice for teacher educators*. Dordrecht: Springer.

Stepniowski, I. (2001). Nauczyciele w roku 2000/01 [Teachers in the school year 2000/01]. Warszawa: Wydawnictwa CODN.

Tharp, R. G. and Gallimore, R. (1988). *Rousing minds to life: Teaching, learning, and schooling in social context*. Cambridge: Cambridge University Press.

Ustawa o systemie oświaty z dnia 7 września 1991 roku z późniejszymi zmianami, Dz. U. 2004, Nr 256, poz. 2572. [Education System Act of 7 September 1991 with further amendments. *Journal of Law, 256*, item 2572].

Ustawa o szkolnictwie wyższym z dnia 12 września 1990 roku z późniejszymi zmianami, Dz. U. 1990, Nr 65, poz. 385 [Higher Education Act of 12 Sept. 1990 with further amendments, *Journal of Law, 65*, item 385].

5 Swedish teacher education and the issue of fragmentation: Conditions for the struggle over academic rigour and professional relevance

Björn Åstrand

TEACHER EDUCATION REFORM AND EDUCATIONAL FRAGMENTATION

A fragmented and atomised education system?

In May 2015, the OECD delivered a special report on the Swedish school system.[1] The PISA results of 2012 had caused Sweden to call for the OECD's assistance in understanding what had gone wrong with the Swedish education system. Andreas Schleicher, director of *Education and Skills* at the OECD, strongly emphasised during his presentation of the report that the Swedish education system was 'atomised' and 'fragmented'.[2] One recommendation for improving schooling in Sweden is to 'address the current highly-fractured state of initial teacher education'.[3] Perhaps we are witness to the advent of another teacher education reform. The question is – will that reform finally produce the desired high-quality programmes? Will it be the remedy, or yet another reform that only adds to the problem?

During the past three decades, Sweden has reformed teacher education three times. Yet still, according to international OECD experts, these programmes are perceived to be fragmented, without focus and sufficient quality. Will another round of reforms improve teacher preparation – or will it add to the maladies? Could one part of the problem be the recurrent reforms themselves as they regularly move shifting ideas on educational issues from above and down, and from the outside in? This chapter on the recent history of Swedish teacher education deals with teacher education reforms in a critical perspective. It does not deny that these programmes are and have been in need of improvements.

However, as the critique concerning the supposed inferiority is not exactly backed up by evidence from randomised and controlled tests, we cannot take these claims for granted and cannot avoid asking critical questions about the idea of traditional reform.

The point of departure here is a seemingly counterintuitive approach, discussing reforms not as cures but as a kind of illness, tentatively arguing that it might be the case that Swedish teacher education suffers from too many reforms instead of too few. Can fragmentation in teacher education be better understood in the light of the reforms as a fragmenting force rather than the opposite? To add to the picture, two other conditions for high-quality teacher education are also addressed, namely the importance of proper models of governance and the importance of strong research cultures.

Fragmentation and teacher education reforms

So, what then is fragmentation in education? Tentatively, and for the purpose of this chapter, fragmentation can be described as situations in which gaps and disconnections, on several levels, dominate the perceived picture and/or experience of the education system under consideration, and do so with a negative impact.[4] This chapter concerns Swedish teacher education from the perspective of coherence and congruence, which is understood as the opposite of fragmentation.[5] Through the years, a number of reforms have been launched that regularly included ambitions to overcome fragmentation. The more pressing the perceived need for advancement in education is, the more important it has become to reform teacher education. But can such initiatives also be part of the problem? Reflecting upon the fact that every teacher education reform redirects, restructures and reorganises key elements of the daily efforts in teacher education, it might be the case that reform heritage is part of the problem.[6]

The term *reform* comes from the Latin *re-formatio*, which literally talks about two aspects of change, making new and making better.[7] Reforms come with the idea to 'wipe the institutional slate clean and start again', but as Tyack & Cuban noted, 'that has rarely happened. Instead, reforms have tended to layer, one on top of another.'[8]

Teacher education is a mass enterprise and is as political as schooling is. School reformers, and reformers of teacher education, can be assumed to act with the best intentions. However, the assumption that outcomes of reforms are always in line with the intention has to be questioned. A working hypothesis here is that there is a relationship between teacher education reforms and the existence of fragmentation in teacher education as well as the understanding of fragmentation. This chapter takes a historical approach, outlining recent change in Swedish teacher education from the perspective of fragmentation. The study focuses on three aspects of importance: reforms, governance and research.

Swedish teacher education – a varied landscape

Studies suggest that powerful teacher education programmes share features such as:

- a vision of good teaching
- well-defined standards
- a core curriculum taught in the context of practice
- extended clinical experience
- teaching methods that apply learning to real problems of practice
- strategies that challenge students' prior beliefs and make them insightful regarding their own learning
- shared beliefs among school- and university-based faculties.[9]

These aspects of excellent teacher education programmes reinforce the belief that reduced or eliminated fragmentation is a key issue of high-quality programmes.

The landscape of teacher education in Sweden is pretty diverse. However, programme structures are determined nationally, as are the overarching content and learning outcomes. This national framework is locally crafted into particular programme designs responding to, for example, the national regulation of content in the education core, the number of weeks of clinical experience and the overarching objectives and degree requirements.

The local execution of these programmes is offered at more than 25 higher-education institutions (HEIs) with locally designed organisation and overarching ideas and notions on teacher education. Hence, the providers of teacher education in Sweden differ in their organisation, character and size. Today's teacher education organisations are, to a smaller extent, self-standing institutions with low levels of integration into other faculties or schools. More common is deep integration into general HEIs, with an umbrella organisation running teacher programmes via faculty organisations.[10] Institutions typically have a general profile and a broad provision of programmes but some are specialised in, for example, physical education or music. The three largest institutions admit over 800 students annually while the smallest enrol cohorts of fewer than 50 students. Some providers are relatively recently inaugurated; others have historical roots dating back to late medieval times. This diversity may also be recognised in a perspective of fragmentation.

Overarching aspects of the importance of understanding teacher education in Sweden

The development of teacher education displays both change and continuity, and the diversity entailed in a school system will also colour the design and execution of teacher education. Reform is the focus of this chapter on the fragmentation of, and in, Swedish teacher education, but we will start by recalling some other aspects of the issue.

To understand the gaps and disconnections, namely the fragmentation in teacher education, we must bear in mind that the close relationship between the nation state and schooling has shifted in form but not in distance and importance. Due to the radical decentralisation of schooling in Sweden since the 1990s, teacher education has become an even more important tool for the centralised steering of schooling – but simultaneously in a more indirect and less visible way.[11] This is important within the perspective of fragmentation as it indicates that pedagogical insights, educational purposes and ambitions might not always be the first priority of national policy on teacher education.

A second essential aspect is the structure of the school system and the profound dual and parallel character of the older Swedish school system: 'From the beginning there was not any connection between the national grammar school and the municipality based common schools.'[12] These detached traditions have historically influenced teacher education separately and been open for politics and larger political puzzles. In addition, there are some concerns that the professional preparation of teachers does not fully seem capable of forming teacher recruits along with set priorities. Unfortunately, initiatives to provide schools with suitable workforce have usually historically come after school reforms or, at best, at the same time.[13]

If educational cultures are important for the existence and understanding of fragmentation in education, then school structures and the gaps between levels of education qualify as well. It might be so obvious that it is not necessary to mention but the existence of levels easily causes gaps (which become echoed in teacher education), and the Swedish school system has historically strong traditions of relative separate school levels.[14] Strong distinctions between levels in the school system create similar gaps and disconnections in the teacher education programme.[15]

Finally, gender division in its shifting forms must also be kept in mind while reflecting upon fragmentation in teacher education. Nation-building, persistent school structures and gender division may be understood as overarching aspects of the importance of fragmentation in teacher education. These phenomena are shaped by forces other than education policy and teacher education and, due to that, they are difficult to deal with in teacher education, and might directly or indirectly cause fragmentation. The focus of this chapter is primarily on other aspects, those more internal to the educational sphere. However, these three aspects need to be kept in mind.

This study is mainly anchored in an analysis of policy documents but also draws on other empirical records.[16] Also to be mentioned is my personal involvement in teacher education. In the early 1990s, I started teaching history to teacher students at Umeå University. At the time, a new-teacher education programme for the comprehensive school had just been implemented and I taught courses in this programme. At the end of the decade, when I was involved in the process of reforming teacher education, and later, as director of studies in my department, I had to figure out how our programmes should be changed. In 2007, then as dean, I took part in, as a governmental expert in the process, yet another reform, which was carried out in 2011. All of these reforms were national but I took part in the local launch in three roles: as a teacher educator, as a director of studies and as dean. And the most crucial part was not to produce syllabuses and so on. It was to merge the new and the old, and to retain things that had worked well and get rid of the ballast – in the midst of a tussle between a range of priorities, persons, prestige and internal competition, typically the more malign features of the academic context.

TEACHER EDUCATION REFORMS IN SWEDEN – AN OVERVIEW

Teacher education is a particularly interesting field for studies of educational change. Education is an inherently political activity and 'questions about the nature and purpose of education are ultimately questions about what it is to be, and about how we understand what it is to be, human'.[17] So, it is a field of many constituencies and they all deserve a legitimate say in teacher education issues. A grand challenge for society is to agree upon priorities on what desirable futures might look like – and to bring these ideas into coherent teaching and learning – in a meaningful way.[18] Consequently, education (including teacher education) is also a field of tensions, visible in internally produced policy as well as in nationally produced policy handed down to institutions.

Overarching developments in the education system are essential to understanding the trajectory of teacher education, and the following are of particular importance:

- the mid-twentieth-century introduction of a democratic comprehensive school that profoundly rested on an idea of a merger between the two educational cultures related to the common school and the grammar school

- the profound decentralisation and deregulation of schooling since the 1980s increased the importance of teacher education as a governmental means for steering Swedish schools,[19] and

- the late twentieth-century expansion of higher education and the allocation of teacher education programmes to an increased number of institutions.[20]

Historical phases in Swedish teacher education

Teacher education is a centrally regulated business in its main features. The national level has exercised a firm grip on how teachers have been educated, at least since the formalisation of schooling.[21] The most recent national teacher education reforms of 1988, 2001 and 2011 are in focus in this study.[22] But also they had a pre-history and Swedish teacher education reforms can be described in two periods, before and after 1945. The change in the role, scope and size of education in society has impacted on teacher education. With the common school reform of the 1840s also came the growing importance of the grammar school for the elite. Consequently, a seminar-based teacher education for teaching in the common school was established and the academic tradition became reinforced as preparation for teaching in what is nowadays secondary schooling.

A key feature of the late nineteenth- and twentieth-century development of teacher education is the emergence of a national regulated system for teacher preparation.[23] When the common school was introduced, no proper teacher preparation was launched in advance. As similar schools existed widely prior to its mandatory implementation, the teacher training at hand was private.[24] The latter part of the nineteenth-century and early twentieth-century development was a period of institutional development of teacher education.[25] Teacher seminars become organised and impressive buildings were erected. Preparation for teaching mainly involved two types, either organised around a school in which the prospective teacher was learning the job more or less in an in-service model, or a more institutional-like model in which the prospective teacher was engaged in taking classes in preparation for teaching.[26]

During this period, preparations for teaching in secondary school also became more formalised. For a teaching position in the mid-nineteenth century, up to seven years of academic studies were required.[27] However, the recognised need for an introduction to the 'teaching' part of the teaching profession (on top of the 'knowing part') resulted in the 1870s in a probationary year that was later followed by classes and coursework. The probationary year disappeared in the 1960s with the advent of the higher teacher seminars. The upgrade of teacher education at the time was, however, accompanied by reduced academic requirements.[28] The secondary-school tradition of employing teachers with PhDs was more or less terminated in the post-war period.[29]

Overall, Sweden has revised these programmes (and their preconditions) in a number of reforms since late 1960s, including two general higher-education reforms with a great impact on teacher education.[30] (Table 5.1) As mentioned, in the late 1950s the Higher Teacher Education Seminars were established on the tertiary level but in general outside the regular higher-education system. This was the first significant attempt to academically upgrade the education of teachers for the common school but also for other categories.[31] A general higher-education reform at the end of the 1970s merged key vocational, post-secondary education such as nursery, social work and teacher education into higher education. From a teacher education perspective, this can be understood as a second attempt to provide an academic upgrade. The reform had a diverse impact on programmes as students in programmes for secondary school teaching already had approximately ¾ of their studies located in higher education. It has to be noted that this reform also introduced the overall idea of studies organised into programmes; hence, this was the advent of more comprehensive programmes for teaching in secondary education.[32]

In addition to these upgrading reforms, since late 1980s Swedish teacher education has gone through three reforms directly targeting the content and form of teacher education programmes, and one general higher education reform impacting teacher education. In the late 1980s came a teacher education reform designed for the preparation of professionals for the comprehensive school (a reform launched in the 1950s and 1960s). That model was not a decade old before governmental directives established (1997) an inquiry into a reformed model. According to that model, a new programme was launched in 2001. Six years later, in 2007, directives for yet another reform were established and new programmes were again launched in 2011 – while, in between, Swedish teacher education, together with the rest of higher education, had been revised due to the Bologna protocols.

Table 5.1 Overview of reforms of teacher education or affecting teacher education

Year	General HE reform	Particular TE reform	Content (name)
1956/ 1968		X	Establishment of higher teacher seminars from 1956 and termination of the common schools' seminars in 1968
1977	X		Academisation of all professional preparation, including the merger of all teacher education institutions into higher education (H77)
1988*		X	Launch of new national programmes for teacher preparation for the comprehensive school (Grades 1–9)
2001*		X	Launch of new national programmes for teacher education for all schooling up to grade 12 (including preschool) (LUK)
2007	X		Implementation of Bologna structure in HE (BP)
2011*		X	Launch of new national programmes for all school forms

*These three reforms are analysed as the key reforms below.[33]

If the history of Swedish teacher education is to be understood in phases before and after the Second World War, then the latter period is characterised by frequent and in-depth redesigns.[34] And currently, a new design for programmes for lower-secondary teaching is proposed and in 2015 the OECD proposed major changes of the teacher education system.[35] The frequency of teacher education reforms is daunting, yet there are also other reforms, like the recently introduced teacher certification system and large-scale pilots on teacher-training schools, that affect teacher education.[36]

Three reforms and three decades of struggle for cohesion and congruence

As indicated above, a working hypothesis is that reforms themselves may also promote fragmentation. They might, for example, create 'fuzz' in organisations, disrupt structures and due to layering, cause notional vagueness on key terms and uncertainties on teaching approaches. In the following, we will look into three aspects of teacher education affected by the three reforms of 1988, 2001 and 2011.

Reformed number of degrees and programmes – coming full circle

In 2011, a new national structure for teacher education was launched in Sweden. In an international comparative perspective, the model might seem ordinary but its foundational structure represented a significant break away from the two previous reforms (1988 and 2001) (Table 5.2) The programme division of 2011 is fourfold, in total providing seven specialisations directly corresponding to the structure of the school system.[37]

In Swedish educational history this reform must be perceived as quite a sharp historical turn, if not a U-turn. A more unified teacher education model came onto the agenda together with ideas of a unified and comprehensive school. However, teacher education for this school model continued to be highly diverse. A teacher education reform for the comprehensive school (introduced during the 1960s) was launched as late as 1988. Prior to that, at least seven programmes and programme versions for the teaching of classes were at hand.[38] The number of programmes and degrees was reduced by the reform to two, intentionally overlapping for educational purposes.[39] For a full picture of teachers' preparation for the public school system one has to take into account the separate programmes for professionals in preschools, leisure-time centres, upper secondary school, vocational training and for music, arts and physical education.

If the reform in the late 1980s took a first grip on the split of teacher education for the comprehensive school, the second, the reform of 2001, took a firm grip on the whole system and reduced eight programmes and degrees to one teacher degree. The reform did not implement one identical education for all teachers but one degree that was awarded with specialisations due to students' voluntary and sequential choices of studies.

Table 5.2 Changed number of degrees/programmes 1988–2011

Years of reform	Reform encompassed	Prior number of degrees/programmes	Reformed number of degrees/programmes
1988	Grades 1–9	Seven	Two*
2001	All	Eight	One
2011	All	One	Four

*This reform did not affect all of teacher education, for example not preparation for teaching at the upper-secondary level.

On a structural level, in the 1980s Swedish teacher education started a process of reducing the number of gaps and breaks in between different teacher programmes and specialisations.[40] Given this trajectory, the reform of 2011 can be viewed as a return to an older structure. The shift signalled more than a shift in how teacher preparation technically relates to the school structure. The process during preceding periods was part of the ongoing professionalisation and formation of teaching as a profession, why it became important to focus on teaching as a single profession with specialisations.

The new directions initiated and implemented in 2011, under a liberal-conservative government, is perceived by some as a sobering turn, by others as a conservative victory entailing progressive development and a model that finds the future for teacher education in a return to older notions of teacher education. The direction teacher education took in 2001 was applauded by some and feared by others, as was the model of 1988. Whatever reform and interpretation, one can assume that structural changes like these required a great deal of work to ensure the successful implementation of each novel structure.

For each of these centrally developed and established models, local institutions had to develop new curricula and syllabuses, new internal models of collaboration together with assuring that all engaged teachers in each institution understood how these new structures were intended, how the content taught in one class draws upon others while creating stepping stones for the next and so on. And, on top of that, they had to inform and educate collaborating schools and their teachers so they could fulfil their crucial part as well. What we are witnessing is a dual challenge: it is frequent and it is significant. Now we leave this aspect of structure and focus on how content is organised and understood.

Teacher education content and the conceptualisation of teacher education

Reforms do not occur in a vacuum, which is why a short note on the development prior to 1988 is required.

Content and purpose in the post-war years

How content is organised in teacher education relates to ideas on the purpose of teacher education. In this section, we expand the historical perspective for the purpose of describing underlying purposes and conceptualisations. The post-war idea was clear: 'The emphasis [in teacher education programmes] has of course to continue to be focused on the key task for teachers: the art of teaching'.[41] However, the post-war years also came with strong democratic ambitions that coloured education: 'The task for the democratic school is to develop free individuals, for which collaboration is a need and a joy'.[42] Hence, the focus was on providing prospective teachers with opportunities to become 'familiar with different teaching methods', to gain 'personal experience' to be able to 'develop [teaching] methods that suit him best'.[43]

The very key idea of the comprehensive school reform of the 1950s and 1960s, the push for equity in terms of outcome and hence individualised and compensatory teaching, required a particular kind of teacher education.[44] The purpose of teacher education programmes became to help teacher students promote their students' personal development, their capacity for collaboration and respect for human dignity and their capabilities to collaborate and contribute to the development of schooling.[45]

Teacher education was perceived to essentially rest upon a kind of *general studies* (studies in subjects, not predominantly in education, but common to all teachers and partly related to the German tradition of Bildung), in-depth *studies in subjects* (to a level necessary for the development of a critical and scientific mindset), studies of educational subjects (the field is described as wider than the academic discipline of education, also containing studies in psychology and teaching methods/didactics) together with the practical experiences during the internship.[46]

On a more technical level, teacher education was understood as constituted by studies in subjects, education, methods and the clinical experience.[47] A key point had to do with the integration of these four constitutive elements (which we discuss here from the perspective of fragmentation); '*What* is it that shall be integrated and *how* shall that be done?'[48] The distinction applied brought together educational studies, studies of teaching methods and students' internship as the 'practical' and 'applied' part of teachers' education, while studies in academic subjects or disciplines were perceived as the 'theory'.[49]

The struggle of how to combine and integrate these areas of studies became more articulated in this period. Here it was stated that it was 'self evident' that a 'profound integration' could be counterproductive as students first need to have acquired 'significant insights' in their subject before it becomes useful to train how to teach.[50] An integration that was too extensive (as a way of increasing the professional relevance) could also risk students becoming superficial in their approach to knowledge. Too little integration, on the other hand, was understood to make students foreign to their forthcoming professional tasks, explaining why a balance was sought. The tradition from the common school seminars and the academic tradition were understood as each other's opposites in this respect, one with too much integration, the other overly separating. The question at stake, it was argued, was not about how the structure connects; rather, it was perceived to be the existence of inner connections that have the potential to create 'a meaningful relation to professional practice', an issue of no less importance today.[51]

Another issue addressed at the time was the problem of internal coherence and congruence within classes and the regular mismatch or misalignment in teacher education between university disciplines and school subjects.[52] For the fragmentation issue the insufficient congruence is just as important as the previously mentioned problem of integration. However, here it is important to note how these problems were identified as consequences of the chosen design of the teacher education programme.

To sum up, the reform ideas of the 1960s display a duality that held future implications. On one hand, it represents a continuation of the traditional teacher education models, albeit with increased scientific ambitions.[53] On the other hand, it clearly represents a change in the perspective of a more nuanced and emphasised problem analysis and a more in-depth description of desirable content and how the programme should impact students. Conceptually, it brought forward integration and congruence as key aspects of teacher education. When it comes to the purpose of teacher education, a widened idea surfaced, pointing towards the societal purpose of education.

The reform of 1988:
A teacher education for fulfilling the comprehensive school

The teacher education reform of 1988 emphasised that it was necessary to view the comprehensive school 'as a whole' and not as earlier, in three stages, each consisting of three years of study, which was the Swedish tradition.[54] The division into stages or levels was seen as an 'obstacle in the role of the comprehensive school as a unity' and that it would be beneficial if 'the fragmented work organisation that students nowadays encounter could be diminished'.[55] The gap between Grades 6 and 7 was perceived as a main problem and particularly harmful as it occurred in 'a sensitive stage in students' development'.[56] Hence, teacher education had to bridge the gap.

Ideally, according to the reform, students should have the same teachers for all grades, but such a model was not perceived as feasible mainly because the appropriate preparation in all school subjects would be inappropriately extensive.[57] A reform for teacher education that deliberately draws upon 'the school system and its structure' had inevitably to challenge the academic subject-based teacher education system and its culture (as the existing teacher education for Grades 7–9, lower secondary, was one and the same as for Grades 10–12, upper secondary).[58] The traditional notion of teacher education as consisting of subject studies, educational studies, studies of teaching methods and clinical experience was recognised as content that 'all qualified teacher education programmes have to cover' and these parts have to be significantly interconnected.[59]

In an ambition to create professional programmes with common features for the whole comprehensive school, a deliberate attempt was made to conceptualise these programmes, not in the traditional four-element model but in an alternative two-element model.[60] Studies in education, teaching methods and the internship were merged together into 'practical education' (as had been envisioned in 1965), a move that intended to increase the cohesion of the studies, traditionally labelled *true professional education*.[61] At the same time, one can assume that such an arrangement still left some gaps and disconnections in relation to the subject studies unaffected due to giving priority to administrative concerns rather than educational ambitions.[62]

So, in sum, with this reform in 1988 came a revised purpose (to support the comprehensive school reform), a change in the structure and a reconceptualisation of the elements of teacher education. It was argued that the 'design of teacher education has [to] give teachers a readiness to actively deal with questions on actual work in schools, on desirable models and how change can be obtained'.[63] In addition to these changes, and as a consequence of the reform, subject teacher education (for secondary school) was split, and a new gap emerged for teacher education to bridge.

Reform 2001:
To learn and to lead, yet another reconceptualisation of teacher education[64]

In the advent of the new millennium, the parliamentary committee for the renewal of Swedish teacher education (1999) emphasised the rapidly changing society and its consequences for the role of teachers. The reformation of teacher education had, according to its investigators, to ensure that teachers were able to:

- act in a learning society
- work in multicultural contexts
- endorse a generation with new questions and values
- earn its authority
- create environments for learning
- utilise a diversity of ways of expression
- endorse, gain and promote a new agenda for knowledge and learning.[65]

This understanding of what teaching is about and what it requires of teachers' education differs from notions expressed in the post-war years, but draws upon and amplifies ideas touched on in the previous reform. However, the reform of 2001 had a radical tune, focusing on teachers as people who lead others in their search for knowledge rather than transfer knowledge. It downplayed the idea that it is 'teachers' task to deliver content and to be in control of teaching', favouring a notion of teachers who 'supervise students and to provide prerequisites for them to evaluate and review, to critically inquire of information and to transform information into useful knowledge' on top of engaging 'students participating in lesson planning'.[66] A strong emphasis was placed on teachers as leaders of the learning processes, as knowledge 'does not exist in a pre-packed format, easily transferred from one to another, instead it is something an individual acquires', which is why teachers have to 'promote that process'.[67]

The reform elaborated this ambition in relation to the concept of competencies, it came with an extended understanding of subjects, and proposed a changed structure, a change based in new understandings of what constitutes teacher education.[68] It tackled the question of theory and practice in a different way compared to previous reforms and made a 'deliberate attempt' to move away from the 'traditional categorisation'.[69] The new structure operated by drawing a distinction between university-based and school-based education and claimed that each of these represents both theory and practice.[70] In this perspective, it represents a changed notion compared with previous models, which had understood that studies at university were the 'theory' of the programme and that what was done in schools was the 'practice'.

The reform changed the programmes' structures into three areas of study: a general field of education, an educational area with an emphasis on particular subjects, and a specialised educational area, a conceptualisation different from the past that also merged internship periods into other courses, such as educational content like maths education into maths courses.[71] This merger was due to the focus on professional knowledge, knowledge perceived to entail more than mastering disciplines or even being insightful in learning issues. Professional knowledge also included knowledge about schools and society, and their interdependence, as well as knowledge development and how knowledge can be perceived differently over time – together with insights into how students' own production of knowledge is supported in the best way.[72]

The reform of 2001 entailed some profound changes, the most important of which contained a changed notion of theory and practice, a division of programme structures into university-based and school-based, together with a conceptualisation of teacher education in three novel areas of study. In addition, one should not underestimate the importance of establishing one single teacher degree.

Reform 2011:
Teachers as experts – aiming for sustainability by returning to traditional approaches

The reform of 2011 intended to provide a more sustainable model for teacher education, emphasising the different types of teaching expertise, an approach resulting in a return to separate teacher degrees, the termination of the integrated internship and, once again, new structures.[73] The focus was also on increased studies in subjects as a foundation for teachers to become experts in their respective field.[74] An overall approach in the public inquiry that preceded the reform was to refine and narrow the responsibility for teachers.[75] The previous reform had merged eight degrees into one teacher degree. That model allowed students to make independent choices to profile their degree. National regulations were to secure the appropriate levels.

In 2011, teacher education took another direction, stressing teacher education as an academic business. The one-degree model was abolished and four degrees (which, with specialisations, offer seven alternatives) took its place. Together with some options for specialisation, the result was more or less a return to the degree structure of the 1970s, when the Swedish school system had been organised on four levels of three years each.[76] The preceding inquiry recognises the long tradition of efforts to increase collaboration between teachers for different parts of the school system but argues that this is not an end in itself and that 'it is hard to motivate a need for collaboration between preschool teachers and secondary school teachers'.[77]

The structure with studies in three different areas was also abandoned in favour of a more traditional conceptualisation with pre-set studies in subjects, low levels of optional choices and separate internships. It also replaced the preceding model, with studies in a general field of education with *a core of educational sciences* whose content was clearly set and defined nationally, no longer up for local deliberation and design.[78] Another novelty was that each programme had to, in an integrated mode, address historical and international perspectives as well as scientific and critical perspectives and information technology as a resource for learning.[79]

Changed notions of teacher education

In education, ideas come and go. Currently, there is a call to reduce the number of teacher education institutions, introduce aptitude tests before admission to teacher education programmes, increase the requirements placed on teacher students, and increase the accountability and direction of teacher education programmes. These ideas are regularly brought forward as a new means for improvement but they were in fact already voiced in parliamentary debates in Sweden in the 1850s![80] Even in the shorter perspective applied here, ideas come and go. Since the Second World War, Swedish teacher education has operated with diverse notions of teacher education, and its constitutive parts, once new, become old-fashioned and return as novelties n probably not the most favourable conditions for congruence and consistency.

Table 5.3 Constitutive elements of teacher education in Sweden, 1940s–2010s

Period	Purpose	Constitutive Elements	Organisation/Division
1940s–1970s	The art of teaching	A fourfold model that included studies in: • subjects • education[1] • teaching methods and the clinical experience (internship).	• A high degree of diversity and several ways to qualify for teaching, over time partly reduced to four main types, referring to Grades 1–3, 4–6, 7–9, 10–12.[2] • A main distinction was made between subject studies and true professional training.
1980s–1990s	Teaching in a developing school – and in support of change	A twofold model including studies in: • subjects, and • practical education.	Separate programmes for: • preschool • comprehensive school (a unified programme with two overlapping (1–7 and 4–9) • upper secondary school.[3]
2000s	Teacher as a leader of students' learning	A threefold model with studies in: • a general field of education • an educational area, and • specialisations.[4] • A high degree of integration between the traditional elements and their merger into the three areas of studies[5]	One unified programme (replacing eight previous degrees) for all teachers but with specialisations for work in preschool, comprehensive school and upper secondary. The model also included teachers for leisure-time centres, the vocational programme and study and career guidance).[6]
2010s	Teacher as an (subject) expert	A threefold model entailing studies in: • subjects (including educational aspects) • educational science core,[7] and • clinical experience. • The model prioritised separating these elements.	Four separate programmes for: • preschool • primary school (Grades 1–3 or 4–6) • secondary school (Grades 7–9 or 10–12), and • vocational education.[8]

As described above, the reforms as such, regardless of their intention, may have contributed to fragmentation. An odd hypothesis maybe, but one anchored in observations of reforms being layered upon each other rather than replacing the old with the new.[81] So far, we have outlined two main types of changes to observe. First, obvious aspects like the dramatic shift from eight teacher degrees to one and then back to a diversified model. Second, the more subtle but pervasive changes, like the different notions of constitutive elements within teacher programmes and their supposed inner relationship. The shifting understanding of the intricate relationship between theory and practice, its multiple manifestation and its relation to concepts such as *true professional training* are examples of highly important and enduring issues that appear to be difficult to master and, of importance here, are most likely interpreted differently within the existing parallel, diverse educational cultures, among colleagues in higher education engaged in teacher education, not to forget students and collaborative teachers in schools.

This second type of change might be less transparent and easy to grasp. Concepts are defined differently over time and different meanings are promoted by various discourses (an observation in support of the working hypothesis as such). Redefined concepts and changed perspectives are, of course, to be primarily understood as inherent aspect of progress. But we may differentiate between, for example, exogenously and endogenously caused change, hypothetically with different levels of potential for fragmentation or coherence building.[82]

These types of reform aspect are most likely the ones that layer with reforms and causes dissonances, conceptual gaps and disconnection that can be understood as essential parts of the de facto fragmentation of teacher education. But they can also affect an external understanding *of* fragmentation in teacher education by a wider public, including politicians, parents and the media, which may not be fully aware of the nuances, their implications and having too few insights into the complexity of education systems, such as, for example, knowhow on the conditions for successful reform, and how to promote change without reform.[83]

This section has described how teacher education in Sweden during the past decades has been profoundly changed in its fundamental aspects of foundational structure and conceptualisation as well as in how content has been perceived and organised in relation to notions of the teaching profession.[84] (Table 5.3) A tentative conclusion so far is that it would be surprising if these shifts had not led to bigger gaps and disconnections, i.e. promoted fragmentation. To further deepen the analysis, two additional studies will be presented: on the power over the direction of teacher education, and on research. The two underlying assumptions for this section are that continuity in steering models and strong involvement in research can be understood as beneficial factors for countering fragmentation.

GOVERNANCE, FRAGMENTATION AND THE POWER OVER TEACHER EDUCATION

Organisational models and the need for appropriate directing bodies

Local choices of organisational setup and how the steering mechanism is designed can be perceived as instrumental for the local capacity to direct teacher education in a manner that reduces gaps and disconnections. However, Lainer and Little (1986) observed that fragmentation in teacher education was not an exception, but rather the norm, and that bodies with 'overall responsibility and accountability', adequately empowered and resourced in relation to the importance of these programmes, were often lacking.[85] A similar analysis was presented in a governmental inquiry in Sweden in the late 1990s.[86] This section focuses on how Swedish teacher education institutions are set up and how they are directed.[87]

Teacher education has historically been organised in four models:[88]

1. As separate post-secondary institutions.

2. As integrated into higher-education institutions (HEIs) but operating as separate organisations within each institution.

3. As integrated into HEIs and, to a significant extent, operating separately but also utilising units organisationally detached from teacher education bodies.

4. As integrated into HEIs in the form of an overarching directive body orchestrating units from all over the institution in conducting teacher education.

Historically, the separate post-secondary model (1) has, with one important exemption, not been in use during the past few decades in Sweden.[89] Since the 1970s, only the other three models (2, 3, 4) have been present, which require appropriate steering models.[90] Based on an assumption that problems in teacher education related to a lack of deliberate steering, reports in the 1990s advocated coherent models and structures for decision-making in teacher education for increased programme cohesion.[91] A change in the Higher Education Act (2001) required each institution providing teacher education degrees to have a particular board, a faculty board for teacher education. If the respective institution had the right to award PhD degrees, the board had also to be responsible for research and PhD training of relevance.[92]

To recall, the point of departure was an observation of a lack of governance over teacher education, an observation that sparked a national requirement to establish appropriate bodies. This requirement was understood as entailing problematic interference in internal affairs within higher-education institutions. Let us follow what happened, but let us also include how the use of the organisational models identified above has evolved.

The direction of teacher education in an age of increased institutional autonomy

In 2002, the first review of the requirement to establish institution-wide and fully responsible bodies was conducted.[93] The review identified that such boards had been established in almost all institutions but they regularly had insufficient and inappropriate mandates to fully take on their responsibility. To improve how teacher education was directed, the National Agency for Higher Education wrote in 2002 a formal request to the ministry to open up the field to more powerful but diverse models.[94] A ministerial investigation in 2004 that discussed this issue, among others, provides vital information. As such, it echoes the traditional resistance in academia to the external direction of interior affairs, and a particular board for teacher education was metaphorically described as 'a foreign bird in academia'; the report also perceives the requirement as 'extreme'.[95] But the report is also interesting because it confirms the need for improvement as it proposes increased flexibility to make institutions able to respond to the needs.[96]

The National Agency for Higher Education recognised in 2007 that the possibilities for more cohesive direction and governance of teacher education programmes had been improved by the requirement, at least according to the majority of vice-chancellors.[97] Half of the institutions had established teacher education boards with sufficient mandates, either directly reporting to the vice-chancellor or the board of the institution.[98] As this conclusion de facto revealed that half the institutions were violating the law, it is surprising that the responsible agency did not execute its power and responsibility to ensure that law was being followed. But in the spirit of the coming autonomy reform (below), the accountable agency had come to agree with the critics of the requirement and argued for local decisions on this, explaining why no activities were proposed to ensure the law was being observed.

In the same year, 2007, a governmental inquiry was set up to promote the autonomy of HEIs in Sweden.[99] Consequently, a renewed Higher Education Act was implemented in 2010. What is of interest here is how the increased autonomy affected the direction of teacher education. So, what happened with the organisational setup for the direction of teacher education when academia was once again granted greater institutional autonomy?

In 2007/08, I surveyed the overarching organisational model for Swedish institutions that provided teacher education programmes.[100] The data collection provides us with an opportunity to identify the state of the art when it comes to a teacher education organisational setup, after decades of struggle for the reinstallation of suitable organisational models to create coherence in these programmes – but before the autonomy reform (Table 5.4).

Table 5.4 Organisational models in higher-education institutions (HEIs) of teacher education (2008)

25 HEIs that provided teacher education programmes in 2008 were studied.		
2 HEIs had no faculty, school or other top-level, overarching board in the institutional structure for the purpose of directing these programmes.[1]	**23 HEIs had** a faculty, school or other top-level, overarching board in the institutional structure for the purpose of directing these programmes.	
	15 HEIs had an integrated and horizontal organisational setting for utilising the best and most relevant competence within the HEI, irrespective of location.[2]	**8 HEIs had a separate or semi-separate and mainly vertical** organisation in forms of a faculty or a school that directs and runs the programme.[3]

Source: Survey of HEIs' websites in January 2008[101]

In 2008, more than 20 institutions provided teacher education.[102] As observed in 2002 and 2007 by the National Agency for Higher Education, in the end almost all institutions had observed the law and established the required boards.[103]

There is no clear-cut distinction between the more integrated and more separately organising models. A tentative distinction has been used here to identify institutions with models that are primarily matrix organised (integrated and horizontal) and institutions with models that have distinctive features of detachment (separate and vertical). An indication of the latter could be that the organisational model includes some departments/units within the respective institutions, there is a responsibility for the particular teacher education board (or a faculty/ school) and that these units have teacher education as their only or main area of activity. Given these distinctions, it may be possible to conclude that, on an organisational level, the period after introducing the requirement for particular teacher education boards resulted in the establishment of such boards, that the majority of institutions had chosen matrix-like models but that a significant proportion (one third) of institutions provide teacher education as a more separate business.[104]

In 2015, some years after the autonomy reform, the picture has changed and most institutions have no overarching body for the governance of teacher education (Table 5.5).

Table 5.5 Organisational models of teacher education in 2015

28 HEIs provided teacher education programmes in 2015.		
18 HEIs have no faculty, school or other top-level, overarching board in the institutional structure for the purpose of directing these programmes.	**10 HEIs have** a faculty, school or other top-level, overarching board in the institutional structure for the purpose of directing these programmes.	
	5 HEIs have an integrated and horizontal organisational setting for utilising the best and most relevant competence within the HEI, irrespective of location.	**5 HEIs have a separate and vertical** organisation in forms of a faculty or a school that directs and runs the teacher education programme.

Source: Web survey (June 2015) of institutional organisational charts[105]

The point of departure for this analysis is an assumption that, for the development of congruency in programmes, it is essential that the organisational set up either entails a strongly mandated, high-level and university-wide body or a relatively separate and self-standing one. This cannot be claimed to be an empirical fact; rather, it is to be understood as a rationally based argument.

Taken together, this overview indicates that teacher education during the past decades has undergone profound shifts in policy on governance.

- Up until the 1960s, independent institutions had a high degree of self-governance.

- From 1977, institutions merged with higher education, particular 'programme boards' for the governance of programmes.

- After 1993 and the first autonomy reform, these programme boards were dissolved to a large extent or their mandates were reduced.

- In 2001, particular teacher education boards were installed via legislation

- After 2010 and the second autonomy reform, teacher education boards were largely dissolved, moved to lower levels and/or their mandates were reduced.

Consequently, the direction of teacher education as a particular academic business has been weakened, a condition probably contributing to increased fragmentation or, at least, causing obstacles to the countering of gaps and disconnections. We might have in mind how Andreas Schleicher has emphasised, in the context of fragmentation, the importance of a programme being run in institutions where it is '. . . not at the margin of what the university does, but is the core business . . .'[106]

One might also reflect upon what caused this pendulum, from separate to integrated models and from first-level issues to second-level ones. Is it the very traditional structures of high- and low-status business in academia, as pointed to by David Labaree, that has been in play?[107] Or is the enduring power struggle between the academic 'tribes and territories' that Becher and Trowler described to blame?[108] Or is it politics that continues to launch top-down reforms in academia and is repeating decentralisation moves without proper reviews of earlier attempts and their consequences? Anyway, it is striking that teacher education is nowadays less organisationally visible and hence a less prioritised area of study in Swedish higher education, a situation clashing with the institutional rhetoric and the public debate on schooling and education, which stresses that high-quality teacher education is the most valuable tool for a successful school.

Historical circularity and the pendulum swing seem to follow general teacher education reforms and how the power to direct teacher education is organised. In the latter case, it might be more appropriate to understand the trajectory as a resistance strategy within academia against external and political steering. If teacher education were like schools of engineering, business or even medicine – regularly well-maintained and cherished businesses with well-respected graduates – we might perceive this as a sign of valuable integrity. Whether that is the case here is questionable; there might be other rationales at play.

For the final part of this study of Swedish teacher education, we turn to the impact of research. Research is the prestige activity in academia, signalling institutional dedication, and among other positive outcomes it promotes a distinctive vocabulary for each domain, hence contributing essentially to educational clarity and coherence.

FRAGMENTATION AND RESEARCH: THE IMPORTANCE OF RESEARCH FOR EDUCATIONAL COHESION

The level of research orientation in teacher education is important for coherence and congruence. It is not primarily about the type of research; rather, it is about the existence of a research culture. The relationship between teacher education and research has long been debated, hence here we will devote some space to describe the situation.

It is not unusual that teacher education, schools of education and education become compared with medical schools and medicine. This juxtaposition holds some relevance but one particular important difference relates to professional language. The clinical practice of medicine early on developed a precise language for professional work, for example on body parts as well as symptoms and diseases. Before the Flexner Report in 1910, American medical education was severely underdeveloped. The reforms in the wake of the Flexner Report also brought medical education into a close relationship with clinical research. As a consequence, on top of the raised educational quality, clinical research as well as basic research expanded, which in itself promoted scientific and professional language.[109] Despite many similarities, such a trajectory has not occurred in the field of education.

Research funding is probably key to the occurrence of such developments. A lively research culture in a field can be assumed not only to produce new knowledge but also to promote understanding of how parts and fields of knowledge relate to each other. That endeavour is also beneficial for promoting overarching understandings and disciplinary-based languages, both of which are vital for the cohesion of a field. The existence of research funds also makes an academic area attractive for pursuing careers in. Historically, teacher education in Sweden has had difficulties in accessing research funding, locally and nationally. It was not until the early 2000s that a special branch of the Swedish Research Council was designated to the educational sciences and today there is still a shocking difference in teacher education as the largest educational sector in higher education (and currently most likely the largest public societal investment) and the tiny research funding that is allocated to the area.

For 2016, the Swedish Research Council has received EUR 630 million and the parliament allocated an additional EUR 270 million for clinical research.[110] The research council is not the only governmental research funding agency but it is the only one with designated resources for educational science, a fact that makes it interesting to look into which proportions of research funds are allocated by the council under the strict direction of the parliament.[111] In 2015, the governmental directive for allocation to the stipulated four research areas distributed the funding as follows (Table 5.6):

Table 5.6
Areas for the distribution of research grants (Swedish Research Council, 2015)[112]

Area of research	Proportion (%)
Science and Technology	44.5
Medicine and Health	37.0
Humanities and Social Sciences	11.8
Educational Science	6.7

The picture is illuminating. Only 6.7% of research funding at the national level is directly allocated to educational science (it is of importance to also note that all educational science research is not primarily related to teacher education). Teacher education benefits from research in other areas as well, but the point here is that designated funding for research directly related to professional needs among teachers not only contributes to increased scientific grounds for teaching but also to the fact that the coherence and knowledge accumulation comes with a scientific language of the profession.

But the overall picture is even worse. Sweden invested 3.4% of GDP in research and development in 2013. Approximately 1.1% is public; the rest is private.[113] Educational science research is almost entirely funded by public funds. The public share of the total national investment in research and development (FoU) is estimated at EUR 4.4 billion (1.1% of GDP) for 2015.[114] The share of the public investment allocated to the Swedish Research Council is 14%, roughly half of which is spent on project funding in the four specific domains described above. Of that part, educational science receives 6.7% – a share in striking contrast to the fact that education is one of the largest societal activities.

Shifting from a national- to local-level examples, we now look at the situation facing two large teacher education providers, Linköping University and Umeå University, both with stronger national research funding from the government than most teacher education providers and both with more extensive educational science research than the average teacher education institution.[115]

The governmental funding for institutions comes earmarked for education and for research but, in general, there are only marginal directions for the further allocation, so it is largely up to the board to allocate the research funding internally.

These two institutions have close to 30 000 students each. They are relatively young institutions, established as universities in the 1960s and 1970s but with a century-long engagement in teacher education at the time of their inauguration. Both of them praise themselves for being young enough to be more adaptive to society than the older and more traditional universities. For the three-year period 2012–2014, on average 8.3% and 10.6%, respectively, of their business was teacher education in financial terms.[116] During the same period, just 3.6% of the research funding in each institution was allocated to educational science.[117]

The figures provided here are not encompassing and sufficient enough to securely inform on the situation in the whole country but, together with a general experience among teacher educators, these examples may indicate that Swedish HEIs appear to significantly underfund research in the teacher education field. A probable consequence of this tendency is less capacity-building in the area and less well-established prerequisites for congruency in teacher education programmes.[118]

These examples, from the national and local levels, show how the national higher-education system fails in its responsibility to provide adequate and sufficient resources for the development of teaching and the teaching profession. We started this section by recalling the frequent comparison between medicine and education and found historical differences in relation to research, while we hypothesised that research and research funding could be essential for the development of a professional language in support of coherence in professional training. On the national and local levels, we found that educational science is seriously underfunded.[119]

For a long time in academia there has been a cherished ideal of having a close relationship between teaching and research as a model to ensure high quality. If, over time, institutions do not allocate resources proportionally to educational assignments, they erode or neglect the building of essential prerequisites for high-quality education in the field. A high level of research within an educational field also historically creates a certain kind of autonomy, intellectual- and status-wise, which is important for crafting coherent programmes.

What is displayed here is probably a complex situation for teacher education within academia. The Stanford scholar, David Labaree, emphasised that:

> ... the relationship between the university and teacher education has been an uneasy one for both parties. There has been persistent ambivalence on both sides. Each needs the other in significant ways, but each risks something important by being tied to the other. The university offers status and academic credibility, and teacher education offers students and social utility. But in maintaining this marriage of convenience, the university risks undermining its academic standing, and teacher education risks undermining its professional mission.[120]

This phenomenon of an 'uneasy' relationship between teacher education and academia appears to influence how teacher education programmes are executed – and thereby impacts upon the issue of fragmentation.

CAUSES, CONDITIONS AND FORCES – CONCLUSIONS AND RECOMMENDATIONS FOR COUNTERING FRAGMENTATION IN TEACHER EDUCATION

Historical amnesia in education?

An article in a central educational journal in Sweden in 1868 poses three questions regarding maths teaching in schools: Has it taken advantage of the progress in mathematical knowledge that has occurred during the past century? Is Swedish school teaching on a comparable level to maths teaching in other countries? Which measures would be best for use in improving the teaching of maths in schools in Sweden?[121] Today's discussions concerning schooling on scientific foundations, PISA scores and efficient teaching models echo similar ambitions. Of course, there are enduring challenges that each generation has to face and strategise for, but in the educational-reform business it is hard to avoid an impression of a deficit of cumulative progress and a surplus of uninformed repetition of ideas.

It might not be wrong that we still address these questions as demands are changing. But if we do not remember what has been done, in which circumstances and in relation to which purposes and so on, we risk ending up with fragmentation. Swedes have had an enduring inclination to borrow inspiration from the United States and international educational policy.[122] An interesting example of how presumably novel reform ideas have in fact been available for decades relates to the famous Sputnik shock in the USA in the late 1950s and a bestseller in education.

The Soviet launch of Sputnik sparked American distrust in US education, which is why an elite academic group was called to gather in Woods Hole on Cape Cod with the mission to outline 'how education in science might be improved in our primary and secondary schools'.[123] The conference produced a report that became an educational bestseller read, if not by all teacher students, then by many since the 1960s, including in Sweden.[124] It also identified a need for the general advancement of teacher quality and the conference thus presented some recommendations:

> Better recruitment and the possibility of better selection, better substantive education in teacher training institutions, on-the-job training of younger teachers by more experienced ones, in-service and summer institutes, closed-circuit television to continue the education of teachers, improvement of teacher salaries – all of these must

obviously be pursued as objectives. But equally important is the up-grading of the prestige of the teaching profession.[125]

With the exception of closed-circuit television, today replaced by other technologies, all of these policies are present in the contemporary discussion five decades later – as new and fresh ideas. In fact, some of today's top educational policy proposals in Sweden – on reducing the number of teacher education institutions, on raising admission qualifications for teacher studies and on the establishment of teacher-training schools – were, as mentioned above, voiced for the first time in the Swedish parliament already in the 1850s.[126] There seems to be a continuous discourse in contrast to variation in practice within the field under critique.

It has been argued that one of the great gains of human development is the emergence of a historical consciousness.[127] The act of mind to revisit human experience and for intentional contemplation on its capacity to inform contemporary identities, decision-making and strategising can be perceived as essential for the sustainability of society. However, there are signs of historical amnesia in the field of education policy. Unfortunately, what has been claimed in the American context, that one of 'the most notable characteristics of the contemporary teacher education reports is their lack of historic consciousness', could well apply to the Swedish debate as well, a conundrum in itself and well worth an in-depth study, but, for now, it is a sad fact to take into consideration in the search for clues to fragmentation as an educational problem.[128]

As a consequence, a non-aligned reform praxis relating to different generations of educational reforms has not only come to co-exist but also to a large extent come to constitute the Swedish education system, at least the preparation of teachers. The merger between the new and old, and/or between diverse elements, is in fact not unlike learning; new ideas and perspectives have to be understood and internalised. The layering aspects of reforms can be understood as a kind of unsuccessful learning that might result in what Schneuwly (2011) called attention to as sedimented practices, for which one antidote might be a historical memory.[129] The high frequency and high degree of turnaround in the reforms of teacher education together with the disunity of the profession, diverse local conditions and organisations, and with the impact of political tides in other sectors on the realisation of reforms, appear to have created situations favourable to educational fragmentation.

Teacher education in academia – a less favourable localisation?

Are universities the best site for teacher education?[130] Here we only address the question from the narrower perspective of fragmentation. David Labaree describes teacher education and academia as having an 'uneasy relationship'.[131] In what way is it uneasy? In this chapter, we have studied teacher education reforms, approaches to the governance of teacher education in academia as well as the funding of research in teacher education. It appears as if academia in the latter two aspects has failed in its responsibilities for the education of teachers. In a study on higher learning in the United States, Derek Bok (1986) outlines some key features of professional schools in medicine, law and business.[132] His analysis is also of interest for schools engaged in the education of teachers. According to Bok, for every professional school, what the relationships between these schools and their 'interested parties' look like is important: 'to the academy, the students, the profession, and the larger society'.[133] Bok provides interesting observations of importance for the situation of teacher education.

For a professional school, the relation to the respective profession is particularly important. Professionals in medicine, business and law have, according to Bok, had a strengthening impact on the particular professional schools.[134] The practical orientation among professionals, and their emphasis on utility, has been channelled into these schools (as has the appreciation of teaching excellence) through interventions like grants, accreditation and certification. The situation seems profoundly different for teacher education. The teaching profession has not held such a prestigious position in Sweden for long, if ever. Instead, schools and teacher education have been on the media agenda as an area in need of substantial reform. And such reforms have been launched frequently and with diverse orientations.

To teach in a professional school is to belong 'to a community of scholars', sharing a set of 'values, priorities, ways of defining excellence and status'.[135] A key question for a professional school is what stance it takes on these. Bok's description of the American academy in the 1980s probably also holds true for contemporary Sweden. In the academy, 'intellectual achievement' is number one. This is displayed in the high value attributed to theoretical and abstract understandings and a focus on researching areas 'for their own sake'. It is less important to focus on practical issues and investigations geared toward application and utility. Success, judged along these priorities, is visualised in research papers. Consequently, a minor emphasis is placed on teaching but so too is promoting teaching to be preoccupied with general insights rather than practicalities.[136]

Up to the early 2000s, these values seem to have permeated teacher education primarily through the requirement that the education of teachers should be research-based. In two national evaluations in 2005 and 2008, it was shown that the average teacher educator in universities or university colleges did not hold a PhD, explaining why change was called for.[137]

During the past few years, these values and priorities have affected teacher education through international rankings. The average Swedish teacher education programme is not conducted within an institution that struggles to be mentioned among the top 100 or so institutions on the Shanghai ranking but, as the national policy for funding HEIs has changed into increasingly allocating resources according to bibliometrics and other aligned research performance promoting models, teacher education providers have had to endorse these values and priorities.

This change can be understood as a final aspect of the integration of teacher education into academia in the sense that teacher educators are becoming required to hold the same profiles as other university teachers. This has long been a national priority and a central aspect of the strategy to upgrade teacher education during the post-war period. However, it has to be noted that this change also comes with a another – from regarding teaching as the prime assignment to understanding research production as holding that position. This may be true for all professional schools – but there is only one professional school that has the promotion of excellence in teaching as its professional field, explaining why this change seems more profound and challenging than in other professional schools. And it is problematic because the field is notoriously underfunded.

The priority of research and its tendency to favour disciplinary-oriented, pure and basic research is clearly very important in a perspective of knowledge production. However, for a professional school, and particularly for schools engaged in the education of teachers, other priorities cannot be neglected. When Clark Kerr, the famous architect of the grand plan for the Californian university system, in the early 2000s produced the fifth edition of his 1963 Godkin Lectures, *The Uses of The University*, he pointed to the surprising fact that no higher-education institution has distinguished itself by its support for primary and secondary education.[138] What he reports is most likely just another aspect of what Harry Judge, David Labaree and others have noted, namely that the high-prestige competition in academia results in an avoidance of contacts with assumingly low-status enterprises like schooling and teacher education. The question is not whether universities are the best localisation for teacher education, but whether institutions will be able to rethink the situation and understand teacher education as its prime interface with society – and that the key profession to team up with is teachers.

Conditions for the coherent education of teachers – findings and recommendations for policy, practice and research

Initially, this chapter briefly touched on some conditions for education that are important in the perspective of fragmentation: the relationship between the nation state, the church and education; gender division; and the relationship between teacher education and schooling. In addition, historical amnesia can tentatively be ascribed with importance as well and the picture might be widening to allow the inclusion of the different education traditions in the field, but that approach would raise other issues, which is why here only some final remarks will be provided, emphasising the provisional findings in this chapter, together with some recommendations for institutional leaders, institutions, agencies in charge, as well as politicians.[139]

The first argument in this study is, though, that teacher education reforms are essential for understanding fragmentation in teacher education. The point made here is that the frequencies and profoundness of these reforms as such can be assumed to have caused increased instances of ambiguity, gaps and disconnections in teacher education. We opened up this inquiry into the issue of fragmentation in Swedish teacher education by considering national teacher education reforms. We found the occurrence of three reforms during less than three decades and identified sharp turns in their direction, entailing a profound restructuring and reconceptualisation of key aspects of these respective programmes.

To give a glimpse of what the frequency is about, an example will be provided. Let us say that an institution admitted students to teacher programmes for upper-secondary teaching in autumn 2001. These programmes are, at a minimum, five years long and, regularly, the final semester would consist of students writing their degree thesis, after having completed their final internships. For both of these activities to be successful, the institution might have planned to introduce students to this in the first semester and then followed this up in a progressive structure of activities. When the first students graduated in spring 2006 and when the institution had its first authentic opportunity to evaluate the full process, already then politicians had advocated a complete overhaul of teacher education – and a year later, in July 2007, after a year of waiting, a public investigation was announced, resulting in a governmental proposition in spring 2010 with the ambition to have new programmes up and running by January 2011. For a teacher educator, this means that after 2006 and before 2010 it was hard to make substantial changes as such work would risk coming into conflict with the national priorities to come.[140] Accordingly, the frequency of reforms might prevent internal systematic review and tends to be an obstacle to internally driven and step-by-step executed reforms.

The scope of the reforms, aiming in different directions, causes similar problems, but that also takes the problem up to another level. Changes in models for degrees, programme structure and reconceptualisation of the content and preferred outcome are highly complex challenges as they encompass intricate distinctions of constitutive elements. Teacher education engages a great number of teachers who have to be educated regarding all novelties, and many of the classes are either run in collaboration with other programmes or other cohorts of teacher students.

The second argument is that governance models of teacher education can be assumed to be of great importance for the endeavour to increase congruence and cohesion in teacher education. Models of governance relate strongly to issues of localisation, levels of independence and autonomy, modes of integration in HEIs and, hence, to ideas on utilisation of competence.

Two essential aspects of the Swedish trajectory for teacher education are notable: the process of establishing independent and separate institutions for teacher education, and its culmination in upgrading these institutions to higher-education seminars in the 1950s and 1960s. The independence and self-governance most likely provided opportunities for strong inner connections in the programmes offered – together with a high level of professional relevance. The striving for increased academic input in these programmes and the stronger academic formation of the teacher workforce soon resulted in the merger of all teacher education institutions into the general higher-education sector. Teacher education institutions went from independent and separate to becoming integrated into the national system of general HEIs.

In this situation, a second aspect of the trajectory becomes poignant, namely, how teacher education is becoming organised within its new environment, traditional academia. The process leading up to national legislation, demanding that all HEIs providing teacher education must establish particular and powerful boards for the direction of teacher education, is revealing, as is the reversed process after the general autonomy reform in higher education. The fact that teacher education seems to have generally become degraded thereafter by the HEIs into more marginal modes of governance may indicate fewer opportunities for strategic handling of the trade-off situation that appears to be colouring teacher education nowadays: how to secure increases in both the academic level and professional relevance.[141]

Third, it is argued that the insufficient provision of research funding may be interpreted as contributing to the difficult situation of teacher education in academia, 'the uneasy relationship' on at least two levels.[142] The lack of research funding has resulted in the insufficient development of knowledge and research of central importance for the education of teachers; furthermore, it might have reinforced the idea that such programmes are practical in nature and that professional formation as such is not a researchable area. Second, as research is the prestige activity in academia, the lack of research funding might have caused a centrifugal shift of research-oriented teacher educators away from these programmes, rather than being a desirable centripetal force, gathering research excellence around key topics for the profession.[143] On another level, it is hard to avoid perceiving the lack of willingness, in national and local HEIs, to fund such research as a de facto indication of the status and value ascribed to the area – at least in relation to other areas.

The pace of change in teacher education that has been addressed here appears, in comparison with other professional programmes, to be quite unique. A possible explanation is that in an age of decentralised school systems (during the past decades Sweden has developed a highly decentralised school market model of a relatively unique character), teacher education is one of the few remaining modes for exerting a governmental influence on schooling. The situation might be perceived as particularly vulnerable due to the strong political role and the assumed weak research base. The development shows features that might also signal that education remains, however surprisingly, a field under development, for which it is still questioned as to whether it is possible to establish scientifically grounded knowledge and expertise.

Recommendations for policy, practice and research

Conditions for congruent and coherent teacher education have to be improved – and this can be done through a change in policy and practice – and through research. What we have learned during the recent decades of reforming teacher education is how complex these activities are and how dependent they are on faculty members endorsing all constitutive elements of the programmes being run. That experience alone is highly demanding for policy-makers, practitioners and researchers.

It was argued above that the localisation of teacher education in traditional academia might have contributed to fragmentation, or at least been an obstacle for countering the kind of educational mismatch we tend to term fragmentation. So, what is to be done? Are we to understand the overall teacher education upgrade attempts through merger into higher education as a failure and an avenue to be abandoned? No, definitely not. But higher-education institutions must learn from the past. To face the reality, much points to the fact that academia has not been the best of contexts. But what has been does not necessarily dictate what is to come.

The fact that academia has strong traditions, strict priorities and harsh internal competition does not condemn teacher education to an eternal marginal business that these institutions do not nurture sufficiently. In fact, if higher-education leaders were to engage in realisation of the current rhetoric, making teacher education and related research into key strategic objectives, much improvement would be made. If institutions took that stance, and if they negotiated with local governance structures for the sole purpose of ensuring high quality in teacher education programmes and related research, and with mandates to advance these activities without today's obstacles, fragmentation in teacher education would disappear like a bad memory.

A key prerequisite for a brighter future for Swedish teacher education is, however, a change in national politics in education. With the high frequency of school and teacher education reforms, turmoil, tension and career politics in educational fragmentation are inevitable. By establishing clear standards for teacher education, providing sufficient resources and space for local modelling, there is no doubt that Swedish HEIs will be able to deliver.

Focusing on teacher education reforms, their frequency and the magnitude of their shifting scope, on governance of teacher education and on research funding, this study indicates the need for:[144]

Higher-education institutions

- To review to what extent the overall resource allocation for research is aligned with the importance ascribed to the educational sphere.

- To inquire into whether recruitment and staffing are adequate for making teacher education the most advanced high-quality education in the institution.

- To prioritise teacher education as the main interface with society.

- To secure interinstitutional arrangements that clearly promote excellent conditions for learning in teacher studies.

Teacher education bodies

- To develop proactive and independent approaches to both the development and review of programmes. To establish powerful strategies with clear objectives, together with systematic monitoring of progress. Reforms, like educational ideas, will come and go. The question is whether each institution can develop its own models and excellence.

- To engage collaborative schools and teachers deeply in programmes. Only if they are fully involved can it be assured that their opinions on relevance, coherence and academic rigour are sufficiently grounded. And only then will their competence and engagement contribute fully.

- To analyse the local institutional setting with the ambition to find the best opportunities to realise the relative advantages behind the model choice. Much effort is spent on designing organisation, less on releasing its potential. Not only reform layers and many advantages become trapped in organisations living in past models.

Researchers

- To further make teacher education, teaching and learning in teacher programmes key research areas.[145] Medicine has benefitted enormously from clinical research, and the strong push for similar developments regarding teaching and learning in schools has to be combined with such an approach to teacher education.

Policy-makers

• To address the higher-education community concerning the importance of institution-wide engagement for schooling and teacher education as a prime obligation. Patents and innovations are of great value but most valuable is the education of the coming generation.

• To secure adequate prerequisites for high-quality teacher education in higher education. To deliberate how the largest enterprise in higher education, the mass teacher education business, can be resourced and empowered to fulfil the high expectations set. Rhetoric is insufficient; money talks.

• To engage teacher educators in envisioning how teacher education can improve, and to require clearly outlined, step-by-step plans for enhancement, sufficient monitoring models and steady improvement.

Note about translation

The author made his own translation of the quotes from the Swedish public records.

NOTES TO TABLES 5.3 AND 5.4

Table 5.3

1 It has to be noted that this is not the academic discipline of 'education' (pedagogik) but a wider area of studies.

2 It should be noted that this division is not identical to the later four-track model; also, for example, teacher education for what later corresponds to lower secondary was not one programme – rather, there were seven roads for teacher qualification in this respect. It should also be noted that preparation for a career as a kindergarten teacher (later preschool teacher is not included here; nor are vocational teacher education and particular programmes, such as for music teaching).

3 As in the period before, particular programmes are left outside the picture here, for example, teacher education for vocational training.

4 The model included a degree thesis, contained either in subjects or within the educational area.

5 The model includes a degree thesis that is integrated into either the general field of education or within studies in subjects.

6 All types of teacher education are included. It should be noted that the overlapping model was mainly preserved as a general model.

7 A degree thesis is required but conducted within studies in subjects.

8 The model includes some specialisations and mainly mirrors the traditional Swedish division of the school system into four separate three-year periods of study.

Table 5.4

1 KTH, LU.

2 GU, HB, HDa, HIG, HH, HKr, HiS, KaU, LiU, LTU, MDH, SU, SH, VxU, OrU.

3 HJ, HiK, HV, LHS, MaH, MiU, UmU, UU.

NOTES

1 OECD 2015.

2 Statement by Andreas Schleicher, presentation (4 May 2015) of the OECD report at Rosenbad with Ministers Fridolin and Hadzialic, then later the same day at the same venue for an invited audience, and, finally, at the national broadcaster (Aktuellt). At the ministerial presentations, he several times described the education system in these terms. In the interview with the national broadcaster, Schleicher said the following: 'The initial teacher training is highly fragmented in Sweden; you have 28 institutions all trying their best but what is lacking is a coherent education system for both the initial part and the continuous professional development. Most high performing education systems would have one or two institutions that are really very, very, good at what they do and that teacher education is not on the margin of what a university does but is the core business, and that something – to achieve a more consolidated approach to teacher

development – seems very important to us'. However, the word 'atomised' is not in the report and 'fragmented' is only mentioned in the context of teachers' professional development (119, 120, 124). The report uses the term 'fractured' instead.

3   OECD, 2015, 111.

4   The term 'fragment' has been used in Swedish since the seventeenth century. The term fragmentation has its roots in Latin and the term *fragmentum*, denoting a piece that is detached from something of which it originally and intentionally was a part. *Frangere* means to break, to break loose, the act that results in the occurrence of *fragments*, parts that have been fragmented. Such an act is something undesirable, the detachment, the disconnection is unintended as both the whole and the part have lost something of its original meaning. In addition, the word has a connotation of vulnerability and fragility (Svenska Akademiens ordbok). But there is another important aspect to bear in mind: the connection to discovery! An archaeologist brings fragments together and, even if not all the original parts are at hand, he/she can more or less accurately arrange the fragments into tentative structures representing the once lost whole. A once unintended occurrence, which led an intentional whole into separation, disconnection and a loss of function and meaning, can in another sequence in its resulting fragments be perceived as the most precious and essential clue to understanding something not yet understood. I.e. fragmentation has to do with parts and their belonging to a whole. It has a negative connotation but also a positive one as it has to do with possibilities of finding connections and discovery, which in an educational perspective relates to learning.

5   For a general discussion of the fragmentation of academic work, see Jones (2013).

6   In this chapter, teacher education reform refers to a national and political decision on change. Reforms are also conducted locally and, not to forget, with each teacher change, daily! Beach (1995) provides an in-depth study of a key teacher education reform in Sweden but from a much more concrete, consequence-searching approach than applied here.

7   Ekbohrn, 1904; Sahlenius, 1916; *Svenska Akademins ordbok*; Östergren, 1981.

8   Tyack and Cuban (1995, 76). In this seminal study on school reforms, it is argued that the proper question to be asked is not what school reforms do to schools but the opposite – what do schools do with reforms?

9   Darling-Hammond (2012, 138f). Cf. Darling-Hammond (2006); in *Transforming Teacher Education. Reflections from the Field*, another but related set of key points is brought forward, namely that a serious teacher education programme must: 1) 'address the central task of learning to teach', 2) 'continually work to develop in each student a new adult and professional identity as teacher committed to the growth of children and to knowing and teaching subject matter in intellectual engaging ways', 3) have teacher educators that 'help prospective teachers develop intellectual habits and a capacity for judgment that will allow them to embrace and negotiate tensions and dilemmas in their work', 4) have teacher educators that can 'create structures and a culture that support ongoing learning of all who work with prospective teachers, mentor teachers, graduate students and faculty teaching in the programme, 5) work for localising 'experiences in schools … at the core of the prospective teacher's learning of teacher education' (Caroll et al., 2007, 3f).

10   University College of Malmö is the most prominent example today of a self-standing teacher education institution after the termination of the Stockholm Institute of Education in 2007. That institution, formally known as *Högskolan för lärarutbildning i Stockholm* (HLS), was inaugurated in 1956 as the first Higher Teacher Seminar in Sweden, later followed by another five institutions (Richardson, 2010, 118). All of these except HLS were merged into other higher-education institutions in the late 1970s. The decision to terminate HLS in 2007 was made by a liberal-conservative government and all programmes were also physically allocated to Stockholm University, an interesting political move in terms of teacher education reform and in an age of a politically emphasised discourse on the autonomy of academic institutions.

11   Cf. Gov. Prop. 1984/85:122: 'Teacher education is a tool to realise the societal intention with schooling. From that perspective it is natural with a more detailed direction of teacher education compared with other academic programmes. The instruments used to direct teacher education shall, for example, contribute to the assurance of quality and comparability of programmes at different sites in the country' (9) and 'Teacher education is a tool for society to exert influence on desired change in schools...' (38); SOU 1999:63: 'The assignment for teacher education entails

three aspects: to be an academic programme, a professional programme and a tool for the national direction of the school system' (109). Cf. Gov. Prop. 1999/2000:135, 16.

12 Richardson (1978, 21). It might be noted that the term 'grammar school' is partly incorrect if it is understood as the narrower British term. Here it refers to the existing school tradition preceding the common school and which prepared for either the degree offered at *gymnasiet/gymnasium* or further studies at universities. It may be better to use the term *secondary school* but that term comes with the hierarchisation of different educational levels and assumes students' progression from primary (or elementary) school to secondary (and tertiary), which is not fully historically correct in this context.

13 Yet it has to be mentioned that four models of teacher education were tentatively discussed in close relation to the introduction of the common school in the 1840s (Skog-Östlin, 1984, 24). But schooling as such was not a novelty; the common school reform expanded education and made it mandatory. The reform that introduced the nine-year comprehensive school was decided on by parliament in 1950 but was not provided with a teacher education model designed for that particular school model before 1988.

14 Five levels: preschool, three periods in Grades 1–9 (1–3, 4–6, 7–9) and upper secondary; historically mainly organised in different schools and buildings. During the 1990s and early 2000s, ambitions of the unified comprehensive school caused an increase in integration, a development that after 2006 became less prominent.

15 Cf. Askling, who emphasised in the early 1970s that 'through the division of teacher education in separate programs [are] obstacles for coordination created to a level that makes such coordination highly marginal' (Askling, 1977, 7).

16 For the study of governance, the official websites of higher-education institutions were used, and charts describing the internal organisation were accessed, and so on. For the study of research funding, governmental decisions and instructions were utilised, together with both personal communication and institution-specific information for the institutions used as examples.

17 Standish, 2003, 231.

18 Cf. Darling-Hammond, 2008.

19 Cf. Gov. Prop. 1984/85:122, which comments that teacher education is a governmental 'tool for realising societal ambitions with schooling' (9), and the governmental inquiry on teacher education from 1999: 'Teacher education has a threefold assignment: to be an academic programme, a professional education and a tool for the state steering of schools' (SOU 1999:63, 109). Cf. Linné, 1996, 335.

20 Other changes, such as, for example, the profound marketisation of the Swedish school system and combined privatisation, impact on teacher education but appear to only marginally add to the complex issue of fragmentation (cf. Åstrand, 2016).

21 Cf. Linné, 1996, 52f.

22 National reforms have to be locally implemented and the importance of that process for fragmentation and cohesion should not be underestimated.

23 One argument for such programmes was the prestige that could come with a central, government-assured training of teachers (Skog-Östlin, 1984, 119).

24 Cf. Linné, 1996, 42; Bertilsson, 2011, 162.

25 Cf. Skog-Östlin, 1984, 22.

26 Hartman, 2005, 97f; Bertilsson, 2011, 162f; cf. Lundgren, 2006, 77.

27 Bertilsson, 2011, 161.

28 The model came to be three full-time semesters of studies in two academic disciplines (totalling three years) followed by a probationary year including practical and pedagogical courses (1 year) (SFS, 1968: 318, §31–36). The model, originating in the inquiry on teacher education from the governmental inquiry, confirmed and continued the dual context for teacher education; the academic tradition and the teacher seminar tradition as this duality also came to be decisive for the new higher teacher seminars. At the time of the merger of teacher education with Swedish higher education (H77), more or less 20 teacher education programmes became reorganised in the new context (The sector for programmes for professional educators ('Sektorn för utbildning för undervisningsyrken'): Barnavårdslärarlinjen, Bildlärarlinjen, Folkhögskollärarlinjen, Fritidspedagoglinjen, Förskollärarlinjen, Grundskollärarlinjen, Handels- och kontorslärarlinjen, Hushållslärarlinjen, Idrottslärarlinjen, Industri- och hantverkslärarlinjen, Musiklärarlinjen, Slöjdlärarlinjen,

Studie- och yrkesorienteringslinjen, Textillärarlinjen, Vårdlärarlinjen, Ämneslärarlinjen (in practice divided into three (SFS, 1977, 263, Annex 11). Cf. Hartman, 97f; Bertilsson 2011, 162f; cf. Lundgren, 2006, 79; *Läroverks-och Folkskoleöverstyrelsernas förslag till ny provårsstadga* (1915). An older critique of the probationary year is summarised in SOU (1948, 27, 368f).

29 Of the 1751 teaching positions in upper-secondary schools in 1946/1947, there were 462 lecturers holding significant research degrees (of whom approximately 60 served as principals). In addition, 62 were holding doctorates in teaching posts other than lecturers and 178 teachers held a lower research degree (licentiate) (SOU, 1948:27, 393f.) Taken together, these figures indicate that approximately 40% of the upper-secondary teachers at the time held this higher qualification. Today, after significant investments during the last decade there are approximately 250 teachers out of close to 270 000 teachers in the whole Swedish school system with such degrees. (www.skolverket.se/statistik-och-utvardering/statistik-i-tabeller/snabbfakta-1.120821)

30 In addition, two 'autonomy reforms' occurred in higher education in 1993 and 2010, as briefly addressed in the section on governance below.

31 These institutions existed for more than a decade parallel to the older teacher seminars for the common school (Bertilsson, 2011, 168; cf. Richardson, 2010, 118).

32 The reform impacted primary and secondary teacher education differently as these new institutions became fully responsible for teacher preparation for primary school but only for the pedagogical and practical preparation of secondary teachers.

33 This overview provides a partially false picture as it assumes that the only and essential reforms in teacher education come from the national level. In fact, there are continuously ongoing local reforms as well. In addition to improvements as such, they can be understood as forms for local institutions to take ownership, operationalise and make sense out of national reforms, hence, possibly countering fragmentation.

34 Cf. TemaNord, 2010, 533, 36. In addition to the frequent reforms, it is essential to also note the frequency and timing of the national evaluations and reviews. After the reform of 1988, a major review was published in 1992 while, after the 2001 reform, teacher education was reviewed in 2005 and 2008. Prior to the start of new programmes arising from the reform of 2011, all institutions had to apply for reaccreditation of all separate programmes and another round of evaluations is currently planned for autumn 2016.

35 OECD, 2015, Ch. 3.

36 In 2006, the liberal-conservative alliance proposed a national system for teacher certification which was put in place in 2011 and became fully effective from 2015 (SFS, 2011:326). The reform launched in 2010 once again required that teacher students should do a probationary year after graduating from a teacher education programme to become eligible for employment as a teacher. According to a governmental investigator, this was even understood as more important than the teacher certification system than was the overarching reform (personal communication). It is to be noted that a particular ordinance (Övergångsbestämmelse 13.a) opened for the validation of eight years of unqualified teaching experience, i.e. work as a substitute teacher, as equal to the required preservice training in a teacher education programme. This is an interesting example of an educational reform coming full circle: introduced in the 1870s, reformed in the early 1900s, terminated in the 1960s, reintroduced in 2010 and again in practice recently terminated due to a teacher shortage and a dysfunctional system. The Swedish National Agency for Education now informs teacher students on the process and rules for acquiring teacher certification as follows (June 2015) at its website: 'You can apply for certification directly after graduation. The parliament abolished in 2014 the requirement of the one-year introduction year as well as the requirement of a letter of recommendation' (my translation) www.skolverket.se/kompetens-och-fortbildning/lararlegitimation, C.f www.svd.se/tunga-instanser-sagar-ny-lararlegitimation.

37 One programme for preschool teaching, one programme entailing two specialisations for Grades 1–3 and 4–6 (with some profiles), one for subject teaching in either Grades 7–9 or 10–12 (specialisations) and finally a fourth programme preparing for teaching in vocational programmes in upper-secondary education.

38 For Grades 1–3, two separate programmes of two or three years depending on prior studies. For Grades 4–6, degrees were awarded by both the older teacher seminars relating to the common school and the new higher teacher seminars. The former was delivered in either two or four years

according to students' prior studies. Teachers prepared for upper secondary school via subject studies and the one-year degree (filosofisk ämbetsexamen) were also eligible for lower-secondary school (Grades 7–9). Teachers prepared for Grades 4–6 could also qualify for Grades 7–9 via a particular programme (SOU, 1965:29A, 242, 276, 309). In addition, certain programmes existed for music, physical education, the arts and so on.

39 For Grades 1–6 and 4–9.

40 However, one has to bear in mind that the 2001 reform came with a dual approach, reducing the number of degrees but increasing the number of possible individual choices. The overarching impression is, however, the dominant desire to increase the commonalities and reduce fragmentation.

41 SOU, 1948:27, 358.

42 SOU, 1948:27, 4.

43 SOU, 1948:27, 5. It is worth observing that the teacher in this report is always a 'he'. Cf. above on gender issues in teacher education. The post-war years did not bring about a teacher education reform due to being occupied with restructuring the school system, however desirable (SOU, 1948:27, 15, 76–79, 355ff, 377f, cf. 495–498) later, in the 1960s, a pressing teacher shortage impacted on the situation, as did an ongoing reorganisation of higher education (SOU, 1965:29A, 20–21, 486ff.) Please take into consideration the existence of a queue into teacher education due to the lack of sufficient capacity in the provision of professional preparation for students with general degrees ('provårskö', 20). Cf. how the Swedish situation was perceived as an international phenomenon: 'Teacher shortage is present all over the world' (68); also how the inquiry reflected on the need for a much more coherent structure for teacher education and how that could be supported with organising teacher education institutions inside higher education and with full responsibility for these programmes. However, it was assumed that in such a model for teacher education these programmes would most likely be perceived for a very long time as second-class programmes (487).

44 SOU, 1965: 29A, 76.

45 SOU, 1965: 29A, 98, 102.

46 SOU, 1965: 29A, 87–100.

47 SOU, 1965: 29A, 103, 668 (the proposed Teacher Education Ordinance). The degrees proposed were class teachers for Grades 1–3 and 4–6. In addition, a special education degree for these grades and two subject-based teacher degrees for Grades 7–9 and 10–12 (670–673).

48 SOU, 1965: 29A, 204.

49 SOU, 1965: 29A, 205. In addition, the traditional dualism between the two main teacher education cultures was understood as a main obstacle and an overarching distinction in teacher education (SOU, 1965: 29A, 17, 574).

50 SOU, 1965:29A, 205.

51 SOU, 1965:29A, 206f.

52 SOU, 1965:29A, 207–212. Cf. SOU, 1965:31, part 5.

53 Cf. the ordinance for higher teacher seminars, SFS, 1968:318, 1 §, in which the higher teacher seminars' first obligation is to ensure education on 'scientific grounds'.

54 Gov. Prop. 1984/85:122, 4. A study in the early 1990s found that teacher educators in one programme were still strongly coloured in their educational understanding of the different educational traditions (Carlgren, 1992, 74).

55 Gov. Prop. 1984/85:122, 5–6.

56 Gov. Prop. 1984/85:122, 6.

57 Gov. Prop. 1984/85:122, 9f.

58 Gov. Prop. 1984/85:122, 4, 8. Cf. Wickman, who points out that already the investigation in the 1960s was inclined to split the old subject-based teacher education into two tracks, one for classes 7–9 and one for Grades 10–12. But the idea was realised. The tradition was too strong and respective teachers were prioritised to be qualified for all these grades through one programme and degree (Wickman, 1997, 8).

59 Gov. Prop. 1984/85:122, 11. As described above, this reform also brought about a change in the teacher education structure as it entailed one teacher education programme with two overlapping teacher degrees, one for Grades 1–7 and another for Grades 4–9.

60   Gov. Prop. 1984/85:122, 39f. As proposed by SOU 1978:86 and pointed to in SOU 1965:29A, 205.

61   In a report in the early 1950s arguing for the establishment of higher teacher seminars, it was claimed that some parts of teacher education should be common for all teacher categories (SOU 1952:33, 41–42) and with this idea a distinction between teacher education studies in general and what became labelled as *true professional training* became established (SOU 1952:33, 19–23). The acquisition of 'general knowledge and particular insights in subjects' was assumed to precede *true professional training*. This distinction came to be highly important and an underlying and recurrent issue of later teacher education reforms. While pointing out this part, it also opens up the perception of this as common ground. It is also stressed that this part of teacher education has a practical purpose. It is claimed that it is not possible to gain 'teaching excellence' only by planning and the capacity to use some craftsmen's tools. Instead, the period of study of *true professional training* has to support prospective teachers in understanding their prior studies from the perspective of children and youth (SOU 1952:33, 22). This distinction continues or reinforces a kind of learning hierarchy in two senses: a sequential one and an epistemological one. But it also affected not only which periods of study should be understood as teacher education but also who should be identified as a teacher educator. A governmental report as late as in the 1990s points out the fact that 80% of a teacher education programme is not recognised as such (Ds 1996:16).

62   Gov. Prop. 1984/85:122, 30, in agreement with SOU 1978:86. Cf. the evaluation of these programmes in the early 1990s (UHÄ-rapport 1992:21, 24–25) acknowledged the existence of collaboration between pedagogy and classes on teaching methods but also commented that educational/learning aspects did not direct the design of programmes, but rather administrative priorities. Kallós and Lyxell (1992) confirm the strong ambition to increase the collaboration between the constitutive elements (subjects) in the programmes but also emphasise the problematic low levels of understanding of the differences between university disciplines and school subjects (38–39, 153–160).

63   Gov. Prop. 1984/85:122, 30, in agreement with SOU 1978:86.

64   The two main documents were the governmental inquiry SOU (1999:63) and the following governmental proposition (1999/2000:135).

65   SOU 1999:63, 49–59.

66   Gov. Prop. 1999/2000:135, 9f.

67   Ibid.

68   SOU 1999:63, 71f, 85, 123f; Gov. Prop. 1999/2000:135, 16–20. Cf. governmental fact sheet on the reform at www.unesco.org/education/uie/pdf/country/Sweden_app8.pdf.

69   Kallós, 2003, 4.

70   SOU 1999:63, 79.

71   SOU 1999:63; Cf. Åstrand, 2006.

72   SOU 1999:63, 78, 84.

73   Cf. SOU 2008:109, 20 where the inquiry outlines its interpretation of sustainability in this respect. The inquiry was later followed by governmental proposition 2009/10:89.

74   SOU 2008:109, 56f.

75   SOU 2008:109, 188.

76   The inquiry in fact proposed a two-degree model, one for primary school and one for secondary school (cf. SOU 2008:109, 24f.) but the governmental proposition became a four-degree model, for preschool, primary school (with specialisation in Grades 1–3, 4–6 or the leisure-time centre), secondary school (with specialisation in Grades 7–9 or 10–12) and for a vocational education (Gov. Prop. 2009/10:89, 9–30).

77   SOU 2008:109, 189.

78   SOU 2008:109, 197ff; Gov. Prop. 2009/10:89, 35ff. The core entailed classes on: The organisation of education and its conditions, Curriculum theory and didactics, Theory of science, research methods and statistics, Development and learning, Special-needs education, Social relations, conflict management and leadership, Assessment and grading, and Evaluation and development work (SOU 2008:109, 27; in the final model these eight were merged into seven areas).

79   SOU 2008:109, 192ff.

80   Cf. Linné, 1996, 53, and Skog-Östlin, 1984, 25f.

81   It should be noted that no empirical studies of classroom practice and teachers' conceptual under-
     standings, and so on, were presented here in support of the hypothesis. Instead, what is pre-
     sented is a rereading of some key aspects of teacher education reforms, indicating how central
     elements and aspects have changed over time.

82   The increasingly internationalised educational community is further not only benefitting from
     the option of policy borrowing but also vulnerable due to a weak professional language that might
     give rise to conceptual ambiguity and confusion. Cf. 'The commonality of concepts in education,
     often through a process of Anglicization, disguises the lack of consensus on their cultural mean-
     ings: the use of accountability or 'learning', all key terms today, overlooks their lack of transla-
     tion or univocal meaning across cultural contexts. Borders are crossed by new global or at least
     European members, bearing a new magic of words. New terms – knowledge society, quality assur-
     ance, knowledge economy, learning economy – while economizing the language of education and
     signaling important new directions, have to bear the weight of local incomprehension' (Lawn &
     Grek, 2012, 7f). Examples of conceptual ambiguity are given in Åstrand (2015).

83   Cf. Cuban, 2013.

84   The empirical material used consisted of governmental bills and preparatory inquiries of impor-
     tance – hence this section has been a study of continuity and change on a discourse level, not a
     study of how teacher education is executed.

85   Lanier & Little, 1986, 565.

86   SOU 1999:63, 369.

87   Different organisational models are also understood as indicative of the organisers' commitment
     to teacher education.

88   Cf. NOKUT, 2006, 65–67.

89   A general higher-education reform of 1977 merged key professional preparation into the higher-
     education system and, in that process, all institutions such as traditional teacher seminars were
     closed. This was also the case with the relatively recent higher teacher seminars. The Stockholm
     Institute of Education, however, remained until it became merged with Stockholm University
     in 2008. In the elections in 2005, the leader of the Liberal Party had a profound focus on school
     reform and called for the closure of Lärarhögskolan i Sthlm (Lejonborg et al., 2005). Stockholm's
     lärarhögskola was consequently terminated by a political decision of the conservative-liberal gov-
     ernment and was closed in January 2008 (Gov. Prop. 2007/08:1, 122).

90   With the exemption named above.

91   The inquiry of 1999 noted that 'their organizational models chosen among the majority of higher-
     education institutions were inappropriate as they were insensitive to governmental direction and
     influences from the surrounding society. In addition, they lack capacity to collaborate with ex-
     ternal organisations' (SOU 1999:63, 369f). Cf. Andrén, 2013, 85–88, and Ds 1996:1. An inter-
     national observation on the governance issue was provided by Lanier and Little already in the
     1980s: '… teacher education is practically everyone's, and yet no one's obvious responsibility or
     priority' (Lanier & Little, 1984, 9).

92   Gov. Prop. 1999/2000:135, 44f.

93   Högskoleverket, 2002. (Report no. 41, incorrectly referred to as no. 22 in the report from 2007).
     In spring 2006, all Swedish higher-education institutions with teacher education had to respond
     to the National Agency for Higher Education on a number of questions regarding the requirement
     to have these particular teacher education boards in place (Högskoleverket, 2006). The responses
     are interesting; for example, the response from Umeå University clearly articulates the ambitions
     that these boards are supposed to hold the programme together and to coordinate it to produce
     greater cohesion.

94   Cf. Högskoleverket, 2002, 10. The National Agency for Higher Education had, however, ar-
     gued against the model with mandatory teacher education boards in the late 1990s (Gov. Prop.
     1999/2000:135, 45).

95   Stening, 2005, 12, 33.

96   Stening, 2005; cf. Högskoleverket, 2007, 11.

97   Stening, 2005, 17, 21.

98   Stening, 2005, 25. The agency at the time clearly supported this kind of faculty equal or superior
     organisational position (27).

99   Självständiga lärosäten, SOU 2008:104. The first autonomy reform in the early 1990s did not end up with the desired change. A general impression is that when the central and detailed directions on organisational arrangements in each HEI were abolished, a similar model became decided upon locally; cf. Andrén, 2013, 97–110.

100 Data were collected during autumn 2007. Acronyms and institutions are listed in Annex 1.

101 Åstrand, 2008.

102 Three of them were particularly small and specialised in, for example, music, which is why they were not included in the study at the time.

103 The one identified here without such boards was one very small music-teacher-preparation unit (approximately 30 students) in a very large university and another was a recently initiated business at the prestigious Royal Institute of Technology for preparing teachers in maths, science and technology (approximately 60 students).

104 The matrix organisational structure in higher education is nowadays often associated with neo-liberal efficiency reforms and a shift from traditional research universities to assumingly more future-oriented entrepreneurial universities (cf. Pinheiro & Stensaker, 2013). It has been argued that the introduction of matrix models represents 'a considerable departure from the traditional ways in which university structures and activities were organized' and it is among other things about a focus on internal collaboration and precision in steering and direction (Pinheiro & Stensaker, 2013, 500). A key argument for the use of matrix models has been their capacity to coordinate capabilities in a large organisation with multiple strategies and purposes (Pinheiro & Stensaker, 2013). However, in a wider higher-education perspective it is interesting to note that the implementation of matrix models is predominantly associated with a shifting model of the whole institution as matrix models *for* teacher education *in* higher education have been introduced for the purpose of an expanded and advanced research base for teacher education programmes, for bringing these programme *into* research universities. Yet there seems to exist an experience-based but quite un-researched notion of a trade-off situation between an increased academic level (meaning the stronger research foundation and orientation of these programmes) and professional relevance and associated cohesion. Such a trade-off is not a priori but, experience-wise, it appears to be the case that the matrix model with its dual or multiple assignments and associations for faculties causes tension over values and identities. This concern, taken together with findings of the low status of teacher education in academia and how that plays out in faculty strategies, points to the very likelihood of this problem and how it can reinforce, if not create, fragmentation (cf. Labaree, 2004; Cuban, 1999). For understanding the position of teacher education in particular and for a general picture on status issues in academia, see Judge (1982) and Becher and Trowler (1989/2001). However, it must also be recognised that such organisational forms can also be perceived as strategies for countering fragmentation as these types of bodies regularly have an institution-wide task to promote the advancement of these programmes.

105 Each university college that provides teacher education programmes was asked which organisational model is used for teacher education. Almost all higher-education institutions, with a very limited number of exemptions, offer the first-level access to comprehensive and relevant information in text and in the form of organisational charts that clearly inform about the overarching organisational units (faculties, academies, schools, institutions) and directive bodies. A difference to be noted is that the small teacher education providers that were excluded from the survey in 2008 due to the purpose of that study are included in this picture. This and other minor differences, such as, for example, that Lund University has launched teacher education programmes together with the University College of Kristianstad, does not significantly alter the overall comparison.

106 Cf. reference no. 2 above.

107 Labaree, 2004.

108 Becher and Trowler, 1989/2001.

109 The approach in the Flexner Report sheds light on its notion of medicine as a scientific discipline: 'The modern point of view may be restated as follows: medicine is a discipline, in which the effort is made to use knowledge procured in various ways in order to effect certain practical ends. With abstract general propositions it has nothing to do. It harbors no preconceptions as to diseases and their cure. Instead of starting with a finished and supposedly adequate dogma or principle, it has

progressively become less cocksure and more modest. It distrusts general propositions, *a priori* explanations, grandiose and comforting generalisations. It needs theories only as convenient summaries in which a number of ascertained facts may be used tentatively to define a course of action. It makes no effort to use its discoveries to substantiate a principle formulated before the facts were even suspected. For it has learned from the previous history of human thought that men possessed of vague preconceived ideas are strongly disposed to force facts to fit, defend, or explain them. And this tendency both interferes with the free search for truth and limits the good which can be extracted from such truth as is in its despite attained' (Flexner, 1910, 156).

110 Gov. Prop. 2015/16:1, Annex 16, 26. In Swedish currency, SEK 5 766 449 000 and SEK 2 461 782 000 (exchange rate as at 1 January 2016). The allocation also covers administration within the council.

111 In 2015, a particular institute (Skolforskningsinstitutet) was established with the dual purpose of: a) the translation of research and dissemination of research to schools and teachers; and b) to fund clinical research in the field of schooling. The institute is allocated EUR 4.4 million (SEK 40 000 000), an amount corresponding to approximately 0.5% of the allocation to the Swedish Research Council.

112 These figures come from the governmental directives for 2015; however, they do not deviate significantly from year to year (*Regleringsbrev för budgetåret 2015 avseende Vetenskapsrådet*).

113 Gov. Prop. 2015/16:1, Annex 16, 148.

114 SEK 40 billion; ibid.

115 In Sweden, resources for public universities are distributed from the government to the institution in two separate channels, one for education and another for research.

116 Figures are not comparable between institutions since they come from different types of sources as no shared data set is available that produces these figures in a comparable way. On the other hand, no two types of source indicate a similar situation in these institutions (Linköpings universitet, 2015, Table 6:15, 90–91), UmU: personal communication (150318), Ann Nordström, Umeå School of Education, Dean's office.

117 It would be illuminating to compare the relationship in HEIs between the proportion of research funds that the given institution allocates to research in relation to each main educational area or programme. However, the accessible data do not easily provide opportunities for such comparisons, which is why another strategy is applied here. Instead, we take as an indicator the status of and the importance ascribed to teacher education, the relationship between teacher education as an educational area and teacher education as a research area. It should be taken into account that these two institutions are most likely among the universities in Sweden to have the strongest institutional support for research relevant to teacher education. There are examples in other institutions, where teacher education research receives a higher proportion of research funding, for example 8%–10%, but in these cases the teacher education share of programmes might exceed 25%. (At Karlstad University, teacher education programmes are above 20% of all programmes (in financial terms; in terms of the number of students, the figures are higher) and the share of the institutional research funds is 10% (cf. Karlstads Universitet, 2015, 32, 46). That institution has taken an internal decision to allocate 10% of its research funding annually to teacher education research.

118 Of course, one can question whether there should exist a strict correlation between the allocation of funds for research and education. That is, however, not the question at hand here. The point is that these figures might indicate that these institutions, despite being some of the most prominent sites for education science research in Sweden, seem to value other sectors higher. A reasonable interpretation is that these figures do show that these institutions have not been able to allocate (or reallocate) funding according to expressed critique against this area as being all too weakly anchored in research, or convinced about the importance of doing so.

119 What could be added to the picture is that there exists a general agreement between the government and public employers that provides opportunities for clinical research in medicine to a value that is more than ten times of what is provided for all educational science research via the Swedish Research Council. This agreement raises SEK 1700 million annually for clinical research in medicine compared with a total of SEK 157 million for both applied and pure research in the educational field. These agreements are in translation named 'Agreement on medical education and research'; cf. Lövtrup, Ett nytt ALF-avtal är klart, *Läkartidningen*, 11 September 2014.

120 Labaree, 2008, 290.

121 Bergius, 1868.

122 Cf. Waldow, 2008; Waldow, 2009.

123 Bruner, 1963, VII.

124 Published in 1960, in Swedish from 1970.

125 Bruner, 1963, 89.

126 Skog-Östlin, 1984, 25f, and Linné, 1996, 53.

127 Luckacs, 1994, 5.

128 Liston and Zeichner, 1991, 3. A tentative hypothesis could be that the political level has been successful in establishing dominant and hegemonic discourses on imagined or real problems but not insightful enough to be able to identify and implement appropriate change, explaining why the system ends up in a situation of unfulfilled ambitions (cf. Lidensjö & Lundgren, 2000, 171ff).

129 Hudson, 2016, 115. Cf. Schneuwly's comment that 'didactics without history is nonsense'. Cf. Tyack and Cuban, 1995, 76.

130 Cf. Zeichner, 2008.

131 Cf. Labaree, 2008.

132 Bok, 1986, 72–113.

133 Bok, 1986, 75.

134 Bok, 1986, 78.

135 Bok, 1986, 76.

136 Cf. Becher and Trowler, 1989/2001. In addition, it has been argued (A. N. Whitehead) that necessary and required competencies for the performance of professional skills may in fact counter competencies required to direct the exercise of these skills. Bok comments: 'Alfred North Whitehead once remarked that the kind of intelligence needed to *perform* professional skills might actually destroy the kind required to *direct* the exercise of the skills' (Bok, 1986, 77).

137 Högskoleverket (2005) and Högskoleverket (2008). The percentage of teacher educators holding a PhD was also interpreted as indicative of the academic level of these programmes.

138 Kerr, 2001, 218f.

139 Diverse traditions do not necessarily have to bring about fragmentation in a field. The question that arises when bringing in that perspective is why diversity in some fields seems to have contributed to progress and cohesion, and in others it is used to explain the opposite (cf. Hartman, 2005).

140 It can be noted that, for example, Umeå University did take a chance and launched a thorough local reform during the period and ended up in failing in almost all its accreditations for a short but painful period (N.B. the author of this chapter was the dean responsible for teacher education at the time).

141 Cf. how David Labaree outlines an extended historical perspective on this (but also from another perspective in the direction of recent developments): 'Ironically, although teacher education was a latecomer to the university [...] it was the core of the original form of the university that emerged in medieval Europe. Early in this institution's history, an advanced liberal arts education was primarily intended to prepare teachers. The university was then constituted as a craft guild for teachers, whose highest degrees (the master's and doctorate) were badges of admission to the status of master teacher and whose oral examinations were tests of the candidate's teaching ability. [...] But over the years teacher education was gradually pushed from the center to the periphery of higher education, which is where it was found in the early nineteenth century when [it] started its long march back' (Labaree, 2008, 290).

142 Cf. Labaree, 2008, and Lanier and Little's comments in the 1980s: 'Universities have never made and do not now make investments in teacher education that are commensurate with talk about the importance of teacher education' (Lanier & Little, 1984, 132).

143 Arreman (2005) provides an interesting account of the past decades of struggle for the development of research in relation to teacher education.

144 These recommendations relate primarily to the Swedish context as the study focuses on conditions for teacher education in Sweden. However, a number of them may be applicable in an international perspective as well.

145 Cf. Zeichner, 2005.

REFERENCES

Andrén, C-A. (2013). *Visioner, vägval och verkligheter. Svenska universitet och högskolor i utveckling efter 1940*. Lund: Nordic Academic Press.

Askling, B. (1977). Stadieindelning och lärarnas specialiseringsgrad. En historisk, utvecklingspsykologisk och kunskapsteoretisk analys av lärarutbildningens specialiseringsgrad, Ds U 1977:1, rapport utarbetad på uppdrag av 1974 års lärarutbildningsutredning.

Åstrand, B. (2006). Aspects of recent reforms of teacher education in Sweden. In P. Zgaga, (ed.), *Modernization of study programmes in teachers' education in an international context*. Ljubljana: University of Ljubljana.

Åstrand, B. (2008). *Organisationsmodeller – lärarutbildning/utbildningsvetenskap vid svenska lärosäten*. A report to the vice-chancellor of Umeå University (2008–01–29, unpublished manuscript, with the author).

Åstrand, B. (2015). Conceptual understandings of democracy and values as aspects of teacher quality – the case of teacher education in Sweden. In G. K. LeTendre and A. W. Wiseman, (eds), *Promoting and sustaining a quality teacher workforce worldwide. International perspectives on education and society, Vol. 27*. Bingley: Emerald Group Publishing Limited.

Åstrand, B. (2016). From citizens into consumers: The transformation of democratic ideals into school markets in Sweden. In F. Adamson, B. Åstrand and L. Darling-Hammond, (eds), *Global education reform – how privatization and public investment influence education outcomes*. New York: Routledge.

Beach, D. (1995). *Making sense of the problems of change: An ethnographic study of a teacher education reform*. Göteborg: Acta Universitatis Gothoburgensis.

Becher, T. and Trowler, P. R. (1989/2001). *Academic tribes and territories. Intellectual enquiry and the culture of disciplines*. Milton Keynes and Bristol, PA: The Society for Research into Higher Education and Open University Press.

Bergius, A. T. (1868). Om skolundervisningen i Mathematik, *Paedagogisk tidskrift*, fjärde årgången, första avdelningen, 1868.

Bertilsson, E. (2011). Lärarutbildning. In E. Larsson and J. Westberg, (eds), *Utbildningshistoria – en introduction*. Lund: Studentlitteratur.

Bok, D. (1986). *Higher learning*. Cambridge: Harvard University Press.

Bruner, J. S. (1963). *The process of education*. Cambridge: Harvard University Press.

Carlgren, I. (1992). *På väg mot en enhetlig lärarutbildning. En studie av lärarutbildares föreställningar i ett reformskede*. Uppsala: Pedagogiska institutionen, Uppsala universitet.

Caroll, D. et al. (2007). *Transforming teacher education. Reflections from the field*. Cambridge: Harvard Education Press.

Cuban, L. (1999). *How scholars trumped teachers. Change without reform in university curriculum, teaching and research, 1890–1990*. New York: Teachers College Press.

Cuban, L. (2013). *Inside the black box of classroom practice – change without reform in American education*. Cambridge: Harvard University Press.

Darling-Hammond, L. (2006). *Powerful teacher education: Lessons from exemplary programs*. San Francisco: Jossey-Bass.

Darling-Hammond, L. (2008). Teaching and learning for understanding. In L. Darling-Hammond et al., (eds), *Powerful learning. What we know about teaching for understanding*. San Francisco: Jossey-Bass.

Darling-Hammond, L. (2012). Teacher preparation and development in the United States. A changing policy landscape. In L. Darling-Hammond and A. Lieberman, (eds), *Teacher education around the World. Changing policies and practice*. New York: Routledge.

Ds 1996:16, *Lärarutbildning i förändring*, Utbildningsdepartementet, Stockholm: Norstedts.

Ekbohrn, C. M. (1904). *60 000 främmande ord och namn m. m. i det svenska språket, tillika med deras härledning och uttal*. Stockholm: Albert Bonniers Förlag.

Erixon Arreman, I. (2005). *Att rubba föreställningar och bryta traditioner – Forskningsutveckling, makt och förändring i svensk lärarutbildning*. Umeå: Umeå universitet.

Flexner, A. (1910). *Medical education in the United States and Canada. A report to the Carnegie Foundation for the Advancement of Teaching. Bulletin Number Four*. New York: Carnegie Foundation for the Advancement of Teaching

Gov. Prop. 1984/85:122. *Om lärarutbildning för grundskolan, m.m.* (governmental proposition).

Gov. Prop. 1999/2000:135. *En förnyad lärarutbildning* (governmental proposition).

Gov. Prop. 2007/08:1. *Budgetpropositionen för 2008, Förslag till statsbudget för 2008, finansplan, skattefrågor och tilläggsbudget m.m. Utgiftsområde 16, Utbildning och universitetsforskning* (governmental proposition).

Gov. Prop. 2009/10:89. *Bäst i klassen – en ny lärarutbildning* (governmental proposition).

Gov. Prop. 2015/16:1. *Budgetpropositionen för 2016 Förslag till statens budget för 2016, finansplan och skattefrågor, Utgiftsområde 16: Utbildning och universitetsforskning* (governmental proposition).

Hartman, S. (2005). *Det pedagogiska kulturarvet. Traditioner och idéer i svensk undervisningshistoria*. Stockholm: Natur & Kultur.

Hudson, B. (2015). Didactics. In D. Wyse et al., (eds), *The SAGE handbook of curriculum, pedagogy and assessment*. London: SAGE.

Högskoleverket. (2002). *Högskolornas särskilda organ för lärarutbildning*, Högskoleverkets rapportserie 2002:41R.

Högskoleverket. (2005). *Utvärdering av den nya lärarutbildningen vid svenska universitet och högskolor*, Del 1–3, Högskoleverkets rapportserie 2005:17R.

Högskoleverket. (2006). *Särskilda organ för lärarutbildning*, remissvar 2006–03–03, (Reg. Nr 31-695-06).

Högskoleverket. (2007). *Vad är kvalitet i distansutbildning? Utvärdering av lärarutbildning på distans*. Rapport 2007:41R.

Högskoleverket. (2008). *Uppföljande utvärdering av lärarutbildningen*, Högskoleverkets rapportserie 2008:8R.

Jones, G. A. (2013). The horizontal and vertical fragmentation of academic work and the challenge for academic governance and leadership. *Asia Pacific Education Review*, 14(1), 75–83.

Judge, H. (1982). *American graduate schools of education: A view from abroad*. A Report to the Ford Foundation. New York: The Foundation.

Kallós, D. (2003). Teachers and teacher education in Sweden. Recent developments. Paper presented at the International Meeting 'La formazione iniziale degli insegnanti in Europa. Percosi attuali e futuri', organised by CIRE (Centro Interdipartimentale di Richeche Educative), Università di Bologna, 24 January.

Kallós, D. and Lyxell, T. (1992). *Linjenämnden och grundskollärarutbildningen*, UHÄ:s utvärdering av grundskollärarreformen, Delrapport 6, UHÄ-rapport 1992:19.

Karlstads universitet. (2015). *Karlstads universitets årsredovisning 2014*.

Kerr, C. (2001). *The uses of the university*, 5th ed. Cambridge: Harvard University Press,

Labaree, D. (2004). *The trouble with ed schools*. New Haven: Yale University Press.

Labaree, D. (2008). An uneasy relationship. The history of teacher education in the university. In M. Cochran-Smith; S. Feiman-Nemser and D. J. McIntyre, (eds.), *Handbook of research on teacher education. Enduring questions in changing contexts*, 3rd ed. New York: Routledge.

Lanier, J. E. and Little, J. W. (1986). Research on teacher education. In M. C. Wittrock, (ed.), *Handbook of research on teaching. A project of the American Educational Research Association*. New York: Macmillan Publishing Company.

Lanier, J. E. and Little, J. W. (1984). *Research on teacher education*. Occasional paper no. 80. East Lansing, MI: Institute for Research on Teaching, Michigan State University.

Lawn, M. and Grek, S. (2012). *Europeanizing education: Governing a new policy space*. Oxford: Symposium Books.

Lidensjö, B. and Lundgren, U. P. (2000). *Utbildningsreformer och politisk styrning*. Stockholm: HLS Förlag.

Linköpings universitet. (2015). *Årsredovisning 2014*.

Linné, A. (1996). *Moralen, barnet eller vetenskapen? En studie av tradition och förändring i lärarutbildningen*. Stockholm: HLS Förlag.

Liston, A. P. and Zeichner, K. M. (1991). *Teacher education and the social conditions of schooling*. New York: Routledge.

Lövtrup, M. (2014). Ett nytt ALF-avtal är klart, *Läkartidningen*. Retrieved from www.xn--lkartidningen-bfb.se/Aktuellt/Nyheter/2014/09/Nytt-ALF-avtal-klart/.

Luckacs, J. (1994). *Historical consciousness – the remembered past*. London: Transaction Publishers.

Lundgren, U. P. (2006). Utbildningsvetenskap – kunskapsområde eller disciplin? In B. Sandin and R. Säljö, (eds), *Utbildningsvetenskap – ett kunskapsområde under formering*. Stockholm: Carlssons.

Lejonborg, L. et al. (2005). Lägg ned Lärarhögskolan och satsa på universiteten. *Dagens Nyheter*. Retrieved from www.dn.se/debatt/lagg-ned-lararhogskolan-och-satsa-pa-universiteten/.

Läroverks-och Folkskoleöverstyrelsernas förslag till ny provårsstadga, *Pedagogisk tidskrift*, Femtioförsta årgången, 1915.

NOKUT. (2006). *Evaluering av allmennlærerutdanningen i Norge 2006*, Del 1: Hovedrapport, Oslo.

OECD. (2015). *Improving schools in Sweden: An OECD Perspective*. Paris: OECD.

Östergren, O. (1981). *Nusvensk ordbok*. Stockholm: Wahlström & Widstrand.

Pinheiro, R. and Stensaker, B. (2014). Designing the entrepreneurial university: The interpretation of a global idea. *Public Organizational Review, 14*(4), 497–516.

Regleringsbrev för budgetåret 2015 avseende Vetenskapsrådet (Regeringsbeslut III:43 av den 22 dec 2014).

Richardson, G. (1978). *Svensk skolpolitik 1940–45. Idéer och realiteter i pedagogisk debatt och politiskt handlande*. Stockholm: Liber Förlag.

Richardson, G. (2010). *Svensk utbildningshistoria. Skola och samhälle förr och nu*. Lund: Studentlitteratur.

Sahlenius, A. G. G. (1916). *Latin-svensk ordbok*. Stockholm: Aktiebolaget Hiertas Bokförlag.

SFS 1968: 318. *Lärarhögskolestadgan*.

SFS 1977:263. *Högskoleförordning*.

SFS 2011:326. *Förordning om behörighet och legitimation för lärare och förskollärare*.

Skog-Östlin, K. (1984). *Pedagogisk kontroll och auktoritet: en studie av den statliga lärarutbildningens uppgifter enligt offentliga dokument kring folkskollärarutbildningen, läroverkslärarutbildningen och lärarhögskolan*. Malmö: Liber förlag.

SOU 1952:33. Den första lärarhögskolan, betänkande utgivet av 1946 års skolkommission, Stockholm, 1952.

SOU 1965: 29A. *Lärarutbildningen, 1960 års lärarutbildningssakkunniga, IV:1*, Stockholm: Ecklesiastikdepartementet.

SOU 1965:31. *Specialundersökningar om* lärarutbildning, 1960 års lärarutbildningssakkunniga, V, Stockholm: Ecklesiastikdepartementet.

SOU 1978:86. *Lärare för skola i utveckling, betänkande av 1974 års lärarutbildningsutredning*, Stockholm: Utbildningsdepartementet.

SOU 1999:63. *Att lära och att leda. En lärarutbildning för samverkan och utveckling*, Stockholm: Utbildningsdepartementet.

SOU 2008:104. *Självständiga lärosäten, betänkande av Autonomiutredningen*, Stockholm.

SOU 2008:109. *En hållbar lärarutbildning, betänkade av Utredningen om en ny* lärarutbildning, Stockholm.

Standish, P. (2003). The nature and purpose of education. In R. Curren, (ed.), *A companion to philosophy of education*. London: Blackwell Publishing.

Stening, A. (2005). *Försöksverksamhet med ändrad organisation inom högskolan*, Utbildningsdepartementet, 2005 (without identification number (dnr)).

Svenska Akademins ordbok. (1893–). Lund: Gleerupska universitetsbokhandeln.

TemaNord 2010:533. Rekrutteringsproblematiken på nordiska laereruddannelser, Nordic Council of Ministers.

Tyack, D. and Cuban, L. (1995). *Tinkering toward utopia – a century of public school reform*. Cambridge: Harvard University Press.

UHÄ-rapport 1992:21. *En grund att bygga på – utvärdering av utbildningen av lärare för grundskolan*, UTGRUNDS:s slutrapport, UHÄ 1992.

Waldow, F. (2008). *Utbildningspolitik, ekonomi och internationella utbildningtrender i Sverige 1930–2000*. Stockholm: Stockholms universitets förlag.

Waldow, F. (2009). Undeclared imports: Silent borrowing in educational policy-making and research in Sweden. *Comparative Education*, 45: 4.

Wickman, P-O. (1997). Grundskollärarlinjens framväxt – LUT 74, *Häften för didaktiska studier* 61, Stockholm: HLS Förlag.

Zeichner, K. (2005). A research agenda for teacher education. In M. Cochran-Smith and K. M. Zeichner, (eds), *Studying teacher education. The report of the AERA panel on research and teacher education*, Washington, DC: American Educational Research Association.

Zeichner, K. M. (2008). Settings for teacher education. In M. Cochran-Smith et al., (eds), *Handbook of research on teacher education. Enduring questions in changing contexts*, 3rd ed. New York: Routledge.

ACRONYMS, SWEDISH HIGHER-EDUCATION INSTITUTIONS AWARDING TEACHER DEGREES (2007/8)

Göteborgs universitet, GU – www.gu.se
Högskolan Dalarna, HDa – www.du.se
Högskolan i Borås, HB – www.hb.se
Högskolan i Gävle, HIG – www.hig.se
Högskolan i Halmstad, HH – www.hh.se
Högskolan i Jönköping, HJ – http://ju.se
Högskolan i Kalmar, HiK (merged 1 January 2010 with Växjö universitet to Linnéuniversitetet – https://lnu.se)
Högskolan i Kristianstad, HKr – www.hkr.se
Högskolan i Skövde, HiS – www.his.se
Högskolan Väst, HV – www.hv.se
Högskolan på Gotland, HGo – (merged 1 July 2013 with Uppsala universitet – http://uu.se)
Karlstads universitet, KaU – www.kau.se
Kungliga tekniska högskolan, KTH – www.kth.se
Linköpings universitet, LiU – http://liu.se/?l=sv
Linnéuniversitetet, LNU – https://lnu.se
Luleå tekniska universitet, LTU – www.ltu.se
Lunds universitet, LU – www.lu.se
Lärarhögskolan i Stockholm, LHS (merged 1 January 2008 with Stockholms universitet – www.su.se)
Malmö högskola, MaH – www.mah.se
Mittuniversitet, MiU – www.miun.se
Mälardalens högskola, MDH – www.mdh.se
Stockholms universitet, SU – www.su.se
Södertörns högskola, SH – www.sh.se
Umeå universitet, UmU – www.umu.se
Uppsala universitet, UU – http://uu.se
Växjö universitet, VxU (merged 1 January 2010 with Högskolan i Kalmar to Linnéuniversitetet – https://lnu.se)
Örebro universitet, OrU – www.oru.se

6 The professional standing of teaching in Europe: Regulation or relegation?

Anthony Finn

INTRODUCTION

The essence of professional status lies in an appropriate balance between trust and accountability. *Good professionals*, be they doctors, lawyers or teachers, deliver a good service to those who rely on their professionalism, and also therefore on their skills, knowledge and expertise being up to date and relevant to their needs. Good professionals seek to improve standards, wherever possible, taking account of the specific needs of those clients for whom they have responsibility, always conscious of the interface between their own professionalism, the needs of their clients and the public interest, and constantly seeking to uphold in practice the agreed values that characterise their profession. In turn, *good professions* have mechanisms in place to secure and maintain high standards, and, in the event that the practice or conduct of an individual member should fall below an acceptable standard, to take appropriate action to protect the public and the standing of the profession.

Traditionally, those professions that have the highest professional status comply with these high expectations. Medical and dental practitioners, lawyers and other professionals take as normal an expectation that they will be registered with a professional body, which has the responsibility to set standards for entry to their professions and for the protection of professional status throughout their careers. In short, they are suitably regulated.

Parents, politicians and teachers regularly use the word 'professionalism' to indicate an expected standard of learning, practice or conduct within teaching. The word can also be overused in reports on issues that, while relevant to teaching, may not directly impinge on professionalism. In addition, teachers sometimes argue that changes to curriculum and assessment or to salaries and conditions of service constrain their professionalism. An example can be found in the negative response of Scottish trade unions (EIS, 2011) to the publication of the McCormac Report, 'Advancing Professionalism in Scottish Teaching'. Although the report's title suggests a focus on professionalism, unions argue, perhaps with justification, that it is more about flexibility in employment.

What, however, is professionalism in teaching? Can it be defined? If we wish teaching to be considered as a profession like, for example, law and medicine, what steps do we need to take to achieve this? Can teaching be promoted to or maintained in the top league of professions? Or is there a risk that some current developments could relegate it to a lower status?

PROFESSIONALISM AND PROFESSIONAL STATUS

As indicated above, teachers generally seek endorsement of teaching as an important profession. Conversely, however, some argue that their professional status is now lower than in a past when teachers were, they considered, respected members of a high-status profession.

It is worth considering when this past might have been and examining the conditions of teachers at that time. In Scotland, for example, it is widely believed that the 'dominie' of the post-Reformation period was a highly respected figure. There is certainly evidence to support the view that Scotland was among the first countries to give priority to the creation of local schools in every parish and the consequent development of educated young people ('the lad o' pairts') who could make their way in society and gain access to university. However, it took many years before access to education became a universal right (Smout, 1986) and it seems that teachers' rewards were also applied inequitably, with wide variations in payment between different genders and social or religious groups. So, while there may be evidence about respect for education, it is less clear that this produced a well-paid, valued professional workforce.

What then is the current status of teaching, when compared to other professions? In research conducted in Cambridge, teachers and others involved in education, including parents, were asked to grade and rank teachers within a group of 16 professions. The findings (Table 6.1) show that others generally perceived teachers' status to be higher than did teachers themselves.

Table 6.1 Perception of the status of teaching when compared with other professions (adapted from Hargreaves et al. 2007)

	Views of teachers		Views of others	
	Grade	Rank	Grade	Rank
Surgeons	6.6	1	6.73	1
Barristers	6.4	2	6.43	3
Doctors	6.3	3	6.45	2
Solicitors	5.6	4	5.50	6
Vets	5.6	5	5.55	5
Secondary headteachers	5.0	6	5.56	4
Accountants	5.0	7	4.91	9
Primary headteachers	4.6	8	5.29	7
Management consultants	4.5	9	4.22	13
Police officers	4.5	10	4.97	8
Secondary teachers	4.0	11	4.69	10
Nurses	3.9	12	4.63	11
Web designers	3.8	13	3.70	15
Primary teachers	3.7	14	4.53	12
Social workers	3.3	15	3.87	14
Librarians	3.1	16	3.22	16

Similar findings in other surveys indicate that the perception of, and respect for, teachers as professionals is generally quite high. *Dolton and Marcenaro-Gutierrez (2013)*, for example, looked at the status of teachers compared with that of 14 other professions across 21 countries. Their results (Figure 6.1) indicate that teaching is generally given relatively high status in most developed countries:

Figure 6.1 Perception of the status of teaching in developed countries

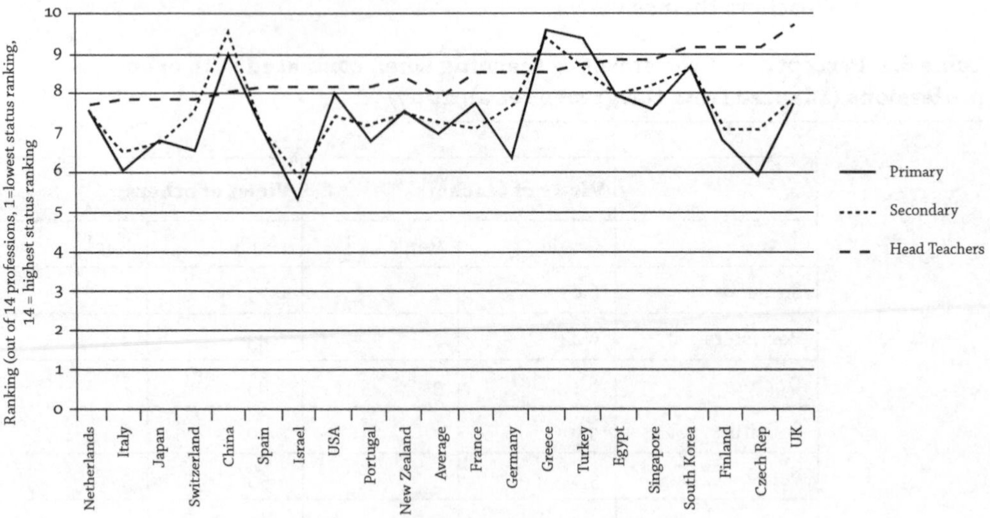

By considering these findings, we can reach a tentative conclusion that teaching would feature in a major professional league if judged by its users. However, this evidence measures client reaction and is an insufficient indication of what constitutes teacher professionalism. A wider understanding of professionalism, and particularly of teacher professionalism, is necessary.

PROFESSIONS AND PROFESSIONALISM

Perhaps the earliest reference to professions may be rooted in the medieval period, when study in universities generally implied learning theology, medicine and law. Interestingly, these *ancient or learned professions* are still widely respected, and mostly well-regulated, today.

The concept of professions within society has developed significantly over the past 150 years. By the beginning of the twentieth century, a number of other employment areas were emerging as both respectable and, indeed, professional. These *newer professions* (for example, accountancy, architecture, civil engineering, dentistry) were mostly full-time occupations that required both some form of study at university and the endorsement of a national body that introduced codes of ethics and governance.

It is arguable that teaching might be considered as one of these newer professions since, at least in countries with well-developed education systems, it had similar features to other professions. However, this was not universally the case across European countries. In some, teacher professionalism was restricted by the lack of political support for policies that required teachers working in schools to be suitably qualified and experienced; and the difficulty of recruiting teachers in some countries led to the employment within schools of unqualified, or underqualified, teachers. Even today, this practice, which would be unthinkable in medicine, can still be found in some countries.

Consequently, there is probably a stronger argument that the professional status of teaching became formally recognised later in the twentieth century, when there developed a better understanding of the need to employ teachers with suitable teacher education and qualifications. In Scotland, for example, Glasgow MP William Hannan criticised the minister for delays in implementing the Wheatley Report (1963), asking:

> ... despite the repeated warnings of my Hon. Friends and myself, will he take steps to reassure the teachers on the question of the uncertificated members in their midst and give some reassurance to parents that the teachers will be as qualified as the doctors and dentists who examine their children? (*Hansard*, 17 June 1964)

Significantly, the Wheatley Report led to the passing of the Teaching Council (Scotland) Act 1965 and the creation of what is believed to be the world's first (and certainly oldest) professional body for teaching, the General Teaching Council for Scotland. However, even in Scotland, it took some time to deliver the expectations anticipated by Wheatley and to achieve acceptance by teachers and parents (cf. Mathieson, 2015).

Teaching may therefore be considered as one of a third group of *modern professions*, perhaps including those engaged in nursing, social work and librarianship, from the middle of the twentieth century.

While established professions have generally reached their own assessments about what professionalism should mean for them, the public use of the term might either extend or restrict understanding of what professionalism might signify. For example, common usage might permit a conclusion that *professionalism* can be conferred on individuals due to:

a) *their receiving payment, often in sport or music:* Professional musicians or athletes normally receive payment for their performance. This status does not increase or fall with the level of payment and it is not uncommon to find examples of individuals being described as both good players and good professionals. Football also throws up the quite twisted example of the 'professional foul', which applies when a player deliberately commits an offence to prevent an opposing side gaining an advantage.

b) *their manner of performance:* Any tradesperson who does a serviceable job and leaves a workplace tidy and well-protected may be deemed to have done a professional job. This describes an attitude to work as professional by indicating that the way it was undertaken has shown a professional commitment. In some circumstances, it might also refer to an individual who demonstrates an impressive degree of competence in a particular skill or area of work.

c) *their being a member of one of the 'professions' and following its guidelines:* More relevantly, this description normally refers to those professions that are well-understood or commonly believed to be professions.

   It is probably fair to assume that this is the traditional view of professionalism in developed nations. In essence, it describes highly educated workers, generally salaried and with earnings perceived as being comfortable, who enjoy considerable working autonomy, and are usually employed in creative and intellectually challenging work.

d) *their being a member of a professional association or a professional body:* This category may seem to be similar to that in (c) above and there are now a growing number of professional (or quasi-professional) bodies across the world. However, it is also confusing as it can be used to describe different types of organisation, including regulatory bodies, professional-development bodies and trade unions.

e) *having relevant expertise or qualifications:* This is a looser definition that addresses some of the issues covered in (c) above.

These definitions are only partly helpful in consideration of the status of teaching. Since the word 'professionalism' is used in a variety of contexts, it is not surprising that there is confusion about its meaning. However, if the teaching profession wishes to be recognised as a profession, or to be in the big league, it needs to act like other professional league players. Consequently, it is necessary to define teacher professionalism; to have agreements in place on the qualifications and formative training required to gain and maintain professional status; and to assess the relevance of issues of conduct and competence.

TOWARDS A DEFINITION OF PROFESSIONALISM FOR TEACHERS

Professionalism is often defined by reference to the specific practice of individuals who practise it. A useful starting base might be the generic definition of professionalism offered by the Australian Council of Professions (1997, 2004):

> A profession is a disciplined group of individuals who adhere to ethical standards and uphold themselves to, and are accepted by the public as possessing special knowledge and skills in a widely recognised body of learning derived from research, education and training at a high level, and who are prepared to exercise this knowledge and these skills in the interest of others.

> It is inherent in the definition of a profession that a code of ethics govern the activities of each profession. Such codes require behaviour and practice beyond the personal moral obligations of an individual. They define and demand high standards of behaviour in respect to the services provided to the public and in dealing with professional colleagues.

This definition clearly points to high standards of knowledge and competence building a foundation for a professional community that is governed within agreed guidelines on practice and supported by a code of ethics.

A number of studies have analysed the professionalism of teaching. For example, MacBeath (2012) argued that there are 12 key features of teacher professionalism. Importantly, these include having high-level knowledge and skills, ensuring induction and preparation for teaching, as well as putting in place a professional code, ethics and regulation system. Like others, he identified the importance of a commitment to public service as particularly significant and added that this 'sets teaching, as a vocation, apart from other and less altruistic professions'. Teachers generally care more about making a difference to children than they do about personal wealth.

Hoyle (1974) saw a difference between 'restricted professionalism' in which teachers see teaching as a craft that is based on their classroom experience, and 'extended professionalism', which involves an analysis of experience and the sharing of professional knowledge and learning. More recently, Pollard (2014), reflecting on Hoyle's work, argued that the 'restricted' model can be used by governments to control and direct teachers. As Harris (2014) pointed out, where teachers are more open to direction, it is easier for politicians to require them to copy a particular approach to teaching. For example, if governments seek to impose curricular solutions or to transfer the 'lessons' of other countries by prescription, the flexibility and professionalism of teachers are restricted.

In addressing the issue of teacher professionalism, a colleague and I looked at a number of different definitions. In the end, we amended Burbules and Densmore's (1991) definition to produce our own expectations of teaching as a modern profession. The 1991 definition was broadly consistent with the Australian generic model in its emphasis on learning, qualification, promotion of the public interest and the concept of individual autonomy. While accepting this approach, we argued that there is now also a related need for self-evaluation, professional development and improving standards of practice; and, like MacBeath, we recognised that education cannot simply be separated from other elements of public service.

Our refined expectations of teachers as professionals are set out below:

- Clearly defined practical and theoretical knowledge
- Systematic education
- Certification of practitioners
- Professional autonomy and accountability
- The prioritisation of service to others before economic benefits
- Commitment to keep learning and improving throughout a career
- Aspiration towards optimal performance
- Collaboration with other professionals (Finn and Hamilton, 2012).

Our view is that it is not sufficient for teachers simply to reach an early professional standard; there is also a need to maintain and improve standards throughout a career. We also anticipate an explicit requirement, observed routinely in the practice of good teachers, to do the best job possible, taking account of the context in which teachers conduct their professional duties and any constraints that these might place on their practice.

This view is broadly consistent with that of Donaldson (2011), who argues that teachers should become 'increasingly expert practitioners whose professional practice and relationships are rooted in strong values, who take responsibility for their own development and who are developing their capacity both to use and contribute to the collective understanding of the teaching and learning process'.

PROFESSIONALISM AND CONDUCT

Any meaningful statement of professionalism, drafted to bring teaching into line with high-status or big-league professions, will inevitably contain clear expectations of the way in which teachers will discharge their duties and include, often in a written code of conduct, clear advice about teachers' conduct and behaviour. On one level, this should ensure that teachers secure, maintain and promote the safety and well-being of their pupils at all times; on another, it will require honesty, fairness, integrity and respect for others. It will also establish parameters of good practice in conduct, relationships, personal benefit and in the expression of and respect for views and opinions.

While the application of such a code of conduct may be easily understood within the classroom, its extension to the private and public life of the teacher is more sensitive. And, yet, teachers must always be conscious of the profession to which they belong, of the demands or constraints that this brings and, in particular, of the implications for the professional standing of teaching in the event that they should act inappropriately. For although teachers, like other citizens, are entitled to a private life and to private views and actions, they must also remember that professionalism is a cloak that provides significant protections, for teachers and for the public, and that therefore brings with it a set of implicit and explicit expectations.

In long-standing professions such as medicine and law, expectations are already well-codified (General Medical Council, 2013; Law Society, 2011). In teaching, any such pattern is less consistently established, being much stronger in those countries in which teaching is already well-regulated (Scotland, Ireland, Wales) than in others in which there is a less defined or structured approach. In most European countries there will be agreement that serious criminal behaviour should lead to a teacher being removed from the classroom. However, there may be less agreement, in principle and in practice, if a teacher is guilty of other offences, especially if that teacher is also an effective and experienced teacher of a shortage subject. For example, cases of fraud, relationships with pupils, extreme political statements or activity and drug or alcohol abuse can be treated differently not only across different countries but even, in the absence of clear guidelines, within countries.

An interesting example of the complexity of teacher professionalism occurs where teachers offer private tuition to students. Now, it could be argued that teachers should be free to engage in private tuition since it allows them to make use of their skills to gain additional income, while protecting students from less scrupulous, perhaps unqualified providers. After all, other professionals, including some doctors, accountants and lawyers, engage in similar forms of practice beyond their contracted duties to an employer. If we accept this argument, teachers should also accept that their private work should not cross a line of professional acceptability, one that might be delineated by a clear expectation that private work did not detract in any way from the proper discharge of their normal duties, did not break any contractual agreements, did not involve their own pupils and did not place teachers or pupils in situations in which there might be a moral or professional risk. In the event that any of these safeguards were not secured, however, private tuition could be a seriously questionable practice.

Soldo and Jokic (2013), in a study of five Eurasian countries, illustrate this particular dilemma within a context in which there is a high level of private tutoring. They indicate that teachers, often earning salaries around or below the national average for their countries, generally use private tuition as a means of supporting their own families and, in some cases, of extending their teaching skills within a less challenging context. However, they also found examples of teachers teaching their own pupils and even, allegedly, creating in their normal classroom work the very circumstances that led parents to believe it to be essential that they engage these same teachers in paid, private tuition. One government department observer commented: 'private tutoring begins to represent a certain form of corruption here', one in which teachers are being paid twice, once by employers, once by parents, to do their normal job.

Although individual circumstances and context must always be considered when questions arise about professional conduct, they cannot be used as a pretext for professional inaction. Consequently, the teaching profession must offer advice and guidance on questions of professional conduct and must also openly address any cases where professional misconduct is in question. This is another argument for professional regulation.

PROFESSIONALISM AND TEACHER EDUCATION

Increasingly, over the past few decades, free-standing teacher education institutions have been integrated into universities. University-led programmes have a focus on linking research and professional practice in the education of teachers; and teaching qualifications are now generally awarded at degree, postgraduate or, increasingly, Master's level. Importantly, this is a strong feature of high-performing countries such as Singapore and Finland.

Despite this apparent consensus about how teacher education can improve teacher quality, there is still a wide debate about the best way forward. In recent years, criticism has been expressed about the quality, understanding of current practice, skills and recent experience of some university teachers, and about the preparation offered by universities for classroom and behaviour management. This scrutiny of the nature of teacher education has encouraged some countries to revise their approach and/or to introduce different routes into teaching. In each case, however, the argument for change is based on a need to improve teacher quality; and Barber and Mourshed's findings (2007) are widely quoted and supported by proponents of change.

As a result, in some countries, higher teacher qualification standards are in place and competition for entry to teaching can be quite intense; in others, there are so many teacher vacancies that 'quick fix' schemes still allow the recruitment of '*teachers*' with limited, formal teacher education; and in other countries (e.g. Sweden, England, parts of America and Australia), the political approach of governments, often quite right-wing governments, has led to changes that, some teachers argue, put teacher professionalism at risk.

While there are a number of new approaches, perhaps the two most significant types are as follows:

- *Hybrid 'clinical model' programmes:* These university-led and research-informed programmes are based in specific, accredited schools with a clear focus on professional enquiry. Examples of this approach can be found in Australia (e.g. the Melbourne M Teach programme), the

Netherlands (opleidingsscholen training schools), Finland (school partnerships with universities) and also in parts of the UK linked to the universities of Glasgow, Strathclyde and Oxford. Early feedback (for example, Conroy, Hulme & Menter, 2013) suggests that this type of programme, when well-constructed and carefully planned, can be successful.

- *School-led or 'craft' approach:* This radical approach is based on a belief that good teaching depends more on an understanding of the craft of teaching and that teachers need to have greater focus on school practice than on university preparation. The resultant programmes are often much more flexible than the traditional model, involving mainly school-based and employer-centred training, with or without a university input. This approach, which is becoming common in England and in parts of the USA, is sometimes confusingly described as 'clinical' because of the time spent observing and interacting with students. It is, however, a very different type of clinical model from that described above, without any guarantee of strong interaction with research and university learning.

In Scotland, however, Donaldson (2011) takes a longer view. He considers that teaching should be seen as 'complex and challenging, requiring the highest standards of professional competence'. He therefore argues for the creation of 'a reinvigorated approach to 21st century teacher professionalism'. He recognises the value of high-quality teacher education and induction and argues that teachers, irrespective of career stage, should have 'high levels of pedagogical expertise, including deep knowledge of what they are teaching'. His emphasis is on enhancing career-long learning by developing, extending and improving teachers' professional standards. This view finds an echo in the work of the 2014 International Teachers' Summit (Asia Society, 2014). The summit brought together political and educational thinkers from across the globe to discuss issues of excellence, equity and high-quality teaching. Some of its main findings are very relevant to the development of teaching as a profession; in (my) very broad summary, these confirm the need for:

- a standards-based profession
- high-quality initial teacher education
- a 'professional learning system' for teachers
- an infrastructure to grow and develop teachers and leaders

- a career ladder for teachers and leaders
- strengthened collaboration in the profession
- promotion of strong partnership across different bodies.

There is a clear emphasis here on improving the professionalism of teaching. Other international summits have drawn similar conclusions, stressing the value of teacher professional development and approaches to leadership.

In recent years, too, various researchers have asserted that teaching is a complex and research-informed activity. Classroom practitioners, they argue, are required to gain a firm, theoretical understanding that will allow them to make relevant, principled decisions and to respond appropriately to the needs of learners (Timperley, 2008; Darling-Hammond, 2005). Darling-Hammond's concept of a teacher as an 'adaptive expert' reinforces this view, confirming the need for early preparation and regular, subsequent development of teachers.

An RSA/BERA study (2014) analysed current developments and provides helpful background information about the strength and weaknesses of different approaches to the preparation of teachers, as well as to the development of their professional skills throughout their career. While its evidence may not be conclusive, it would be difficult not to reach a view that the professional quality of teachers, and therefore their ability to have a strong and sustained impact on the learning of children, is linked to the quality of their professional preparation and subsequent development as teachers.

Overall, therefore, it is suggested that teachers' professionalism is enhanced when their education and subsequent professional development prepare them for the *complexity* of their work in schools. This would provide an understanding of practice that is informed by theoretical and technical expertise and that promotes an ability to reflect, interrogate and analyse experience with a view to refining and improving practice.

A DISUNITED KINGDOM

As different European countries address important issues of teacher professionalism and practice, it would be logical to anticipate some degree of fragmentation in policy and practice across the continent. In the

United Kingdom, however, there is a clear example of fragmentation within one member state.

The UK government makes provision for England but arrangements in the other countries are, at least to some extent, devolved. In Scotland, educational policy and practice were devolved to the Scottish government in 1999 but have been separately governed since the Act of Union in 1707. Indeed, it could be argued that a vote for independence in the 2014 Scottish referendum would have had minimal impact on education: Scotland has its own curriculum, assessment and examination systems and its own approach to teacher education and professionalism.

In these areas, there is wide divergence in approach between Scotland and its nearest neighbour. Much of this can be accounted for by political and ideological differences. The UK Conservative Party, for example, has been in government for over 40 of the past 65 years; in Scotland, however, it has had only one UK Member of Parliament since 2001.

Over the past 30 years, British Conservative politicians have written extensively about education and teacher education, and shown strong, political preferences for unregulated and free-market approaches. Mrs Thatcher, in particular, clearly wished to change the ethos of teacher education: 'The effective monopoly exercised by the existing teacher training routes had to be broken'. She therefore argued against traditional teacher education approaches and sought to maximise recruitment from the controversial Licensed Teacher and Articled Teacher schemes: 'We wanted to see at least half of the new teachers come through these or similar schemes, as opposed to teacher-training institutions' (Thatcher, 1993).

Mrs Thatcher's successor, John Major, took a similar line (1992): 'I also want reform of teacher training. Let us return to basic subject teaching, not courses in the theory of education.' He went on to signal that schools would also be taken out of local authority control, recognising that this would lead to an argument with what he described as 'the educational establishment'.

Throughout this period, Conservative Governments were advised and influenced by a number of right-wing thinkers. One of these, Anthony O'Hear, a well-known English academic philosopher and educational thinker, argued strongly (1989) against the academic formation of teachers. Teaching was, for him, a craft that should be learned on the job:

There is, I suggest, no well-established and comprehensive body of theory covering teaching and learning. For practical purposes, I argue, this would not matter, since teaching is a practical matter, one best learned by doing, under the guidance of experienced practising teachers.

Professor O'Hear still has considerable influence and recently wrote a piece that shows the commitment of conservative thinkers to a market-led and economically driven education sector:

An independent school which fails to satisfy its customers will close in short order. This is not the case with state schools, whose clientele are not customers so much as suppliants, who have to be grateful for what they get. [...] Hardly surprising that too many state schools, not subject to minimal economic discipline, coast along in complacent mediocrity or worse, the damage compounded by the attempts of successive governments to regulate standards by otiose regulation and ideologically driven inspection. (O'Hear, 2013)

In the 2010 Conservative-led government, another freethinker, then Education Minister Michael Gove, implemented many of these ideas in practice. His gurus are of the American Right. In 2013, he asserted that 'evidence shows the best teacher training is led by teachers; that the skills which define great teaching – managing behaviour, constructing compelling narratives, asking the right questions, setting appropriate tasks – are best learnt from great teachers; that the classroom is the best place for teachers to learn as well as to teach'.

As a result of this ideological approach, English schools and teacher education have changed. First, the teaching regulator, GTC England, was abolished in March 2012; rules changed for entry to teaching, and schools were encouraged to train staff on the job. More than 400 'free schools' have been approved in England and more than 4500 schools are now open as 'academies'. These schools are no longer required to hire qualified staff or meet national teacher conditions. In addition, entry to teaching in England is often undertaken through school-led teacher-training courses (e.g. Schools Direct), designed by groups of schools working in school-centred training or with a university, and based on the skills that these schools are looking for in a newly qualified teacher.

In short, teaching in England has become unregulated and is now openly compared to a craft-based occupation. Those supporting these changes argue that teachers will learn more about the key issues of teaching from other teachers than they would in a university course.

The rhetoric behind these changes is powerful and proponents claim that they place priority on improvement in teaching standards. Although there is little empirical evidence to support this judgement, it is likely that some schools will make the system work. However, the driving philosophy behind this development seems to be supported more by political preference than by a research base. At best, it depends on current teachers being able to have secure knowledge of up-to-date developments in learning and teaching and sharing this with new teachers. It is arguable, too, that an approach to teacher education that can dispense with a strong, university-led input puts at risk the perception of teaching as a major league profession.

On the other hand, it is important to acknowledge that teacher education is governed by political choice. The education of our young people is of such significance that politicians will necessarily seek to ensure that it is delivered as well as it can be within the resources available at any given time.

The approaches across the United Kingdom show how differently this imperative can be interpreted; and the claim that policy is built around a quest for improved standards is common in each of these approaches. In Scotland, there is wide acceptance, confirmed by the Scottish government's endorsement of the Donaldson Report (Donaldson, 2011) that teachers should have appropriate academic and vocational qualifications.

GTC Scotland (GTCS), established in 1965, is a key player in determining professional standards in teaching. In 2012, GTCS gained even higher status by being granted the right to become a fully independent professional body. This decision by government showed increasing trust not only in the regulation of but in *self-regulation by* the teaching profession.

GTCS now sets the standards required of all teachers in Scotland: teachers must be qualified to degree standard and have completed a programme of teacher education in a university accredited by GTCS before they can enter the profession. Professional standards (GTCS, 2013) then guide teachers throughout their career and illustrate expectations of growing professional engagement and improvement.

New teachers complete a rigorous but well-supported probationer induction scheme to attain the Standard for Registration and gain an entitlement to become fully registered; they must then engage in professional development throughout their careers, aspiring to the Standard for Career-long Professional Learning and, if they deem it appropriate, to the Standards for Leadership and Management. Finally, they must also use the standards to reflect on their progress and performance, being required to provide evidence to GTCS every five years that they are keeping their teaching skills up to date (Professional Update).

Unlike England, Scotland has a Code of Professionalism and Conduct, which offers clear advice to teachers on the key principles and values of teaching, highlighting the boundaries of professional behaviour and conduct that ensure that trust in teachers is maintained. There is also a Framework on Teacher Competence, which sets out procedures for handling questions of teacher underperformance in a manner that is fair to the teacher, while ensuring high professional standards.

In short, there is a clear understanding among Scottish teachers of the expectations of the profession. Importantly, all of these significant professional changes were profession-led, being introduced by GTCS following lengthy consultation, and are the result of an emerging Scottish consensus about teacher professionalism. In Scotland, there is broad acceptance by teachers, unions and employers of these key tenets of teacher professionalism.

In both Wales and Northern Ireland, different patterns apply. While not enjoying the same devolved power available to Scotland, each has taken its own approach to teaching as a profession and neither has accepted the unregulated provision promoted in England. In Northern Ireland, a process of review of teacher education was initiated in 2003 and revisited in 2010 (DENI, 2010). Despite delays in the implementation of the recommendations, plans are now emerging (DENI, 2013) to grant stronger powers to an independent professional body that may be similar to the Scottish model. In Wales, the General Teaching Council for Wales recently developed into an Education Workforce Council that regulates and sets standards for teachers, FE lecturers and support staff. In addition, a recent report for the Welsh Assembly on teacher education advocates a model that, while set firmly in the context of Wales, is not significantly different from the findings of the Donaldson Report in Scotland. It proposes, for example, 'a form of initial teacher education that is expansive rather than restricted, one that gives teachers themselves the skills, knowledge and dispositions to lead the changes that are needed' (Furlong, 2015).

Overall, there is much common ground between the three smaller nations within the United Kingdom, each setting educational change within its own context, and all taking quite different paths to that of their English neighbours. This fragmentation is perhaps best reflected in a joint statement on teacher professionalism issued in 2013 by the Teaching Councils of Scotland, Wales and Northern Ireland, together with the similar body (Teaching Council Ireland) that operates within the separate state of Ireland. The contrast with the approach adopted in England is clear:

> We view teaching as a complex profession which requires high standards of competence, professional skills and commitment. We consider that high quality teaching is necessary to deliver high standards of learning for our students. We believe that quality teaching is achieved when teachers commit themselves to lifelong learning and ongoing reflection on their professional practice; when they have excellent knowledge of the curriculum which they are expected to teach; when they have deep and detailed understanding of how pupils learn; and when they have the confidence to apply and vary their pedagogical skills to meet the needs of learners in different and sometimes challenging contexts.
>
> ... When assessing the suitability of those who wish to teach within our jurisdictions, we will require that teachers are suitably qualified, both academically and professionally, and that they have appropriate values and a commitment to maintaining and improving their professional practice as they progress throughout their careers.

Although there is a divergence of view about the most appropriate approach to teacher education across the United Kingdom, it is clear that this issue is extremely important to governments and also to the profession. Indeed, despite its political agenda, the UK government has also been open to considering different ideas. It commissioned a review of what, significantly, it calls teacher training (as opposed to teacher education). The report (Carter, 2015) advises government on current developments and adopts a more encouraging stance for those who are most critical of deregulation. Carter suggests, for example, that government should commission a new sector body to take teacher professionalism forward, stating that 'we feel it is critical that a framework is developed by the sector, rather than by central government'. Carter also gives priority to areas such as subject pedagogy, evidence-based teaching and school–university partnerships. Of particular relevance is his suggestion that all those preparing to become teachers should have a 'clear understanding of the professional role and expectations of a teacher'.

Carter's views are consistent with the growing groundswell of support in England for self-regulation by a new College of Teaching (2015) offering professional standards, development and knowledge, as well as a professional code. Perhaps the Disunited Kingdom may yet reunite in a common quest for high standards of teacher education and professionalism.

TOWARDS A MORE UNITED CONTINENT?

A number of European countries have already taken significant steps to demand high standards of those who wish to teach in their jurisdictions, while others are considering or implementing similar steps. In Finland, for example, access to teacher education programmes is highly competitive; there is a clear emphasis on the importance of research-based learning and on Masters' level provision for all teachers; and there is an associated expectation that teachers will have significant professional autonomy in the classroom. It is perhaps not surprising therefore that the profession is valued and, indeed, considered to be similar to that of doctors, engineers and lawyers (Sahlberg, 2015).

In a number of other European countries, a planned approach to incremental professional development can be observed. For example, the Republic of Ireland has recently made significant changes to its approach to teacher education and professionalism. The Teaching Council Ireland (2011) required all university providers to complete a re-conceptualisation of programmes in line with carefully constructed guidelines that address the development of teachers across their careers. The council also subjected all new programmes submitted by providers to an extensive process of review and accreditation (Teaching Council Ireland, 2011a), thus ensuring compatibility with its own expectations and those of the Irish government. Consequently, postgraduate students now follow challenging research-led Master's programmes as the basis for their entry to the profession.

In other countries, the trend is also towards stronger and higher standards, although generally these changes are overseen by government departments (e.g. the refinement of programmes at Master's level in France in 2010 and 2013) rather than by professional bodies. While EU Directive 2005/36/EC ensures professional mobility between member states, this does not imply that teacher qualifications across the community are equal in quality or in academic or professional standards. However, since agreements were reached on the Bologna Process, less diversity in terms of approach and a general direction towards a higher qualified profession can be detected. There is considerable interest in developments in Finland, in Ireland and in Scotland; and the influence of EU policy statements may subsequently lead to greater coherence across the Union.

Despite this good progress, the European Union has a limited role in developing educational policy. All member states are responsible for their own education systems and the Union's main role is to help identify skill shortages and to address shared issues. It offers a useful service by collating data, disseminating statistics and sharing good practice; it publishes helpful advice and guidance on trends or on areas identified as being of common interest; and it can offer funding in support of preferred policy reforms that are in line with EU policy.

Notwithstanding these limitations, the work carried out by the EU is helpful to the development of teacher professionalism. Indeed, the EU and its Commission have consistently emphasised strong links between educational attainment and effective systems of teacher education (e.g. EU Commission, 2007). In 2012, the Commission invited member states to 'revise and strengthen the professional profile of all teaching professions [by] reviewing the effectiveness as well as the academic and pedagogical quality of Initial Teacher Education, introducing coherent and adequately resourced systems for recruitment, selection, induction and professional development of teaching staff based on clearly defined competences needed at each stage of a teaching career, and increasing teacher digital competence'. The Commission, clearly anticipating that states would ensure that high standards could be found in every school, followed this publication with a specific report that looked at competencies (EU, 2013a), offering policy-makers 'practical and reasonable advice that is underpinned by evidence from academic research and from the analysis of current policies in participating countries'.

In its subsequent report (EU, 2013b), the Commission highlighted examples of practice across Europe that, perhaps, show just how much we still have to do to ensure that consistent standards apply. It found, for example, that 17 countries had taken no meaningful action to enhance the teaching profession's attractiveness and, surprisingly, that 18 European countries had no induction scheme for teachers, a feature generally considered very beneficial to new teachers. While emphasising the need for teacher education to have a strong link with experience in the field, the Commission also made clear that practical experience alone cannot provide sufficient training; mentoring and reflection are equally important. The report concludes by making a number of specific recommendations that broadly endorse the need for a higher degree involving research on professional practice, together with approaches that 'professionalise all persons involved in teacher education and training'.

Given the emphasis of the EU's work, it is perhaps not surprising that Xavier Prats-Monné, the Commission's Deputy-Director General for Education and Culture, told a meeting held in Dublin that:

> Teaching Councils of the kind that exist in Wales, Ireland, Scotland and Northern Ireland can be a very interesting model for other Member States to examine. They can play a significant role in the professionalisation of the teaching workforce, in promoting a culture of reflective practice and career-long learning, and in raising standards of teaching. (Prats-Monné 2013)

CONCLUSION: RELEGATION OR REGULATION?

This chapter has considered the concept of teacher professionalism and its development. It has argued that there is good reason for teaching to be perceived as a profession that belongs in the same *league* as medicine or law but that, in order to achieve this status, the practices, qualification requirements and expectations of teaching should be given similar emphasis to those of established professions. This view is reinforced by the second McKinsey Report (Barber et al., 2010), which argued that good education systems could become 'great' by 'shaping the teaching profession such that its requirements, practices and career paths are as clearly defined as those of medicine or law', by increasing the flexibility and autonomy of teachers and by 'establishing mechanisms that make teachers responsible to each other as professionals for both their own performance and that of their colleagues'.

In using the populist language of football, I have opened up a comparison between regulation and high standards in some countries and deregulation and professional relegation in others. This football analogy does have another application, however. The most successful football players recognise that they need to work hard and keep adapting their approach as systems and tactics change; they cannot assume that their contribution to the team is unique or disconnected to the work of other players. Both footballers and teachers are team players and must therefore be accountable in discharging their responsibilities. Good teams ensure that players support each other but are also responsible to each other for their own performance and that of their team. In both teaching and football, inadequate standards or insufficient quality can lead to failure and relegation.

If teaching is a mature profession, the regulation of teaching and teachers is important. Consequently, we must regularly review the success of different systems and encourage the detailed study of effective policy and practice across Europe. In particular, we must address a series of difficult questions professionally.

First, there needs to be clear advice on issues of teacher conduct and behaviour, together with a fair and accountable mechanism to evaluate and adjudicate those cases where a teacher may have failed to act appropriately.

Second, while teaching standards are generally high, one incompetent teacher is one too many, given the potential impact of poor teaching on students. Promoting high standards and addressing incompetence where it does occur are, I would argue, the first requirements of any profession. There should, accordingly, be effective systems to guide, coach and support a teacher who might be experiencing difficulty or who is at risk of becoming incompetent. There must also be agreed mechanisms to measure competence and to support teachers to attain, maintain and improve standards. Where teachers are chronically incompetent, however, we must have a system that measures this failure objectively and that can, if necessary, lead to their removal from the classroom.

Third, a profession must expect high and improving standards from teachers at all stages of their careers. We must anticipate they will have high levels of knowledge and classroom skills, have a strong emphasis on pedagogy and learning and seek to maintain and improve teaching standards and skills throughout their careers. Teachers will therefore accept the responsibility to keep learning and to address any weaknesses they may have; and we must also take steps to support them systemically.

Fourth, although my own country can claim to have taken many of the steps outlined above, there may be different ways forward in other countries. Every country should therefore analyse best practice and find its own solutions, taking account of its context and starting base.

As Xavier Prats-Monné suggested, it might be constructive for EU countries to examine the benefits of introducing professional regulatory bodies or teaching councils. Any such approach would take time and careful planning to balance rights and responsibilities. For, although teaching councils have been adopted successfully in the UK, Ireland, Canada, Australia, New Zealand and Africa, there are lessons to learn from the particular difficulties experienced in England and in British Columbia, which led to the dissolution of the GTC England and the British Columbia College of Teachers. In best practice, however, teaching councils have thrived and led to considerable improvements in teaching standards and teacher professionalism.

In conclusion, I recommend wider research and analysis of the effectiveness of steps taken in Scotland and other countries to develop a new professionalism.

Overall, I argue for a future in which teacher quality in the upper league of professionalism is protected by effective professional bodies with regulatory and professional powers, and with increasing independence from the volatility of other bodies, including government. This is a high level of ambition, especially in those countries where there are no such bodies or where power granted by statute is at best conditional and/ or where the support of teachers and parents has not been confirmed.

In future, teacher professional regulatory bodies would be trusted to act sensibly in the public interest and to take professional decisions that would be supported, or at least respected, by the profession and by the public at large. All such bodies would need to accept that they need to win the right to the trust that would allow them to operate independently, and to remain always conscious that this right could be taken away if they, or their members, should act inappropriately. Trust would therefore be balanced by accountability.

In my view, teacher professional regulatory bodies should be careful to engage only in activities that are professionally relevant to teachers and to teaching; they should take steps to ensure that teaching is seen as a complex, high-order profession with appropriate entrance qualifications and standards; they should set high standards of conduct and competence; develop regulatory processes that are fair and equitable; and act with credible authority in pursuit of the public and the professional interest. And, while they must be willing to stand up for and promote teaching, there must be a clear distinction between that professional role and the responsibilities of a teacher trade union.

Inevitably, education is a matter of great political importance. It is disappointing, however, that discussions about teacher professionalism have sometimes been diverted into ideological political stances that have implications for the professional status of teaching and that can create irretrievable change across the school system. In planning for a professional future, therefore, we need to ensure that there is appropriate external *regulation* but to guard against the unnecessary use of external *control*.

This debate should be about what is best not just for teachers but also for students. The real value of teacher professionalism lies in the assurance that it brings higher standards for learners. Would we risk patients in hospital with surgeons who were unqualified or did not keep their skills up to date? Could a clever, well-informed and educated debater do the job of a lawyer? Could an able bus driver pilot an aircraft? In other professions, practice 'on the job' is seen as important once you have understood the theory that underpins it and this leads to greater security and a higher-quality service. Our students too will benefit from higher standards; perhaps an unregulated profession therefore deserves to be relegated.

REFERENCES

Asia Society. (2014). Excellence, equity and inclusiveness. high quality teaching for all. The 2014 International Summit on the Teaching Profession. Retrieved from http://asiasociety.org/files/2014teachingsummit.pdf.

Barber, M. and Mourshed, M. (2007). *How the world's best performing school systems come out on top* (pp. 16 et seq.). New York: McKinsey & Company.

Barber, M. Chijioke, C. and Mourshed, M. (2010). *How the world's most improved school systems keep getting better* (executive summary, pp. 3–4). New York: McKinsey & Company.

Burbules, C., and Densmore, K. (1991). The limits of making teaching a profession. *Educational Policy*, 5(1), 44–63.

Carter Review of Initial Teacher Training. (2015). London: Department for Education. Retrieved from www.gov.uk/government/publications/carter-review-of-initial-teacher-training.

Conroy, J., Hulme, M. and Menter, I. (2013). Developing a 'clinical' model for teacher education. *Journal of Education for Teaching: International Research and Pedagogy*, 39(5), 557–573.

Darling-Hammond, L. and Bransford, J. (eds) (2005). *Preparing teachers for a changing world: What teachers should learn and be able to do.* pp. 201–231, San Francisco: Jossey-Bass.

DENI (Department of Education, NI). (2010). *Teacher education in a climate of change.* Belfast: Department for Employment and Learning.

DENI. (2013). *Proposals to widen the powers of GTCN and extend its remit to include the further education sector.* Retrieved from www.deni.gov.uk.

Dolton, P. and Marcenaro-Gutierrez, O. (2013). *The global teacher status index 2013.* P16, London: Varkey Gems Foundation.

Donaldson, G. (2011). *Teaching Scotland's future: Report of a review of teacher education in Scotland* (P15, p. 84). Edinburgh: Scottish Government.

Educational Institute of Scotland (EIS). (2011). McCormac review – our concerns. Retrieved from www.eis.org.uk/McCormac/McCormac_Our_Concerns.htm.

EU Commission (2007). *Communication to the Council and the Parliament on Improving the Quality of Teacher Education.* Retrieved from http://www.europarl.europa.eu/RegData/docs_autres_institutions/commission_europeenne/sec/2007/0931/COM_SEC%282007%290931_EN.pdf

EU (2012). *Rethinking education: Investing in skills for better socio-economic outcomes.* Retrieved from http://eur-lex.europa.eu/legal-content/EN/TXT/?qid=1389776578033&uri=CELEX:52012DC0669.

EU (2013a). *Supporting teacher competence development for better learning outcomes.* Retrieved from http://ec.europa.eu/dgs/education_culture/repository/education/policy/school/doc/teachercomp_en.pdf

EU (2013b). *Study on policy measures to improve the attractiveness of the teaching profession in Europe.* Retreived from http://www.ijf.hr/upload/files/file/knjige/Study_on_Policy_Measures_to_Improve_the_Attractiveness_of_the_Teaching_Profession_in_Europe-Vol-1.pdf

Finn, A. and Hamilton, T. (2013). The General Teaching Council for Scotland: An independent professional body. In T. Bryce, W. Humes, D. Gillies and A. Kennedy, (eds.), *Scottish education: Referendum; Edition 4* (pp. 964–973). Edinburgh: Edinburgh University Press.

Furlong, J. (2015). *Teaching tomorrow's teachers.* A report to the Welsh education minister, Cardiff, p. 38. Retrieved from http://gov.wales/docs/dcells/publications/150309-teaching-tomorrows-teachers-final.pdf.

GTC Scotland. (2013). *Professional standards.* Edinburgh Retrieved from www.gtcs.org.uk/standards/standards.aspx.

General Medical Council. (2013). Good medical practice; and also Standards and ethics guidance for doctors. Retrieved from www.gmc.uk.org/publications/standards_guidance_for_doctors.asp.

Gove, M. (2013). *Gov.uk, 5 September 2013*, accessed 6 April 2015.

Hansard. (1964). *House of Commons official report*, UK Parliament, London, 17 June 1964.

Hargreaves L., Cunningham M., Everton T., Hansen A., Hopper B., McIntyre D., Oliver C., Pell T., Rouse M. and Turner P. (2007). *The status of teachers and the teaching profession in England: Views from inside and outside the profession.* Cambridge: University of Cambridge/DfES.

Harris, A. (2014). PISA keynote speech. Scottish Learning Festival, Glasgow, 24 September 2014.

Hoyle, E. (1974). Professionality, professionalism and control in teaching. *London Education Review*, 3(2), 13–19.

Jokic, B. and Soldo, A. (2013) The roles of teachers in the decision concerning the use of private tutoring services. In B. Jokic, (ed.), *Emerging from the shadow: A comparative qualitative exploration of private tutoring in Eurasia* (pp. 115–162). Zagreb: NEPC.

MacBeath, J. (2012). *Future of teaching profession* (pp. 14–16). Cambridge: Cambridge Network.

Major, J. (1992). Speech to Conservative Party conference, 9 October. Retrieved from www.johnmajor.co.uk/page1208.html.

Mathieson, I. (2015). *Milestones and millstones. The General Teaching Council for Scotland.* Edinburgh: GTCS.

O'Hear, A. (1989). *Who teaches the teachers?* London: Social Affairs Unit.

O'Hear, A. (2013). The riddle of the voucher. Conservativehomeblogs, an online blog for Conservative party readers. Retrieved from http://conservativehome.blogs.com/thinkers_corner/2013/01/anthony-ohear.html#more.

Pollard, A. (2014). *Reflective teaching in schools.* London: Bloomsbury Academic.

Prats-Monné, X. (2013). The professional identity of teacher educators. Paper presented at Irish Presidency Conference, Dublin, 18–19 February.

RSA/BERA. (2014). *Research and the teaching profession: Building the capacity for a self-improving education system.* Final report of an inquiry into the role of research in Teacher Education. London: RSA.

Sahlberg, P. (2015). Finnish Lessons. *What can the world learn from educational change in Finland?*, 2nd ed. New York: Teachers' College Press.

Smout, T. C. (1986). *A century of the Scottish people, 1830–1950.* London: Collins.

Teaching Council Ireland. (2011). *Policy on the continuum of teacher education*; and *Initial teacher education: Criteria and guidelines for programme providers.* Retrieved from http://www.teachingcouncil.ie/en/Publications/Teacher-Education/Initial-Teacher-Education-Criteria-and-Guidelines-for-Programme-Providers.pdf and http://www.teachingcouncil.ie/en/Publications/Teacher-Education/Policy-on-the-Continuum-of-Teacher-Education.pdf.

Teaching Councils of Scotland, Wales, Northern Ireland and Ireland (April 2013). Joint Statement. Retrieved from: www.teachingscotland.org.uk/news-and-events/educationalnews/news-teaching-councils-issue-a-joint-statement.aspx.

Thatcher, M. (1993). *The Downing Street years (memoirs).* London: Harper Collins

Timperley, H. et al. (2008). *Teacher professional learning and development.* Brussels: The International Academy of Education.

7   Weaving the fabric: Teaching and teacher education ecosystems

Francesca Caena

INTRODUCTION

Overcoming fragmentation means weaving a consistent, yet flexible fabric of teaching and teacher education to fit swift change – which calls for rethinking education paradigms, with a focus on meaningful learning. This singles out the vital role of collaborative practices and governance as connective tissues for the effective learning and communication of teachers, education professionals and stakeholders in professional communities, institutions and organisations.

However, it also requires an awareness of the peculiarities of teacher education, namely as context-based and embedded in wider systems. An ecological perspective can be helpful for describing the complexity of teacher education – as an *activity system* whose aims and outcomes are shaped by its settings, rules, roles and actors. As such, it is characterised by ongoing change and constant interaction with other systems, reacting to external pressures. The global drive towards effectiveness and coherence – along the continuum of teacher education, across national boundaries – could thus become a catalyst for improvement.

Teacher education is being 'Europeanised'; since it has cultural and historical traits traditionally linked to national contexts, this can sharpen existing tensions, but also boost innovative solutions to issues – such as the one of fragmentation. Views of schooling and citizenship underlying teacher education increasingly reflect a global shift in focus from knowledge input to competence outcomes, with a developmental perspective. At the same time, relationships with other policy areas in education systems (school education, teacher status, quality assurance) flag the importance of context variables, as hurdles or opportunities: the professional profiles of teachers and teacher educators, the autonomy or control of key stakeholders and institutions, governance mechanisms.

In this system perspective of teacher education, partnerships and networks can play a pivotal role for integration, consistency and innovation so as to boost the development of individuals and education communities. This highlights the importance of reflection and collaboration in teacher education as *boundary objects* (shared elements for dialogue and learning across cultural groups), with professional leaders and coordinators as *boundary spanners* (change agents bridging different settings and organisations). To this end, policy support has an important role to play in fostering a culture of collaborative learning and innovation across professional and institutional contexts.

These perspectives foreground the 'messy' but promising potential of current global trends in teacher education policy and practice, across wide national variations in Europe – linking the worlds of schools, higher education, stakeholders and policy-makers for greater consistency; deploying professional and institutional autonomy for enhanced motivation and effectiveness; and enhancing quality control for greater equity.

THE BACKDROP: SOCIETAL TRENDS AND MEANINGFUL LEARNING

Reforms of education happening globally tend to meet two stumbling blocks. The first one is the *glocal* quandary: the tension between global pressures and local priorities – being part of globalisation processes, while keeping distinctive cultural values. The second one is a system issue in education and schooling: how to prepare learners to face new economic and social challenges, in a system that tends to meet those challenges by doing what was done in the past. As Sir Ken Robinson argues, there is an urgent need for a radical change of paradigm, to go beyond 'factory models' and standardisation, in schooling and teacher education.[1]

In Flanders, a 2013 forecast exercise by education experts, who outlined future scenarios for schools in 2030, described a series of contrasting societal trends.[2] One of them is the tension between an increasing sense of collective responsibility and empowerment of social groups on the one hand (seeking bottom-up responses to challenges together), and increasing individualisation, self-reliance, fragmentation and isolation (of individuals and groups) on the other. This highlights the decisive role of collaboration as the stuff of growth for individuals, groups and institutions – first and foremost in school and teacher education contexts as multipliers – with the need to cherish motivation through meaningful learning in education, and harness the potential of creative thinking.

Fullan and Langworthy's report *A Rich Seam* recommends new pedagogies that are able to catalyse pupils' and teachers' excitement in leading their own and others' learning, with three integrated aspects:

1. new learning partnerships between and among students and teachers

2. deep learning tasks that re-structure the learning process towards knowledge creation and purposeful use, and

3. digital tools and resources that enable and accelerate the process of deep learning. (Fullan & Langworthy, 2014, 10)

It is teachers' responsibility to use such pedagogies to set up environments and opportunities for learning experiences that can uncover and boost pupils' capacities. Teachers are called on to be meaningful learning activators, not just facilitators: being creative in choosing from a wide palette of strategies to be mixed and adjusted, adapting to context needs. Mentors who establish trust relationships with pupils, organising individual and group learning; alchemists who mix and match strategies, techniques and resources to produce and spark pupils' learning and creativity; welders who structure and connect bits and pieces of knowledge and activities for a meaningful whole; team players who understand and deploy their own and others' potential to the full – teachers need to encompass and combine such roles in situations. In a modelling and mirroring game, the same features are required in those who prepare and support teachers throughout their careers, that is, teacher educators in initial teacher education, induction and continuous professional development.

However, meaningful learning in schools and tertiary institutions can be hindered by some features that are ingrained in education systems: assessment focused on content rather than mastery, narrow views of evaluation and institutional accountability, an instrumental or limited use of technologies. New pedagogies require consistency between assessment processes and learning tasks – foregrounding learner autonomy, collaboration, facilitation by digital technologies, and outcomes linked to the real world (Fullan & Langworthy, 2014).

Teacher education and professional development need to take stock of this scenario by considering the habits of adult learners as affected by global trends (Figure 7.1). Huge information flows, dwindling attention spans, and social networks' demands all affect adults' learning. Modern professionals are increasingly flexible and self-directed in adapting their own learning to specific needs. They are also more and more bent on processing knowledge by interacting, sharing and collaborating with others. Professional-learning processes tend to be increasingly personalised, untethered and informal since adults have increasing opportunities to meet their specific development needs outside formal contexts. As a consequence, teacher education policy and practice need to consider how to meet the growing demands for collaborative, flexible, tailored modes of professional learning.

Figure 7.1
The modern learner. Copyright © 2014 Deloitte Development LLC.

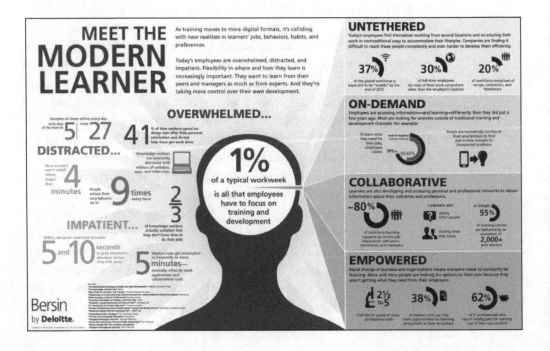

WALKING A TIGHTROPE IN TEACHER EDUCATION POLICY

According to transformational views of globalisation, governments, institutions and social groups need to adapt to the blurring of international and national concerns, which blends economic, political and cultural aspects (Giddens, 1999). In the resulting mosaic of wide *glocal* diversities, there is an interplay of local needs and global policies, the influence of various power organisations on different scales, and tensions between global uniformity and local autonomy (Caena, 2014a).

In teacher education systems, these push–pull dynamics can act as drivers of professionalisation (regulating by state or professional bodies), deregulation (allowing a variety of provision and routes), standardisation (of assessment and evaluation) as well as diversification of provision (Feuerstein, 2011). Balancing these drivers for effective governance, at different levels, means walking a tightrope – with the interplay of government bodies, teacher education providers and the teaching profession (Walker & Bergmann, 2013). Since teaching, schooling and teacher education are largely characterised by their contexts and reflect cultural diversity, tensions between global and local issues might need to be tackled by honing deregulation mechanisms to meet global demands, rather than standardising education and training.

Achieving coherence in teacher education systems can mean striking a balance between control (external accountability) and institutional and professional responsibility (internal accountability) (Looney, 2011). If the focus of teaching and teacher education is on deep, meaningful learning – to develop creative individuals and adaptive professionals who make motivated choices in specific contexts – teacher education is called on to be both accountable and flexible, to promote institutional and professional experimentation and reconcile needs at different levels (European Commission, 2013).

However, teacher effectiveness linked to pupil achievement, and a competitive focus on pupil competencies, can represent joint global drivers towards the standardisation of aims, pedagogies and outcomes (Attard Tonna, 2007). This can have a relevant impact on policy regarding teachers and teacher education (European Commission, 2012). On the other hand, changes on the local level induced by global pressures will often reflect cultural, political or economic priorities of the specific context (Tatto, 2006).

The institutional nature of teacher education can display local variations for a series of factors: historical background, conceptions of teaching and citizenship, learning theories, school technologies, governance
and administration styles, available budget and resources, quality
assurance (Cummings, 2003). National traits of education governance
are linked to the balance between autonomy and trust on the one side
(in education institutions) and control (by education authorities) on
the other. The features of governance levels – local, regional, institutional, governmental – represent another relevant factor (Gambhir et
al., 2008). The degrees of centralisation and decentralisation, along with
the way education and training match job market demands, affect local
solutions for specific circumstances (Bonal & Rambla, 2007).

Accountability mechanisms can vary in relation to purposes (formative or bureaucratic) and the role of quality-control structures, such as
professional bodies and standards as 'quality gatekeepers' (Gordon et
al., 2009). In teacher education, third-level providers have traditionally enjoyed relevant degrees of autonomy, although they have been
increasingly affected by curricula based on professional competencies.
The wide institutional diversity of teacher education providers (related
to size, public or private status, educational philosophy) recommends
flexible, collaborative accountability – with an awareness of the political
dimension of teacher education policy, and potential conflicts between
decision-makers and stakeholders (Stobart, 2008).

In Europe, education systems have moved towards increasing institutional and local autonomy, diversification and flexibility of organisation, delivery and curricula. This has meant a governance shift
towards the devolution of operational control to other system levels,
with the government 'steering by goals and objectives' (Caena, 2014b).
It has been argued that devolutionary modes can increase the efficiency
of decision-making as they are closer to context and more sensitive to
local needs (Green, 2002).

Decentralisation trends in European education systems reflect a huge
variety of national translations. They range from devolved administrative and budget autonomy to institutions (such as in the UK), partial
devolution to institutions paired with central financial control (such as
in France or Italy), devolution to geographical or linguistic areas (such
as in Belgium or Spain), or devolution to the local level of municipalities
(such as in the Nordic countries).

Due to their dependence on government control, education institutions can be both vulnerable to global pressures and resistant to them (Tatto, 2007). For instance, global drives towards systemic education reforms often include external monitoring mechanisms related to standards of teaching and training. Since they often replace local, culturally determined control processes, these external mechanisms might be viewed as endangering professional autonomy. They can spark reactions of 'Sherwoodisation' – resistance and distortion – in social and professional groups that have power in local contexts (Robertson, 2002).

Global processes in teacher education systems can be viewed and deployed as evolutionary opportunities rather than threats to be resisted, and their complexity and contradictions described with spatial metaphors. From this perspective, 'dislocation' can represent an area of development and involvement connecting different elements, in interacting cultural systems (Edwards & Usher, 2008). 'Dislocation' processes can affect local practices in teacher education institutions and professional communities, interacting with national education policies and global trends. Therefore, 'dislocation' processes can involve partnerships and networks, as catalysts of change – providing dynamic spaces for mediations, and opportunities to develop new concepts of teachers, teaching, teacher education and learning environments.

WEAVING THE FABRIC OF TEACHING AND TEACHER EDUCATION

Teaching and teacher education are perforce interwoven, although the potential for reciprocal growth and learning to benefit both worlds could be further acknowledged in policy and practice. Research connects meaningful learning and professional development with collaborative processes of pupils, teachers and teacher educators; it highlights the key role of schools shaped as professional-learning communities, to support professional dialogue and feedback, enquiry and experimentation embedded in ongoing practices (Cordingley & Bell, 2012). Collaboration in education and training contexts is flagged as positively contagious for enhancing motivation, self-efficacy and adaptive, metacognitive, interpersonal competencies (Johnson & Johnson, 2009).

Perspectives about teacher learning and cognition outline an incremental, collaborative, 'work-in-progress' view of teacher preparation and competence development (European Commission, 2013): one that acknowledges the burgeoning, changeable demands befalling the profession as well as the complex intellectual and emotional processes underlying the build-up of teacher identity (Day et al., 2006).

Global policy reform pressure on teacher education has also generated a Hydra-like multiplicity of conflicting trends across national settings: crowded, loaded curricula and intensive, demanding programmes provided by tertiary institutions on the one hand, and a tendency to the diversification of routes and providers on the other (MacMahon et al., 2013). This suggests viewing new teachers as 'budding' professionals whose attitudes and habits of ongoing learning and collaboration are key, and whose qualification represents just the first stage of competence development.

Initial teacher education is an open system defined by its multiple contexts, with a hybrid status spanning the worlds of schools and academia – between the chalkface and the ivory tower (Murray, 2008). The challenge of fragmentation affects teacher education curricula and delivery, its quality and governance (Menter et al., 2010). Once a continuum perspective of teacher education is acknowledged, the issue of fragmentation extends to the whole teaching career – pinpointing potential mismatches or disconnects between initial preparation, support in early career stages, and in-service professional development.

As regards curricula and pedagogies, research foregrounds teachers' learning *for* practice as well as *from* practice, accessing and processing knowledge (Darling-Hammond, 2006a). This means sustained, active involvement with the reality of school contexts, integrated by opportunities for reflection and feedback on practice – experimenting and revisiting beliefs in professional communities (Korthagen et al., 2006). Researchers and professionals agree on the pivotal role of a carefully planned teaching practice that is tailored to fit individual student teachers' needs and development. Darling-Hammond underscores the importance of a field practice where student teachers examine theories and learnt strategies over time, with increasing responsibility and independence in teaching, scaffolded by expert teachers who model how to meet different learning needs (Darling-Hammond, 2006a).

Teachers are asked to prepare pupils with increasingly diverse cognitive and cultural features for ever more challenging work situations: flexibility, creative problem-solving, individualisation, coaching and counselling need to become ingrained professional habits and attitudes, starting from initial teacher education (Persson, 2004). However, the 'powerful' features of teaching practice described above are not enough to maximise student teachers' learning. It is the immersion in the materials of practice, using them to work on particular concepts, that acts as a booster of student teachers' learning, tapping into the potential of action research and case studies – analyses of pupil work and teacher plans; observations, discussions and feedback about teaching in action (Hammerness, Darling-Hammond & Shulman, 2002).

Therefore, the centrality of schools, as an axis around which curricular activities are designed, stands out as a critical factor for effective teacher education. If school institutions function as professional, collaborative learning communities with shared responsibility and values, with a focus on pupil learning and reflective inquiry, they offer a favourable ambience for novice and expert teachers' reciprocal learning and knowledge exchange (Vescio, Ross & Adams, 2008). This flags the importance of whole-school development for creating settings where state-of-the-art practice is the norm, innovation can happen and prospective teachers can learn productively. The quality of supervision and mentoring is also key, which raises the issue of the preparation, recruitment, status and commitment of teacher educators.

Several institutions and bodies are involved in teacher education, with widely different organisational cultures (take the example of time and work schedules in schools and universities) and a multiplicity of actors and processes (teachers, teacher educators, mentors, student teachers, school heads, education authorities). Fragmentation issues represent a major concern that calls for coherence, coordination and communication in distributing power and roles, aligning assessment processes and tools, taking responsibilities for monitoring, evaluation and review. Leadership and consistency could be further endangered by national policy trends, which can downsize the function of third-level institutions in teacher education (such as in England), or multiply alternative, fast-track, workplace routes into teaching (in several countries, globally).

It has been pointed out that consistency and integration are paramount in teacher education. Teaching practice settings need to be consistent with the rationale of teacher education programmes – and reflect pedagogical, organisational and educational climates attuned to visions of teaching and schooling that student teachers have learnt to value (Darling-Hammond, 2006b). This pinpoints the fragmentation issue in the governance and quality assurance of teacher education, and gives partnerships a fundamental role as catalysts of integration, to create vital connective tissue in the fabric of teaching and teacher education.

THE OPEN ECOSYSTEM OF TEACHER EDUCATION

The systems of schooling and teacher education are open (connected to other education subsystems) and characterised by organisations that are 'nested' (embedded) in wider systems, interacting with them. Teachers' practices in the classroom are set in schools, which are 'nested' in local, municipal or regional education systems (under government control). Connections of different kinds tie schools to one another, to tertiary institutions and teacher education providers; national education systems are embedded in the wider global arena (Mueller & Lawler, 1999). The interactions within and across layers can be likened to those of an ecosystem: actions at any level can either facilitate or hinder those in the neighbouring ones (Resnick, 2010).

An ecological model of teacher education conveys an idea of balance for individual and collective advantages, with global processes of mediation and adaptation; it can help understand the layers of teacher education systems in which cultural, social and organisational influences are constantly interacting (Bronfenbrenner, 1979).

Activity theory (CHAT – Cultural Historical Activity Theory) can further help describe teacher education as an open ecosystem. CHAT offers a system unit of analysis to understand cultural practices in education systems through the cultural tools of a community defined by historical, institutional, social rules and roles (Cole & Engeström, 1993). An activity system is defined by six interconnected elements: a shared *object* (that directs activity towards the expected outcome), the *subject* (the individual or subgroup whose perspective is taken for analysis), the *division of roles* (interactions among system members), the *community* (participants in the system, sharing a common object and activity), the *rules* (norms regulating processes in the system), and the *tools* (cultural, material or symbolic instruments that shape the common activity) (Figure 7.2).

Activity systems are characterised by ongoing tensions (*contradictions*) *within* and *between* system elements (Cole & Engeström, 1993).

Primary contradictions describe conflicting aspects – as drivers of evolution and change – *within* each system element, while secondary contradictions arise *between* elements, as a consequence of influences of neighbouring activity systems; new, external elements are processed until they become parts of the system.

Since innovation requires aligning social, cultural and historical aspects (power relations, resources and institutions), it can be useful to understand such aspects as being related to tensions in activity systems (Engeström, 1996). Activity systems can have cycles of expansion and change – which result from reflectively analysing current structures, processing new models and tools for solutions to contradictions – seen as innovations to be later mainstreamed in the system (Engeström, 1999). Therefore, tensions (contradictions) can represent opportunities for learning, innovation and improvement in systems constantly striving for balance (Engeström, 2001).

In the case of initial teacher education in Europe, external influences on activity systems can be the global drives towards the consistency and quality of curricular aims and outcomes linked to the Bologna Process (Caena, 2014a). Within teacher education activity systems, contradictions concern cultural concepts of teachers and teaching, teacher education and schooling: conflicting views of roles and responsibilities, rules and tools, as well as institutional and organisational tensions between local and wider aims or needs (Cole, 1996). If the teacher education curriculum represents a cultural tool in the activity system, its contradictions (leading to change) can be evolutionary elements of 'dislocation' – mediating external influences and multiple priorities. As such, they can relate to the integration and balance between curricular areas, with a focus on the features of teaching practice; this can have a crucial impact on fragmentation issues across settings and institutions.

The innovative potential of contradictions in teacher education activity systems, under the impact of external global influences, can outline opportunities for interesting 'glocal' evolutions (Figure 7.2). A comparative survey of case studies in four European countries (teacher education contexts in England, France, Italy and Spain) seems to support this view (Caena, 2011).

Figure 7.2
Contradictions in teacher education activity systems: evolutionary opportunities

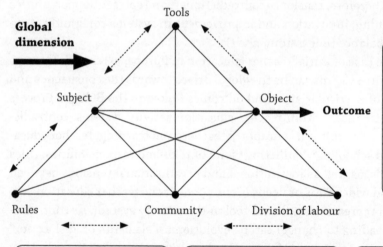

Teacher education providers:

professional

><

academic mission

Curriculum tools:

learning processes

><

learning outcomes focus

Future teachers:

all-round professionals

><

specialists

Global dimension

Tools

Subject

Object

Outcome

Rules

Community

Division of labour

Professional profile:

competences

><

knowledge focus

Activities, pedagogies, assessment:

professional

><

academic requirements focus

Community:

collaboration

><

autonomy culture

Teacher educator's roles:

strategic, social

><

formal, functional focus

In Figure 7.2, primary contradictions (internal to system elements) are indicated by >< symbols; secondary contradictions (between system elements) are indicated by intermittent, double-ended arrows. The *subject's* perspective is that of initial-teacher-education providers, responding to global influences (the European Higher Education Area raising initial-teacher-education programmes to more demanding tertiary-level qualifications). This generates a contradiction between *academic mission* (degree requirements: knowledge base and research skills) and *professional mission* (competence development required by key stakeholders, such as school heads, professional organisations, education authorities).

This contradiction impacts on the length and features of teaching practice and other curricular areas, and their integration; as such, it can sharpen fragmentation issues. It is also connected to context-specific features such as recruitment mechanisms, job market demands and teacher status.

The *object's* contradiction is between a focus on future teachers as knowledge specialists (according to tertiary institutions' practices) and a view of teachers as all-round professionals requiring transversal competencies. Likewise, the contradiction in *outcomes* is about the professional profile – between a focus on content knowledge (in curricula and assignments, shaped by tertiary-level cultures), and a focus on professional skills, attitudes and values (in selection, learning environments and activities, assessment processes and tools).

Such contradictions (in objects and outcomes) are particularly relevant because of the 'masterisation' of initial teacher education, especially in cultural settings that traditionally lay emphasis on either professional or academic aspects (such as England and France).

The contradiction in *rules* is about programme design and delivery (schedules, settings, assessment): regulations, institutional autonomy, resources for teaching practice. In particular, there can be tensions between activities in school and tertiary settings – about formative and summative assessment mechanisms, and professional requirements such as competencies and dispositions.

The contradiction in the *division of roles* lies in the relationships, duties and expectations of teacher educators in schools and tertiary institutions. The formal roles of teacher educators prioritise the acquisition of knowledge bases and skills development – assessing future teachers against expected outcomes. The social roles of teacher educators support the build-up of professional identity, with an emphasis on the formative assessment of competencies in action, in school settings.

Both contradictions (of rules and roles) impact on consistency and integration in teacher education programmes, and can be affected by governance and collaboration cultures.

The primary contradiction in cultural *tools* concerns the curriculum (pedagogies, resources, activities): the tension between a focus on practical theories (theories linked to the practice of teaching), self-assessment and practice-based research in school contexts (for example, with portfolios and reflective writings, to develop professional competencies), and a focus on professional knowledge (for instance, with assignments, examinations, summative assessment). This contradiction has an impact on the expected professional profile – in particular, the attention to professional attitudes and dispositions in initial teacher education.

Finally, the primary contradiction in the *community* (teacher education programme directors and coordinators, school and faculty teacher educators, novice and expert teachers, school heads) is between a culture of collaboration for coherent activities and assessment, and a culture of self-reliance that foregrounds institutional and professional autonomy. This contradiction can have a heavy impact on the quality and equity of teacher education.

An ecological model of teacher education stresses the opportunities offered by contrasting drives and views – if teacher education activity systems function as learning organisations, and strive for ongoing change and improvement. If pupil achievement is linked to teacher education, practice and development, which depend on context opportunities and constraints, it becomes crucial to enhance the *social capital* within and across organisations – the competencies, knowledge, behaviours that are present and shared in professional communities and partnerships (Resnick & Scherrer, 2012).

To facilitate collaboration, innovation and learning across the teacher education system, 'boundary spanners' (agents of change playing multiple roles in different settings) are key. As such, leaders and coordinators (school heads, teacher educators, mentors, middle management in schools) can cross cultural boundaries between institutions, helping build up consistency and improvement within partnerships and networks in the first place (Spillane & Kim, 2012).

PARTNERSHIPS AS LEARNING ORGANISATIONS

Effective, collaborative partnerships between schools and universities can catalyse change in schooling and teacher education – and make a key contribution to tackling the fragmentation challenge. The potential of both school and academic institutions can be leveraged: if collaborative, practice-based research involves teachers, teacher educators, mentors and researchers, it is able to create a virtuous loop of inquiry, theory, knowledge and practice. Such partnership environments, bridging the gap between school and academia, can improve the curricula and practices of both worlds, with innovative effects rippling across system levels (Darling-Hammond, 2005).

Research shows that in these partnerships (such as in Professional Development Schools), reforms and innovation initiatives can be jointly supported by school and local education authorities; an example is represented by teams of university and school educators working on curriculum design, school improvement, and practice-based research (Abdal-Haqq, 1998). University faculty can be involved in teaching or professional development in schools, while school staff can teach as faculty in the teacher education programme, and have regular training to build up mentoring skills. Future teachers can obtain regular supervision and feedback, and find opportunities to learn all over the school environment – taking part in collective planning and decision-making (Darling-Hammond, 2006a).

Even if they are difficult to enact, these partnerships tend to produce more knowledgeable teachers, and expert practitioners report improvements at classroom or school level (Darling-Hammond & Bransford, 2005).

From a wider perspective, collaboration and governance (including quality control) stand out as key aspects in successful teacher-education and professional-development programmes (Lauer et al., 2005). Teachers' impact on pupil learning is found to be linked to collaboration between education faculty, subject faculty, teachers and administrators – to align teacher education and school curricula, related standards (competence frameworks), and expectations. Since regular monitoring of teacher education (assessment of student-teacher preparation, mentors' and administrators' feedback) needs to feed into programme review, providers are called on to design evaluation strategies and gather evidence (for instance, through school heads' focus groups, student teachers' surveys, regular faculty meetings on evaluation results). Consistency of curriculum content, pedagogies and goals of teacher education, across settings, thus goes hand in hand with the use of data for improvement, and shared leadership.

Partnerships can be vital for supporting teacher learning, acknowledging the distinctive roles that each of the actors, institutions and bodies in teacher preparation can play. A series of studies suggests key factors for successful school–university partnerships in teacher education: roles and responsibilities (the *roles and rules* of activity systems) are mentioned, together with time and commitment, leadership and incentives, communication and relationships.

Time is needed to build up commitment to shared values – identifying mutual benefits for all partners (Epanchin & Colucci, 2002). Then all parties are called on to acknowledge cultural differences between school and tertiary institutions with regard to missions, structures, management, policies, politics, leadership and evaluation. A systematic process of cultural learning in the partnership is necessary to actually align assessment, pedagogies and curricula (Ohana, 2003).

The partnership, as a formal yet dynamic organisation that identifies clear roles and responsibilities, needs to devote painstaking attention to relationships, which are the most frequent causes of issues (Kersh & Masztal, 1998). A well-defined plan for communication, with multiple, ongoing channels, can help support an effective network, fostering collegiality and trust (Pugach & Johnson, 2002). Steering structures need to set directions, review achievements and plan developments, using data for ongoing evaluation and improvement. Sharing of leadership and power is advisable among top leaders of partner institutions (Peel, Peel & Baker, 2002).

Resources and incentives are necessary to secure time and support for planning, creating structures, implementing, evaluating, reflecting and revising (California Alliance for Pre K-18 Partnerships, 2004). The commitment of teacher educators also needs to be promoted: alternative paths to an academic career should make working with schools and teachers as worthwhile, for faculty, as research publishing (Epanchin & Colucci, 2002). Finally, joint ownership in powerful partnerships can give participants agency and voice for dialogue and collaboration with policy-makers – to inform about partnership goals and achievements, but also participate in reform consultations, or seek additional resources (Coble, Edelfelt & Kettlewell, 2004).

CONCLUSIONS

An analysis of recurrent tensions in teacher education activity systems – and *glocal* developments that mediate external and internal pressures – can offer food for reflection on how to overcome fragmentation and improve teacher education, considering enablers and obstacles.

The crucial role of governance and partnerships in teacher education, for the development of professionals and learning organisations; the features of effective teacher education, for the meaningful learning of pupils and teachers; the conflicting drivers (global and local) affecting the choices of teacher education institutions – these key aspects for consistent teacher education all highlight the key function of reflection and collaboration as *boundary objects*.

Boundary objects represent shared concepts that are used and meant in potentially different ways by interacting communities, for common practices and activities – but preserve a stable content core that guarantees conceptual integrity and understanding across contexts (Star & Griesemer, 1989). They can have a crucial role for cultural dialogue, mediation and knowledge exchange, as interfaces between different communities with a shared aim; in activity systems, boundary objects are key cultural tools that are able to promote learning and knowledge exchange.

The concept of reflection represents a precious boundary object: cultural variations of the concept can be found in teacher education activity systems across countries and settings – with differences in *rules* (pedagogies and activities) and *roles* (of teacher educators and teachers) (Caena, 2011). In particular, the pivotal aspect of reflection in teaching practice – related to curriculum integration, consistency across settings and roles, and institutional support (resources and policies) – displays the widest array of cultural variations within and across teacher education activity systems.

Reflection, as foregrounded by a continuum perspective of teacher education, is linked to knowledge creation and critical inquiry by professionals and communities. It is crucial for relationships and professional identity, and thus for teacher learning. Further, reflective processes are vital for effective partnerships and governance in teacher education systems – to harness the innovative potential of *glocal* tensions within and across institutions as learning organisations: analysing, monitoring and reviewing action for informed choices about change.

The roles of *boundary spanners* – key agents (such as teacher educators or coordinators) bridging and acting across institutional boundaries – can be valuable not only as gatekeepers of consistency and integration in teacher education, but also as initiators of reflective dialogue and mediation across cultural differences in organisations and stakeholder groups.

Collaboration, as a boundary object, is closely tied to the dimension of values in teaching and teacher education – for professionals, communities and institutions. The concept can reflect marked cultural diversities in teacher education activity systems, especially in the elements of *community* (collaboration underlying a shared vision of teacher education) and *outcomes* (collaborative dispositions in the professional profile of the teacher) (Caena, 2011).

The value of collaboration is decisive, not only in education professionals as learners and social actors for equity and diversity; it is also crucial for teacher education governance and accountability – to develop consistent evaluation frameworks across organisations, and clarify roles and responsibilities for better communication between governance levels. Once again, the figures of boundary spanners – as catalysts of collaborative processes across different institutional cultures – are crucial for promoting shared responsibilities, values and visions, for a common goal of coherence in teacher education.

The relevance of reflection and collaboration as boundary objects also lies in their potential for creating a 'third space': a neutral zone for dialogue and reciprocal learning – exploring assumptions, bridging different cultures and beliefs about teaching, schooling and teacher education.

Third spaces can offer valuable opportunities for reflective dialogue on values in teacher education – involving social groups and stakeholders in taking responsibility and developing agency to pursue common aims. Responsibility and agency can be associated with the Aristotelian concept of ἐυδαιμονια (self-realisation). This could represent common ground for working towards shared values and aims, across cultural variations in teacher education – connecting ethical dispositions to individual and collective learning and improvement.

NOTES

1   www.ted.com/talks/ken_robinson_changing_education_paradigms.
2   www.vlor.be/sites/www.vlor.be/files/rapport_leerlab_eng.pdf.

REFERENCES

Abdal-Haqq, I. (1998). *Professional development schools: Weighing the evidence.*
    Thousand Oaks, CA: Corwin Press.
Attard Tonna, M. (2007). Teacher education in a globalised age. *Journal for Critical
    Education Policy Studies,* 5(1). Retrieved from www.jceps.com/wp-content/uploads/
    PDFs/05-1-07.pdf.
Bonal, X. and Rambla, X. (2007). In the name of globalisation? Southern and
    Northern paradigms of educational development. In R. Dale and S. Robertson,
    (eds), *Globalisation and Europeanisation in education.* Oxford: Symposium Books.
Bronfenbrenner, U. (1979). *The Ecology of human development. Experiments by nature
    and design.* Cambridge, MA: Harvard University Press.
Caena, F. (2011). *Prospettive europee sulla formazione iniziale degli insegnanti secondari.
    Uno studio comparativo.* Lecce: Pensa Multimedia.
Caena, F. (2014a). Comparative glocal perspectives on European teacher education.
    European Journal of Teacher Education, 37, 106–22.
Caena, F. (2014b). Teacher competence frameworks in Europe: Policy-as-discourse
    and policy-as-practice. *European Journal of Education,* 49(3), 311–31.
California Alliance for Pre K–18 Partnerships. (2004). *Raising student achievement
    through effective education partnerships: Policy & practice.* Long Beach, CA: Authors.
    Retrieved from http://calstate.edu/CAPP/publications/Alliance_for_Pre_K-18_
    Partnerships.pdf.
Coble, C., Edelfelt, R. and Kettlewell, J. (2004). *Who's in charge here? The changing
    landscape of teacher preparation in America. Perspective.* Denver, CO: Education
    Commission of the States. Retrieved from www.ecs.org/clearinghouse/54/36/5436.
    htm.
Cole, M. (1996). *Cultural psychology: A once and future discipline.* Cambridge, MA:
    Belknap/Harvard University Press.
Cole, M. and Engeström, Y. (1993). A cultural-historical approach to distributed
    cognition. In G. Salomon, (ed.), *Distributed cognitions: Psychological and educational
    considerations.* Cambridge: Cambridge University Press.
Cordingley, P. and Bell, M. (2012). *Understanding what enables high quality professional
    learning. A report on the research evidence.* CUREE Report. Coventry: Pearson School
    Improvement.
Cummings, W. K. (2003). *The institutionS of education. A comparative study of
    educational development in the six core nations.* Providence, MA: Symposium Books.
Darling-Hammond, L. (ed.) (2005). *Professional development schools: Schools for
    developing a profession,* 2nd ed. New York: Teachers College Press.
Darling-Hammond, L. (2006a). Constructing 21st-century teacher education. *Journal
    of Teacher Education,* 57(3), 1–15.

Darling-Hammond, L. (2006b). *Powerful teacher education: Lessons from exemplary programs*. San Francisco: Jossey-Bass.

Darling-Hammond, L. and Bransford, J. (eds) (2005). *Preparing teachers for a changing world*. Report of the Committee on Teacher Education of the National Academy of Education. San Francisco: Jossey-Bass.

Day, C., Stobart, G., Sammons, P. and Kington, A. (2006). Variations in the work and lives of teachers: Relative and relational effectiveness. *Teachers and Teaching, 12*(2), 169–92.

Edwards, R. and Usher, R. (2008). *Globalisation and pedagogy: Space, place and identity*, 2nd ed. London/New York: Routledge.

Engeström, Y. (1996). Developmental work research as educational research. *Nordisk Pedagogik/Journal of Nordic Educational Research, 16*(5), 131–43.

Engeström, Y. (1999). Activity theory and individual and social transformation. In Y. Engeström, R. Miettinen and R.-J. Punamäki, (eds), *Perspectives on activity theory*. Cambridge: Cambridge University Press.

Engeström, Y. (2001). Expansive learning at work: Toward an activity theoretical reconceptualization. *Journal of Education and Work, 14*(1), 133–56.

Epanchin, B. C. and Colucci, K. (2002). The professional development school without walls: A partnership between a university and two school districts. *Remedial and Special Education, 23*(6), 349–58.

European Commission. (2012). *Supporting the teaching professions for better learning outcomes*. SWD (2012) 374 final. Strasbourg.

European Commission. (2013). *Supporting teacher competence development for better learning outcomes*. Brussels: EC.

Feuerstein, A. (2011). The politics of accountability and teacher preparation. *Action in Teacher Education, 33*, 3–23.

Fullan, M. and Langworthy, M. (2014). *A rich seam. How new pedagogies find deep learning*. London: Pearson.

Gambhir M., Broad K., Evans M. and Gaskell J. (2008). *Characterizing initial teacher education in Canada: Themes and issues*. Toronto: University of Toronto; OISE/Ontario Institute for Studies in Education.

Giddens, A. (1999). *Runaway world: How globalisation is reshaping our lives*. London: Profile.

Gordon, J., Halász, G., Krawczyk, M., Leney, T., Michel, A., Pepper, D., Putkiewicz, E. and Wisniewski, J. (2009). *Key competences in Europe: Opening doors for lifelong learners across the school curriculum and teacher education*. CASE Network Report No. 87. Warsaw: Center for Social and Economic Research.

Green, A. (2002). The many faces of lifelong learning: Recent education policy trends in Europe. *Journal of Education Policy, 17*, 611–26.

Hammerness, K., Darling-Hammond, L. and Shulman, L. (2002). Toward expert thinking: How case-writing contributes to the development of theory-based professional knowledge in student-teachers. *Teaching Education, 13*(2), 221–45.

Johnson, D. W. and Johnson, R. T. (2009). An educational psychology success story: Social interdependence theory and cooperative learning. *Educational Researcher, 38*(5), 365–79.

Kersh, M. E. and Masztal, N. B. (1998). An analysis of studies of collaboration between universities and K–12 schools. *The Educational Forum*, 62(3), 218–25.

Korthagen, F., Loughran, J. and Russell, T. (2006). Developing fundamental principles for teacher education programs and practices. *Teaching and Teacher Education*, 22, 1020–41.

Lauer P. A., Dean C. B. and Nelson, R. W. (2005). *The teacher learning continuum*. Denver, CO: McRel.

Looney, J. W. (2011). Alignment in complex education systems: Achieving balance and coherence. OECD Education Working Papers, 64. Paris: OECD Publishing.

McMahon, M., Forde, C. and Dickson, B. (2013). Reshaping teacher education through the professional continuum. *Educational Review*, 67(2), 158–178. Retrieved from http://dx.doi.org/10.1080/00131911.2013.846298.

Menter, I., Hulme, M., Elliot, D. and Lewin, J. (2010). *Literature review on teacher education in the 21st century*. Edinburgh: Educational Analytical Services, Scottish Government Social Research.

Mueller, Charles W. and Lawler E. (1999). Commitment to nested organisational units: Some basic principles and preliminary findings. *Social Psychology Quarterly*, 62(4), 325–46.

Murray, J. (2002). Between the chalkface and the ivory towers? A study of the professionalism of teacher educators working on primary initial teacher education courses in the English education system. *Collected Original Resources in Education*, 26(3), 1–530.

Ohana, C. (2003). *Partnerships in math education: The power of university–school collaboration*. Portsmouth, NH: Heinemann.

Peel, H. A., Peel, B. B. and Baker, M. E. (2002). School/university partnerships: A viable model. *International Journal of Educational Management*, 16(7), 319–25.

Persson, M. (2004). Learning – perceptions, challenges and strategies. In M. Persson, (ed.), *Towards the Teacher as a learner. Contexts for the new role of the teacher*. Karlstad: The Learning Teacher Network.

Pugach, M. C. and Johnson, L. J. (2002). *Collaborative practitioners, collaborative schools*, 2nd ed. Denver, CO: Love Publishing Company.

Resnick, L. B. (2010). Nested learning systems for the thinking curriculum. *Educational Researcher*, 39(3), 183–97.

Resnick, L. and Scherrer, J. (2012). Social networks in 'nested learning organisations' – a commentary. *American Journal of Education*, 119, 183–92.

Robertson, R. (2002). Opposition and resistance to globalisation. In R. Grant and J. R. Short, (eds), *Globalisation and the margins*. Basingstoke: Macmillan.

Spillane, James P. and Chong Min Kim (2012). An exploratory analysis of formal school leaders' positioning in instructional advice and information networks in elementary schools. *American Journal of Education*, 119(1), 73–102.

Star, S. L. and Griesemer, J. R. (1989). Institutional ecology, 'translations' and boundary objects: Amateurs and professionals in Berkeley's Museum of Vertebrate Zoology, 1907–1939. *Social Studies of Science*, 19, 387–420.

Stobart, G. (2008). *Testing times*. London: Psychology Press.

Tatto, M. T. (2006). Education reform and the global regulation of teachers' education, development and work: A cross-cultural analysis. *International Journal of Educational Research*, 45, 231–41.

Tatto, M. T. (2007). *Reforming teaching globally*. Didcot: Symposium Books.

Vescio, V., Ross, D. and Adams, A. (2008). A review of research on the impact of professional learning communities on teaching practice and student learning. *Teaching and Teacher Education*, 24, 80–91.

Walker, J. and von Bergmann, H. (2013). Teacher education policy in Canada: Beyond professionalization and deregulation. *Canadian Journal of Education*, 36(4), 65–93.

8 Overcoming the fragmentation between research and practice: Managing and mobilising the professional knowledge base for teachers

Sarah Younie and Marilyn Leask

INTRODUCTION

'Must do better' is a refrain educators hear from governments around the globe, and this chapter starts with an overview of some of the calls for improvement faced by educators. There is a considerable body of literature indicating the demand from teachers, governments and international bodies such as the OECD and UNESCO for access to research to underpin practice and policy. In addition, the UNESCO Education 2030 Framework for Action calls on educators to act to improve learners' outcomes worldwide. This contribution provides an overview of these demands for access to research, the challenges in meeting the demand, and potential solutions to these challenges including the use of digital tools to provide innovative solutions and new ways of working. Underpinning the analysis and the proposals in this chapter is the proposition, based on research and supported by both UNESCO and the OECD, that better access to research-based knowledge about effective teaching is likely to lead to more effective teaching in classrooms.

Reports and research calling for improvement in education systems rarely make specific proposals that start with a clearly defined vision of what a successful system would look like and then analysing how that could be achieved, who would need to be involved and so on (OECD, 2009, 2016; McKinsey, 2007; Akyeampong, Chapter 9; Finn, Chapter 6). The quality, extent and accessibility of the professional knowledge base for teachers, which we suggest is what provides the foundation for improvements in practice, appears to be treated as a 'magic ingredient' in these improvement strategies, one that can be taken for granted, one that teachers (or some unnamed third party) will supply and that does not require coordination, discussion, systematic management, renewal, resources or support. We argue that without investment in this 'magic ingredient', attempts to improve learning in classrooms falter. So how might effective provision of the 'magic ingredient', an educational knowledge base, be judged? What might it look like? Our criterion for judging the quality and scope of such a professional knowledge base is that:

> Teachers can access, at the time of need, brief, up-to-date, quality assured, summaries of research and evidence, written with classroom application in mind, to underpin their professional judgement in teaching specific subjects and specific threshold concepts to specific types and age groups of learners.

Such a professional knowledge base requires an openly accessible database and forms of publication focused on impacts on practice. In the medical world, this type of research and publishing is known as 'translational research'. This concept is new in the education sector. A special edition of the *Journal of Education for Teaching* (vol. 5, December 2015) is focused on knowledge mobilisation and translation research and contributions outline how the concept of translational research is being or could be applied in education systems in different countries. Contributors are partners in developing the solutions discussed in this chapter.

In this chapter, we specifically explore the practicalities of knowledge mobilisation and knowledge management (KM) that would provide a system to meet the above criterion. We make no claims for research to be applied undiluted in classrooms. Instead, we understand *evidence-informed practice* (EPIC practice) to come from a combination of *professional judgement*, which includes the teachers' deep knowledge of the context and the learners plus the *research or evidence* (MESHGuides, 2016). See Figure 8.1.

Figure 8.1 Definition: evidence-informed practice (MESHGuides, 2016)

Evidence-informed practice in classrooms (EPIC practice) = professional judgement + research/evidence

In this chapter, initially we look at international and national demands for changes in educational practice both in classrooms and in the training and professional development of teachers. We then look at the challenges for knowledge mobilisation (KMo) and for building and access to a knowledge base for professional practice – for all subjects, all threshold concepts, all types of learners. This section includes a challenge to universities to update their existing practices. Then we discuss theories that provide insights into knowledge mobilisation, knowledge management and whole system change.

The next section focuses on solutions, including an analysis of strengths and weaknesses of current approaches (Figure 8.5). The scope of the task to build and keep updated a professional knowledge base is vast. Based on our analysis of existing textbooks covering teacher pedagogic knowledge, we estimate such a database would hold tens of thousands of entries, which would need to be kept up to date, and of course translation to different languages is essential to make the knowledge freely available to teachers, teacher educators, learners and their parents anywhere. We address issues of quality, funding and updating processes of such an international translational research database in the latter part of the chapter. What we propose could be envisaged as an open database providing a quality-assured, regularly updated version of Wikipedia, a kind of an 'Edupedia' that would include diverse views. We exclude solutions that require extensive funding as our experience is that such solutions are not sustainable in the long term. Instead, we focus on models that more effectively use resources already in the system.

We do hope through this chapter to support a move from rhetoric about evidence-informed policy and practice to a pragmatic realism – for the benefit of learners everywhere.

INTERNATIONAL AND NATIONAL DEMANDS FOR CHANGE IN EDUCATIONAL PRACTICES AND THE 'MAGIC INGREDIENT' OF PROFESSIONAL KNOWLEDGE

Calls for improvement in four main areas – teacher quality, national teacher standards, knowledge management in education, and the creation of a strong evidence base for practice – are regularly published by international bodies as well as national governments.

Improving teacher quality

Reports from international organisations (OECD, UNESCO) and other international studies indicate that improving the quality of teachers is more likely to improve educational outcomes than increased financial investment in other areas of education systems (Akyeampong in Chapter 9; Barber & Mourshed, 2009; Hattie, 2003; Michalak, 2010; OECD, 2003, 2005, 2007, 2009, 2015, 2016; UNESCO, 2009, 2011a,b, 2013, 2015). The United Nations 'Education First' initiative, launched by the United Nations Secretary-General in 2013 to help achieve the UNESCO global priorities, stresses the importance of putting 'quality, relevant and transformative education right at the heart of the social, political and development agendas' (UNESCO, 2013, 10). Teacher education needs to be aligned with this vision if the priorities are to be realised.

Improving the quality of teaching is also clearly a priority for national governments; see, for example, the Australian government (DEST, 2005; DEEW, 2007, 2010), the Indian government (2010 a,b), similarly in China as reported by the China Education and Research Network in 2000 and Ming-yuan (2006), also in America by the US Department of Education in 2006, 2011 and in 2006, by the DCSF in England as well as in the EU (Michalak in Chapter 2; European Commission, 2005, 2007; European Council, 2007; Proton Europe, 2007).

The chapters in this book acknowledge the need for teacher education and teachers' professional learning to be enhanced in order to meet not just pan-European goals but also broader global priorities expressed through UNESCO's Sustainable Development Goals (SDGs) and the UNESCO Education 2030 Framework for Action (UNESCO, 2015). Akyeampong (Chapter 9) and Finn (Chapter 6), the OECD (2005, 2016) and UNESCO (2011 a,b) indicate that progress made in achieving similar goals set in the past has been elusive.

How, for example, can the Organisation for Economic Co-operation and Development's call for the transformation of 'traditional models of schooling ... into customised learning systems that identify and develop the talents of all students' be achieved without major investment in teacher education (OECD, 2009, 3)? And which mechanisms are there to reach all teachers? Many countries have set teacher standards – but these assume the availability of the 'magic ingredient'. Some professions (not teaching as far as we know) require members to demonstrate that a specified number of points for continuing professional education ('CPD points') have been gained before their annual registration is renewed. This system puts an onus on employers to ensure relevant CPD is available, at least virtually.

Changing qualification requirements is one response of governments to the quality challenge. As Finn observes in Chapter 6, there are a number of countries where the teaching profession is qualified to Master's level and there is an expectation that teachers will engage with research. At the other end of the spectrum, in England the government elected in 2010 took an extreme approach and, contrary to international trends to require more of teachers, encouraged schools to take on unqualified people.

Setting teacher standards is another response of governments to the quality challenge.

Improving quality through national or international teacher standards and the 'magic ingredient' of professional knowledge

In the McKinsey Report (2007), Barber and Mourshed make the point that 'the quality of education cannot outperform the quality of its teachers'. To this end, the World Summit on Teacher Education held in New Zealand in 2014 highlighted the need to move to a standards-based profession, where teaching is recognised as a 'professional learning system' that links teachers as practitioners to the research evidence base. Setting teacher standards is a first step in improving quality but, without the foundation of a solid knowledge base being available for teachers to draw on, meeting the requirements can be seen simply as a superficial box-ticking exercise with no external reference points to provide benchmarks.

Donaldson, Finn and Hamilton (2012) update the work of Burbles and Denison (1991) on standards and identify the need for new-teacher standards that address the following three points: a commitment to keep learning and improving throughout one's career; a commitment to collaborate with colleagues and other professionals such as researchers; and aspiring to achieve optimal performance.

Finn (2014) makes the case for developing global teacher competencies to drive up the quality of teaching (UNESCO, 2009, 2011b). In Finn's Chapter 6 discussion on the future of teaching as a profession, he suggests that the professional status of teaching requires a balance between trust and accountability. Trust requires teachers to display appropriate professional conduct alongside also displaying up-to-date knowledge. Finn (2014) argues that there is an interface between professional values and public accountability, with other professions such as law and medicine having a professional status alongside the setting of national standards.

Standards from various countries require teachers to demonstrate that they use research and evidence to underpin practice. The UK's BERA/RSA Inquiry into Research and Teacher Education (2014) found that 'the evidence gathered by the inquiry is clear about the positive impact that a research literate and research engaged profession is likely to have on learner outcomes' (BERA/RSA, 2014, 6). The requirements for Chartered Teacher certification in England (College of Teaching, in press) require teachers to demonstrate the use of research and evidence to underpin judgement and practice and give a recognised professional status to teachers. In England, 'Chartered' status is a recognition of excellence across a number of professions, for example, engineers and surveyors following initial education and the demonstration of effective practice.

The requirements for Chartered Teacher status, however, demand that teachers can access a quality-assured research and evidence base.

Improving knowledge management, the evidence base and professional communities

Significantly, the OECD1 Teaching and Learning International Survey (OECD, 2009) is explicitly critical of knowledge management (KM) in the education sector and challenges governments, academics and practitioners to adopt new ways of sharing and building knowledge:

> ... in many countries, education is still far from being a knowledge industry in the sense that its own practices are not yet being transformed by knowledge about the efficacy of those practices. (OECD, 2009, 3)

The OECD sets this challenge for national systems:

> ... the challenges facing education systems and teachers continue to intensify. This will require the creation of knowledge rich, evidence-based education systems, in which school leaders and teachers act as a professional community with the authority to act, the necessary

information to do so wisely, and the access to effective support systems to assist them in implementing change. (OECD, 2009, 3)

Attempts to move practice in education to a more evidence-informed approach have been documented by many authors from a wide range of countries over many years; for example, BERA/RSA, 2015; Cochran-Smith and Zeichner, 2005 (USA); Campbell, 2014 (Canada); Davies, Nutley and Smith, 2000 (UK); Fazlagic and Erkol, 2015 (Poland); Hattie, 2003 (NZ/Australia), Khan, 2014 (Pakistan); Levin et al., 2010 (Canada); Leask, 2004 a,b, 2011 (UK); Leask and Jumani, 2015 (Pakistan); Leask and White, 2004 (UK); McLean Davies et al., 2015 (Australia); M. Mizukami et al., 2015 (Brazil); Morris and Andrews, 2006 (UK); Oakley, 2003 (UK), Younie and Leask, 2013a (UK); and Zeichner, 2008 (USA). Our analysis indicates that there are many commonalities between countries and that an international knowledge-based resource would be of significant benefit. Research into common problems such as the underperformance of pupils from poor families across different countries (Usi from Malawi, forthcoming; Dragea from Uganda, 2015, Perrin from Australia, 2014) shows similar problems across countries. Sharing this knowledge and interventions that have helped might help others with similar problems target resources more effectively. There is a potentially a lot of benefit from sharing knowledge in the professional communities envisaged by the OECD above. Research commissioned by Leask in her role at the improvement arm of local government in the UK into their online communities of practice initiative (now Knowledge Hub, www.khub.net) showed considerable savings through knowledge sharing across dispersed specialist communities (IDeA, 2009).

The opportunities for professional communities are further discussed under digital tools below.

CHALLENGES FOR KNOWLEDGE MOBILISATION AND THE CREATION OF THE 'MAGIC INGREDIENT' OF QUALITY-ASSURED RESEARCH-BASED KNOWLEDGE

We suggest there are several critical pieces of the improvement jigsaw that have to be in place to achieve the desired educational improvement mentioned above. These provide challenges that need to be met if a step-change in the quality of teaching supported by access to a quality-assured knowledge base is to be provided. Missing pieces include an understanding of the following:

- How to identify research questions that teachers need to answer to improve the relevance of research.

- What the gaps are in the research that is available.

- Which professional and accountability processes might support improvement.

- How dispersed and inaccessible the knowledge base is now with thousands of studies in some areas but little research in others.

- The new systems that are possible with digital tools that can support teachers working with researchers to test out research in practice and feed back their findings in a cyclical process of research development and accumulation of knowledge.

- How the research and evidence base underpinning practice is generated – this is taken as a given; reports seem to assume that someone somewhere is taking responsibility for this. In fact, analysis carried out by the now closed government agency, the Training and Development Agency for schools (2004–2008), indicates that the situation for the generation of research relevant to classroom teaching is chaotic, with a massive duplication of effort and wastage of resources (Leask & White, 2004).

- Cost-effective ways in which teachers can engage with and contribute to research to improve practice.

Our analysis suggests that there is value in coordinated collaboration on knowledge mobilisation involving those who can make changes to practice on the ground: in the UK, these are teachers, local authority/regional advisers, teacher educators and researchers (Jones et al., 2015; Ovenden-Hope & la Velle, 2015; la Velle, 2015; O'Meara, 2015). The Spelling and English as an Additional Language MESHGuides are examples of this approach to knowledge mobilisation (www.meshguides.org). Following the success of these knowledge mobilisation initiatives, a model for the approach is being rolled out across other subject areas.

New systems using digital tools to support evidence-informed practice

Imagine if teachers, parents, policy-makers, learners, researchers and teacher educators could access a quality-assured professional evidence base for effective practice based on cumulative research over years, across settings rather than as is currently the case in many areas of knowledge, being faced with thousands of academic journal articles not written for practitioners, which are small scale, contradictory perhaps, and not strong enough to provide a foundation for practice or policy-making.

Academic journal articles have never been meant for research users; rather, they provide a form of academic conversation, building on the past and reporting outcomes of research for other academics. The British Educational Research Association provided advice about the importance of publishing for research users in 2000. Figure 8.2 sets out the vision in the British Educational Research Association's 'Best Practice in Research Writing Guidelines' for a pyramid of research writings. The one least operationalised by researchers we suggest is the production of the 'professional report' for practitioners, which we see as a 'translational research' report that could usefully be stored in a central 'Edupedia' repository as mentioned previously.

Figure 8.2 Four levels of research publication

Pyramid model of collected writings (BERA, 2000, p. 3)

New digital tools now allow the low-cost updating of documents as new knowledge is created and validated. Digital tools support new ways of working and also support new ways of publishing, including the publishing of alternative viewpoints side by side so that teachers can exercise their professional judgement to make decisions about pedagogic practices for their learners in their context on the basis of evidence. Imagine if a teacher could, in discussions with parents, refer to such a resource when explaining how a child's barriers to learning are being addressed and could show a choice of alternative pedagogic strategies if those currently employed are not effective for the learner in question.

THEORIES OF PROFESSIONAL KNOWLEDGE, CHANGE MANAGEMENT, KNOWLEDGE MANAGEMENT AND MOBILISATION

There are several theories that can be usefully employed to develop a framework for change in the education system. Some specific theories relevant to the ideas in this chapter are mentioned here.

Forms of professional knowledge

Shulman (1987) published a seminal work on the types of knowledge required by teachers to execute their professional practice (see Figure 8.3).

Figure 8.3 Forms of professional knowledge for teaching from www.MESHGuides.org

1. (Subject) Content Knowledge
2. General Pedagogic Knowledge
3. Curriculum Knowledge
4. Pedagogic Content Knowledge
5. Knowledge of Learners and their Characteristics
6. Knowledge of Educational Contexts
7. Knowledge of Educational Ends (Aims)

Source: Adapted from Shulman, 1987; cited in Capel, Leask & Younie, 2016, 18

Improving classroom teaching requires a specific focus on Shulman's Type-2 knowledge, General Pedagogic Knowledge, and Type 4 Pedagogic Content Knowledge, and we suggest that these forms of knowledge would provide the primary focus in the development of an 'Edupedia'-type professional knowledge base.

Teachers can expect to gain subject content knowledge (Shulman's Type 1) from their initial university degree and we acknowledge that keeping up to date in Type 1 is a challenge. We have ideas for how digital tools can be used to provide cost-effective support to teachers in this area but this level of detail is beyond the scope of this chapter.

Curriculum knowledge (Type 3), Knowledge of Learners, Contexts and Aims (Types 5, 6 and 7) are school-, subject-, region- and country-specific and vary depending on the national context for education.

Change management

Meeting the challenges outlined above requires a change in professional practices and there are a number of tried and tested theories of change that can be applied: the need to engage those whose practice is to be changed is considered of prime importance (Campbell, 2014; Leask, 1998; Procter, 2015; Rogers, 1983). Levers for change include those identified in the OECD's TALIS report (2009, 2), which recommends that national systems 'consider the processes in place, the building and accessing the knowledge base for educational practice and policy making and consider the quality of key levers to change in the system, i.e. the quality and extent of the knowledge base and the quality and training of teacher educators'.

A detailed analysis of change theory and how it relates to professional practice in teaching is beyond the scope of this chapter.

Knowledge management

Knowledge management systems in the private sector and in some areas of the public sector using digital technologies are well documented, but not in education (Collison & Parcell, 2006; Davenport & Prusak, 1998; Henley, 2008 a,b; IDeA, 2008, 2009; Leask & Younie, 2013 a).

The OECD above specifically mentions the need for effective knowledge management in education. Effective KM systems (IDeA, 2008) have strategies to support the use, managing, creating, finding and sharing of knowledge by all in the organisation and these five strategies provide a useful analytical framework for judging progress in the education sector. Younie and Leask (2013a) and Leask (2011) provide a detailed argument about KM for education systems and outline a model for professional development based on knowledge management principles.

In brief, the cost of a full KM strategy for education is considerable if each country has to have its own complete strategy, but, as the European SchoolNet (www.eun.org) initiative demonstrates, there is considerable benefit in collaboration across countries. More than 20 countries contribute funds to the EUN and have done so for 20 years. The medical sector's Cochrane Collaboration (www.cochrane.org) and Wikipedia also provide examples of the mass mobilisation of knowledge through engaging individuals who are committed to knowledge in particular areas: might such approaches work in education? Quality assurance is an issue with Wikipedia but the education sector already has models of peer review to moderate the quality of academic article publishing, which could be applied to an 'Edupedia'-type solution.

Professional communities and digital tools

Lave and Wenger's seminal work (1991) and Wenger's later work (1998) and with others (2002) on professional communities and subsequent research in the area (Younie, 2007) demonstrate the value of professional networking and new digital tools supporting new forms of professional communities beyond those envisaged by Lave and Wenger. As Finn highlights in Chapter 6, there is an expectation that teachers will need to collaborate with other professionals in order to keep learning and improving as they aspire towards optimal performance. Such collaboration can be enhanced beyond the local through online networking to international teachers, teacher educators and researchers (Preston, 1999; Mirandanet). Accordingly, digital technologies support a new vision of the relationship between researchers and research users. Researchers could, through adopting new ways of working with teachers (with teachers as users and producers of research, with continual testing and teacher feedback), revolutionise the research lifecycle through collaborative partnerships and rapid publishing of up-to-date knowledge. A number of digital tools could be used to facilitate free online communities for teachers, such as Facebook, Linked-In, ResearchGate, Knowledge Hub, Mirandanet, subject- and professional- association networks. These enable practitioners to network with like-minded researchers and scale up promising small-scale research across countries (see Figure 8.5 for an analysis of the strengths and weaknesses). Twitter is used by many teachers but, among other drawbacks, the knowledge produced is not organised in ways that allow the accumulation of research-based knowledge. What is crucial regarding the development of a global, education knowledge management initiative is the need to connect networks to maximise benefits for all. The current plethora of unconnected networks means that the significant management and development costs are not shared and this can lead to serious challenges regarding sustainability in the long term.

SOLUTIONS TO A FRAGMENTED PROFESSIONAL KNOWLEDGE BASE

We suggest that new working practices are needed at all levels: policy-makers, research funders, teachers, researchers, teacher educators and in university systems with digital tools providing a stimulus to adopt new practices.

Digital tools

Arguably, the current processes involved in knowledge building and sharing of academic practice in the education sector have more in common with the nineteenth century than the twenty-first century. The publishing houses have not radically adapted practices, but have simply moved print to online. Yet digital tools offer much more potential to overcome the fragmentation of knowledge: collaboration between expert groups via online networking, between researchers and teachers and the publishing of research could enable a truly global knowledge base for the profession. The vision set out in Figure 8.4 suggests that we are now living in an era of the 'rapid dissemination of knowledge, globalism, low-cost updating, ease of knowledge building through online communities of practice', which in turn are able to give rise to 'extended professionalism' (Hoyle & John, 1995). These new possibilities could enable the creation of an integrated professional-learning culture to support teachers' education and enable the sustainable development of the profession's knowledge base.

Figure 8.4 New ways of working with twenty-first century tools

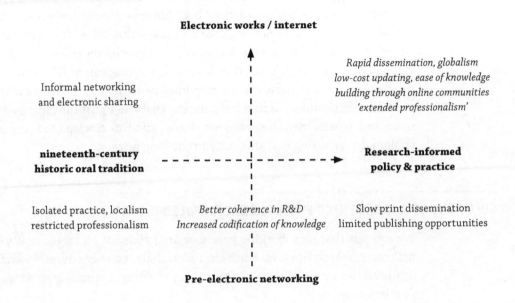

Research funders, university practices and a waste of resources

One problem regarding research in the UK, which may also apply in other countries, concerns the lack of funding for subject specialist research in pedagogy (TDA, 2002); competitive tendering for research tends to favour areas where there are strong researching teams already. In the UK and Australia, there is pressure on academics to publish so, to meet demand, it appears that they undertake research within the resources freely available to them. A consequent problem has been that much reported research is small scale, which then often limits relevance and transferability. Using low-cost digital tools, academics can collaborate with networks of schools engaging in research to scale up promising small-scale research and to move beyond these limitations. This was Stenhouse's (1975) vision of 'synthesis', where small-scale research could be replicated and scaled up, which we argue has the potential to be more effectively realised now, given the digital tools available for networking (teachers and researchers) and publishing online. Hopkins (1989) provides a case study of this approach across schools in one region.

A consequence of the many small-scale case studies, which are hard to generalise from, can be illustrated in the case of research into the teaching of modern foreign languages (MFL) in the UK. Prior to the introduction of MFL in the primary curriculum in 2006/2007, Leask, in her role within the UK government's Training and Development Agency for schools, had commissioned several systematic reviews of the research into specific areas of knowledge. A search of the literature for the systematic review into the most appropriate pedagogy for delivering MFL to primary-age children yielded over 5000 research articles, which, due to the varying methodologies, could not be systematically synthesised to produce a clear evidence base for practice. A rough estimate puts the cost in staff time of conducting so many MFL studies at the equivalent of one person for a thousand years, which is approximately GBP 40 million in salary costs. This example demonstrates the inefficiencies in the system where knowledge creation by individuals (the academic researcher as the lone expert) is arguably flawed. MFL is just one example of many. In the case of autism, one UK charity associated with autism found 18 500 relevant articles (Leask & Younie, 2013a).

It can hardly be beyond the capacity of all those involved in educational research to bring more organisation into the area so that research builds on what has gone before.

A small change in university practices could be the requirement. As part of the submission of a PhD or Master's thesis, we envisage a translational research summary being submitted to the 'Edupedia'-type resource to help contribute to overcoming the issue of the fragmentation of knowledge bases.

Similarly, the expectation that translational research summaries would be produced for research users at the end of major funded projects is not particularly onerous or expensive but could make a major difference to the dissemination of research, particularly if the summaries were stored in a common 'Edupedia'-type repository.

Quality and style of academic journal articles

In addition to the volume of articles, there is also significant variation in the quality of reporting across research papers. During the period of commissioning of the systematic reviews mentioned above, it became apparent that different forms of reporting and inadequate reporting meant that studies which might be relevant had to be omitted from the systematic reviews. Newman et al. (2004) were commissioned to provide advice on this matter and they developed author guidelines (now found on the Internet with a search for 'REPOSE Guidelines') for those who wanted their work to be considered for inclusion in research syntheses. The Ministry for Education in England shared these guidelines in workshops with academic journal editors. The EPPI centre (http://eppi.ioe.ac.uk/) had been commissioned by the government to coordinate the development of a systematic review library for education following the model used in medicine to provide summaries of medical research (www.cochrane collaboration.org).

Relevance

Research by Leask and Preston (2010) into teachers' views of digital tools for future teachers included the kinds of questions that teachers want answering in research, where it was found that these do not necessarily match those that academics are publishing about. Currently, there is no system in the UK for identifying the areas of research teachers want covered, yet this could be easily and cheaply remedied if there were some centralised coordination of effort.

Findability

A national survey undertaken for the UK parliamentary select committee review in 2009 on teachers' continuing professional development found that teachers' access to up-to-date knowledge is patchy (Leask & Younie, 2009). Further, research by Leask and Preston (2010), BERA/RSA (2014) and Procter (2014) highlighted that UK teachers wanted access to recent and relevant knowledge and to also collaborate in the creation of new knowledge specific to the needs of teachers. There are low-cost solutions to these issues, which we address in the next section.

A COHERENT SOLUTION TO FRAGMENTATION? THE MESH KNOWLEDGE MANAGEMENT SYSTEM

The research underpinning our analysis here is listed in Younie and Leask (2013) and has taken place over decades as we have researched the opportunities offered by digital technologies to support teacher professional development and, in the past 20 years, more specifically knowledge mobilisation, knowledge management and evidence-informed practice. There have been major discoveries along the way. Figure 8.5 summarises some of the issues relating to different solutions to the managing and mobilising of the professional knowledge base for teachers.

Figure 8.5 Strengths and weaknesses of selected KMo and KM tools

	Limitations/risks	Mitigating actions
Research newsletters	Relevant articles not easily found at the time of need. Ephemeral. Limited scope in any edition. Costly. Quickly out of date.	Individual articles could be linked to a searchable database giving personalised 'alerts'.
Online communities e.g. Facebook, Knowledge Hub, Mirandanet, European SchoolNet	Many teachers may have more than one major professional responsibility, e.g. they may be school leaders as well as subject teachers. Hence, it may be appropriate for them to be members of multiple professional communities, all with different login details and using different forms of software with different types of functionality. This does not lead to a good user experience. The cost of providing high-quality collaboration software is beyond small organisations such as subject or professional associations. This means freeware is commonly used, leading to multiple solutions and fragmented, unconnected networks.	A directory could be useful so that teachers find the communities relevant to them. An internationally recognised collaboration environment, such as the European SchoolNet but for teacher educators and researchers, would be one solution. There would have to be long-term financial security to make the effort worthwhile for teachers to switch from the fragmented solutions currently adopted. To gain credibility, governance of any provision would need to be seen to be independent by the profession. Fragmentation with different communities using different software is likely to continue. MESH is experimenting with encouraging educators to use the Knowledge Hub educational communities (www.khub.net), which are specifically designed for professional communities. See Preston, 1999; Leask et al. 2008.
Individual databases, e.g. maintained on university/ charity/ organisational websites	Usually not cross-searchable so there is a low chance of a teacher finding what is relevant to them at the time they need it. Once project funding ceases, such databases may cease to be updated. Where they depend on the work of one individual or a small team, the work stops when individuals retire or move on.	Have a universally used tool dedicated to cross-searching specified databases. At least three initiatives are known to us. Two have fallen out of use when funding from the EU, Microsoft and UK government finished. See www.eep.ac.uk; www.eipee.eu/eipee.org and see BERTIE, being developed by Bath Spa University, www.bathspa.ac.uk/static/bertie/bertie.html. Invest in networks that have a remit to become sustainable, e.g. through links with long-standing professional associations. See Leask and White, 2004.

Continued over page

Academic journal articles	Often too local and small scale to provide a solid foundation for practice. Inaccessible style. Length.	They're not intended for research users; more in the style of academic conversations. Research syntheses and research summaries provide a more reliable evidence base for research users.
Specialist search tools	The pilots of such tools have worked well; see individual databases above.	Sustainable funding is essential.
Government-funded and government-held repositories	At risk of closure upon a change in government. Subject to censorship.	There are now many examples of governments not maintaining repositories. In writing this chapter, we came across examples of missing repositories from governments in the UK, India, Australia, Sweden and the EU. Best practice is for government to invest in but the repositories must be independently professionally managed. See Blamires, 2015. Also see EUN.org for an example of long-standing successful collaboration between governments (Leask & Younie, 2001).
Government/ other funded but professional-/ subject- association-held repositories	Sustainability depends on the association paying ongoing hosting costs for resources.	The history of a professional association is an indication of its ability to keep resources available over the long term. Some have a very long history. See, for example, Council for Subject Associations on the web.
Subscriptions for teachers to journal repositories	See 'academic journal articles' above. The volume of possibly relevant articles is overwhelming.	Research syntheses should provide foundations for practice as for the Cochrane Collaboration. See, for example, the Cochrane Collaboration on the web.
Twitter and other social media	Ephemeral. Accumulation of knowledge not easy. Often no quality assurance or stated evidence base.	Useful for communicating new developments with reference to detailed information and evidence behind the brief post.
Professional and subject associations and their communities	Sustained by membership fees and often depending heavily on volunteers. Unlikely individually to be able to commission high-quality online community software for members.	Despite the limitations, in the UK such associations demonstrate a very long-term commitment to developing subject pedagogy and to improving the knowledge base of the members.
Conferences	Not a resource available to all teachers everywhere.	Streaming and creation of virtual conferences closes the access gap but there are issues of payment.
Research synthesis	Existing models may need further development to ensure the usefulness and relevance of summaries.	Sustained long-term development is needed. Could teacher reading groups play a role here?

We were partners in founding the European SchoolNet initiative in 1995 (www.eun.org; Leask & Younie, 2001) and we saw first-hand in the early days of development of the use of the Internet the power of on-line collaboration, which allows ideas to flow freely across international boundaries, and the resulting rapid communal construction of new knowledge (Leask & Younie, 2002). One of the early EUN projects was the conceptualising of a Virtual Teacher's Centre. The work below here has benefitted from that early work.

We have subsequently been developing and testing a similar inter-national model for knowledge sharing and building to link teacher edu-cators, researchers and teacher researchers – the Mapping Educational Specialist knowHow initiative (MESH, www.meshguides.org). One goal of MESH is to have a feedback loop from research users to research producers to support the accumulation of knowledge rather than rep-lication, and a second is providing a research summary library using a model of 'translational research' reporting, i.e. flowcharts giving easy access to specific aspects of knowledge.

MESH is designed to be a knowledge management system supporting the sharing of soundly tested pedagogic knowledge and giving a feed-back loop for the testing and publishing of translational research. The rationale for this particular approach in response to challenges for an improvement in teacher quality and evidence-informed practice is illus-trated in Figure 8.5.

MESH has been specifically developed to address the issues of find-ing, using, sharing, managing and creating research relevant to class-room practice and improving student outcomes, although the model can be applied to all forms of professional knowledge (Figure 8.3). MESH addresses the following issues:

1. Teachers cannot easily access high-quality research syntheses/sum-maries on which to base their practice.

2. Research goes out of date very quickly.

3. Research coverage is patchy. Tens of thousands of concepts would need to be covered to have a comprehensive research summary data-base for teachers of all subjects and phases. Metatagging and index lists of concepts demonstrate the scale of the task. Collaboration and changed ways of working between academics and teachers are neces-sary to curate, accumulate and update such an extensive knowledge base. The scale of the task is such that, at the current rate of major

funded educational research projects in the UK, we estimate it will take 100 years to build this database. And then, even if the research existed about effective teaching of all these concepts, it would need to be updated regularly. We suggest that existing resources in the sector could be mobilised more effectively to realise the goals outlined in this chapter, for example, mobilising knowledge and energies focused on small-scale research in areas already well served, focusing research on gaps, Master's dissertations and PhD theses, as well as the energies in research schools could go a long way to turning theories about evidence-informed practice into practical possibilities.

DIGITAL TOOLS – NEW OPPORTUNITIES

Our research shows that, when combined with knowledge management approaches, advances in digital technologies provide an opportunity to develop highly effective ways of conducting and publishing educational research, particularly new ways of working between researchers and teachers.

Opportunities through online communities of practice

There is an argument for an education form of Facebook. In the MESH initiative, we are using the public-sector online communities' resource, the Knowledge Hub (https://knowledgehub.local.gov.uk/).

New forms of online publishing and updating published materials

MESHGuides use digital technologies and an innovative knowledge-mapping approach to provide research-based advice and just-in-time learning to support teachers in extending and deepening their professional knowledge. Research and evidence links are provided with summaries for those who want to gain in-depth knowledge. Updating can be done quickly as new research is submitted. MESHGuides are quality assured via academic editorial boards and tested with teachers, providing advice linked to research.

SO, IN BRIEF, WHAT IS MESH?

MESH is an international knowledge management strategy initiated by the independent Education Futures Collaboration, which is an education charity set up by universities and other educational organisations that provides governance. The aims of MESH are to: join up the pockets of excellence in teaching and evidence-based practice; improve the quality of teaching and pupil attainment by creating knowledge-rich educators; create a joined-up profession, linking educators regardless of location; provide diagnosis and intervention tools to help educators and learners break through barriers in pupil learning; and the teaching and learning of particular concepts (see www.MESHguides.org for further information).

MESH is specifically a translational research initiative, which takes research published in academic forms and translates it into advice that can be put into practice. (In medicine, translational research takes ideas from bench top to bedside; in education, from concept to classroom.)

The overall aim is to address the fragmentation between theory and practice and to improve the quality of teacher education by:

- mobilising knowledge held by teachers, researchers, teacher educators and regional staff to provide teachers and other educators with quick access to summaries of specialist knowledge (MESHGuides), based on research, to support their professional judgement

- providing a resource to support teachers in demonstrating that they meet the standards required. See Ingvarson (MESH, 2012) on how the need to demonstrate standards will drive the requirement to have an accessible knowledge base; Ingvarson (2012) on teaching standards and MESHGuides (www.meshguides.org)

- providing a place where teacher-research networks and academic researchers are able to disseminate their research in forms accessible to practitioners, teacher educators and policy-makers

- inviting critical scrutiny of current research

- providing a means for identifying research questions that teachers and other educators want answered and communicating this to researchers, and

- signposting current research and gaps in the research base so as to help avoid duplication.

MESHGuides: the demand from teachers

In a three-year study of teachers' attitudes to, access to and use of research in England, Procter (2014) asked teachers how they would use an education website that provided research summaries, like a Wikipedia for education. The research conducted by Procter (2011–14) was in fact the initial testing of the MESHGuides website with teachers, who replied that they would: 'use with trainee teachers'; 'when providing CPD for colleagues', 'this would be great for teacher training and staff CPD to get teachers to understand what evidence says about practice', and 'bring it into peer INSET training'. Teachers were also asked how this approach would fit in with their current practice: 'I can use it to prompt ideas'; 'it would enhance the sorts of discussion about teaching and learning we already have'; 'when part of a working party on "assessment of the learning" or other topics'.

Subsequently, the MESHGuides website has been accessed from 161 countries by tens of thousands of users. This is an initiative with no funding outside the voluntary time of educators and a small subscription paid by the founding member organisations. And the guides are growing steadily in scope, quality and international engagement in their creation – currently, there are 30 of which 20 now have editorial teams. There is no reason to think that this bottom-up initiative, costing a minute amount compared with what is spent by governments, aid agencies and others on research, is not sustainable in the long term for providing translational research to the benefit of all educators and learners.

CONCLUSIONS

In summary, the core challenges that the UN and OECD identify as facing educators in the twenty-first century are:

- the importance of knowledge management
- the need to move to more evidence-informed practice
- the need to improve the quality of research, and
- the need to understand how advances in digital technologies can be used to improve the quality, relevance and timeliness of both educational research and access to that research.

This chapter set out to tackle the problem of how these challenges could be met and how the quality of teaching can be improved by enhancing access to the research and evidence base underpinning educational practice. The gap between research and practice, rhetoric and reality in teacher education was explored and strategies to support evidence/research-informed practice outlined. Ideally, an international standard for publishing translational research would be established so that, regardless of the origin of the research summary, it can be added to a centrally held database.

Our analysis led to the development of the MESH knowledge management strategy to address concerns about career-long teacher development and open access to up-to-date professional knowledge as well as UK-specific current professional concerns (BERA/RSA, 2014) that teachers should engage more actively with research as both the creators and producers of research, as well as consumers who are critically engaged in using research. We suggest that the MESH approach has the potential to address the issues outlined of fragmentation of the knowledge base, as theory and practice are integrated as part of a professional dynamic between teachers, teacher educators and researchers. In this way, teachers and researchers can create and sustain an integrated professional-learning culture to support an enhanced practice.

We invite others concerned with these issues to contact us to take this research and development forward.

Imagine if, for example, researchers, research funders and teachers could easily:

- see gaps in the research base
- see what topics are well researched
- find questions teachers want researched
- cost-effectively network and collaborate across regions to scale up and test out emerging practice in different settings, and
- easily find out research-informed practice in other countries.

The UNESCO Education 2030 Framework for Action calls on all educators to do what they can to improve the education of future generations. We hope the MESH approach outlined here provides a stepping stone or two towards that goal.

ACKNOWLEDGEMENTS

Following consultation with educators from organisations in a number of countries, the Education Futures Collaboration (EFC) was set up in July 2010 and was led by Marilyn Leask, Sarah Jones, Richard Procter and Sarah Younie, with two main strands of work to map educational specialist knowhow – the MESH initiative. The first strand of work is connecting teachers and researchers via online communities, initially using the Education Communities platform in August 2010 and now called MESH Connect-Ed (www.khub.net/connect-ed); the second is a translational research publishing initiative called MESHGuides in 2011 (www.meshguides.org). The EFC is independent of any government or individual organisation and is governed by founder universities, subject associations and other partners (www.meshguides.org/sponsors/). EFC was awarded charity status in 2014. The authoring of MESHGuides, as with medicine's Cochrane reviews, is funded partly through voluntary contributions and, where available, funding for specific projects. The research base underpinning the strategic direction of the EFC is set out in publications by the above authors and partners.

NOTES

1   The OECD is the Organisation for Economic Co-operation and Development – a subscription-based organisation with members from the world's leading economies. 'The mission of the Organisation for Economic Co-operation and Development (OECD) is to promote policies that will improve the economic and social well-being of people around the world'; see www.oecd.org/about.

REFERENCES

Australian Government. (2007). *Quality teaching*. Curriculum Corporation. Canberra: Australian Government. Retrieved from www.deewr.gov.au/Schooling/QualityTeaching/AGQTP/Documents/QualityTeachers.pdf. No longer available online.

Barber, M. and Mourshed, M. (2007). *How the world's best-performing school systems came out on top*. McKinsey and Co. Retrieved from www.mckinsey.com/clientservice/Social_Sector/our_practices/Education/Knowledge_Highlights/Best_performing_school.aspx.

BERA/RSA. (2014). *Research and the teaching profession: Building the capacity for a self improving education system*. Retrieved from www.bera.ac.uk/project/research-and-teacher-education.

Blamires, M. (2015). Building portals for evidence-informed education: Lessons from the dead. A case study of a national portal intended to enhance evidence-informed professionalism. *Journal of Education for Teaching, 41*(5), 597–607.

Campbell, C. (2014). Q & A with Carol Campbell. *Lead the Change Series,* 41, American Educational Research Association (AERA) Educational Change Special Interest Group. Retrieved from http://aera.net/Portals/38/docs/SIGs/SIG155/41_Carol%20 Campbell.pdf.

Capel, S., Leask, M. and Younie, S. (eds) (2016). *Learning to teach in the secondary school: A companion to school experience,* 7th ed. London: Routledge.

China Education and Research Network. (2000). *Teacher education in China (II). Remarkable results of reform and development of teacher education.* Retrieved from www.edu.cn/20010101/21924.shtml.

Cochran-Smith, M. and Zeichner, K. (2005). *Studying teacher education: The Report of the AERA panel on research and teacher education.* Washington, DC/Mahwah, New Jersey: American Educational Research Association/Erlbaum Associates.

Collison, C. and Parcell, G. (2006). *Learning to fly.* London: Wiley.

Davenport, T. and Prusak, L. (1998). *Working knowledge.* Boston, Mass.: Harvard Business School Press.

Davies, H., Nutley, S. and Smith, P. (eds) (2000). *What works? Evidence-based policy and practice in public services.* Bristol: The Policy Press.

DCSF. (2006). *2020 vision: Report of the teaching and learning in 2020.* Review Group chaired by Christine Gilbert, Chief HMI. London: DCSF.

DEEW (Department of Education, Employment and Workplace relations) (2010). *Quality teaching. Canberra, Australia: Australian government.* Retrieved from www. deewr.gov.au/Schooling/QualityTeaching/Pages/Qualityteaching.asp no longer available online.

DEST (Department of Education, Science and Training) (2005). *The emerging business of knowledge transfer: Creating value from intellectual products and services.* Canberra: Australian Government.

Donaldson, G., Finn, A. and Hamilton, H. (2012). *Leading systems change in Scotland – challenges of implementation.* General Teaching Council Scotland Professional update: A GTC Scotland Position Paper. Edinburgh: GTCS.

Dragea, A. (2015). The influence of parental education and literacy skill levels on children's achievement in primary school, Moyo District, rural Uganda. PhD thesis, Trinity College, Dublin, Ireland.

Fazlagic, J. and Erkol, A. (2015). Knowledge mobilisation in the Polish education system. *Journal of Education for Teaching, 41*(5), 541–554.

Finn, A. (2014). The future of teaching as a profession in Europe: Regulation or relegation? TEPE (Teacher Education Policy in Europe) conference, Faculty of Education, University of Zagreb, Croatia, 15–17 May.

Hammersley, M. (2002). *Educational research: Policy-making and practice.* London: Paul Chapman.

Hattie, J. (2003). *Teachers make a difference. What is the research evidence?* Australian Council for Educational Research, October Retrieved from www.det.nsw.edu.au/ proflearn/docs/pdf/qt_hattie.pdf.

Henley Knowledge Management Forum. (2008a). *Building and sustaining communities of practice.* Knowledge in action, 07. Henley: Henley Management College.

Henley Knowledge Management Forum. (2008b). *Sharing knowledge with other organizations.* Knowledge in action, 08. Henley: Henley Management College.

Hopkins, D. (1989). *Evaluation for school development.* Milton Keynes: Open University Press.

Hoyle, E. and John, P. (1995). *Professionalism, professionality and the development of education professionals.* London: Cassell.

IDeA UK: Improvement and Development Agency for Local Government. (2009). *Internal research report: Communities of practice usage year 1.* London: IDeA.

IDeA UK: Improvement and Development Agency for Local Government. (2008). *Knowledge management tools and techniques: Helping you find the right knowledge at the right time.* London: Improvement and Development Agency for local government. Retrieved from www.idea.gov.uk/idk/aio/8595069.

Indian Government. National Council for Teacher Education: A statutory body of the government of India. *Awards to teacher educators in India.* (2010a). Retrieved from www.ncte-india.org/publicnotice/invitation.pdf. No longer available online.

Indian Government National Council for Teacher Education: A Statutory Body of the Government of India (2010b). *Awards to teacher educators in India.* Retrieved from www.ncte-india.org/teacheraward.htm. No longer available online.

Ingvarson, L. (2012). *Teacher standards and MESHGuides.* Education Futures Collaboration charity. Retrieved from www.meshguides.org/mesh-background-2/teaching-standards-and-mesh-guides-lawrence-ingvarson/.

Jones, S., Procter, R. and Younie, S. (2015). Participatory knowledge mobilisation: An emerging model of international translational research in education. *Journal of Education for Teaching,* 41(5), 555–573.

Khan, K. (2014). Building the knowledge base. GED: Global Education Dialogues: South Asia Series (SAS) Research and Relevance, British Council Conference, 6–7 May, Lahore, Pakistan.

La Velle, L. (2015). Translational research and knowledge mobilisation in teacher education: Towards a 'clinical', evidence-based profession? *Journal of Education for Teaching,* 41(5), 460–463.

Lave, J. and Wenger, E. (1991). *Situated learning: Legitimate peripheral participation.* Cambridge: Cambridge University Press.

Leask, M. (2011). Improving the professional knowledge base for education: Using knowledge management (KM) and Web 2.0 tools. *Policy Futures in Education,* 9(5), 644–660. Retrieved from www.wwwords.co.uk/pfie/content/pdfs/9/issue9_5.asp.

Leask, M. (2004a). Using research and evidence to improve teaching and learning in the training of professionals – an example from teacher training in England. Paper presented at the British Educational Research Association annual conference, University of Manchester, UK, 16–18 September. Retrieved from www.leeds.ac.uk/educol/documents/00003666.htm.

Leask, M. (2004b). Accumulating the evidence base for educational practice: Our respective responsibilities. Paper presented at the British Educational Research Association annual conference, University of Manchester, UK, 16–18 September. Retrieved from www.leeds.ac.uk/educol/documents/00003665.htm.

Leask, M. (1998). The development and embedding of new knowledge and practice in a profession. PhD thesis, De Montfort University.

Leask, M. and Preston, C. (2010). *ICT tools for future teachers,* Coventry: Becta.

Leask, M., Preston, C. and Younie, S. (2008). Symposium: Web 2.0, communities of practice and new forms of engagement between policy makers, researchers and practitioners – where are the academics? BERA, Edinburgh.

Leask, M., Rafferty, R. and Younie, S. (2013). Identifying gaps in knowledge needed to improve learning outcomes using digital technologies. International research seminar, OECD, Paris, France, 22 April.

Leask, M. and Jumani, N. B. (2015). MESH Pakistan: Prospects and challenges. *Journal of Education for Teaching,* 41(5), 586–596.

Leask, M. and White, C. (2004). Initial Teacher Training (ITT) Professional Resource Networks (IPRNs) – rationale and development. Paper presented at the British Educational Research Association annual conference, University of Manchester, UK, 16–18 September. Retrieved from www.leeds.ac.uk/educol/documents/00003667.htm.

Leask, M. and Younie, S. (2013a). National models for continuing professional development: The challenges of twenty-first-century knowledge management. *Journal of Professional Development in Education,* 39(2), 273–287.

Leask, M. and Younie, S. (2013b). *Mapping Education Specialist knowHow (MESHGuides); New ways of working.* Research seminar, Homerton College, Cambridge University.

Leask, M. and Younie, S. (2009). *Parliamentary select committee inquiry into initial teacher training and CPD report.* Submission of written evidence to the House of Commons, London.

Leask, M. and Younie, S. (2002). Communal constructivist theory: Information and communications technology pedagogy and internationalisation of the curriculum. *Journal of Information Technology for Teacher Education,* 10(1&2), 117–134.

Leask, M. and Younie, S. (2001). The European SchoolNet. An online European community for teachers? A valuable professional resource? *Journal for Teacher Development,* 5(2), 157–175.

Levin, B., Cooper, A., Mascarenhas, S. and Thompson, K. (2010). Using interventions to increase knowledge mobilisation in Canadian secondary schools. Paper presented at the American Educational Research Association Conference, Denver.

McKinsey Report. See M. Barber and M. Mourshed (2007).

McLean Davies, L., Dickson, B., Rickards, F., Dinham, S., Conroy, J. and Davis, R. (2015). Teaching as a clinical profession: Translational practices in initial teacher education – an international perspective. *Journal of Education for Teaching,* 41(1), 514–528.

MESHGuides. (2016). *Definition of evidence-informed practice.* Education Futures Collaboration charity. Retrieved from www.meshguides.org.

MESH. (2012). *Teacher standards and MESHGuides.* Education Futures Collaboration charity. Retrieved from www.meshguides.org/mesh-background-2/teaching-standards-and-mesh-guides-lawrence-ingvarson/.

Michalak, J. M. (2010). Teacher education in the context of improving quality in higher education in Poland. Conference paper, TEPE, Tallinn. Retrieved from http://eduko.archimedes.ee/files/tepe2010_submission_29.pdf.

Ming-yuan, G. (2006). The reform and development in teacher education in China. Beijing Normal University. Retrieved from www.icte.ecnu.edu.cn/EN/show.asp?id=547.

Mizukami, M., Rali, A. and Tancredi, R. (2015). Construction of professional knowledge for teaching: Collaboration between experienced primary teachers and university teachers through an online mentoring programme. *Journal of Education for Teaching*, 41(5), 493–513.

Morris, A. and Andrews, R. (2006). *Report on the working group on the National Centre for Evidence in Education Nerf working paper 4.1*. DCSF. Retrieved from www.eep.ac.uk/nerf/publicationsnetworks/workingpapers/indexe42d.html?version=1.

Newman, F. and Holzman, L. (1997). *The end of knowing*. London: Routledge.

Newman, M., Elbourne, D. and Leask, M. (2004). Improving the usability of educational research: Guidelines for the reporting of empirical primary research studies in education. Roundtable discussion paper presented at the 5th Annual Conference of the Teaching and Learning Research Programme, Cardiff, 22–24 November.

Oakley, A. (2003). Research evidence, knowledge management and educational practice: Early lessons from a systematic approach. *London Review of Education*, 1(1), 21–34.

OECD. (2016). *Supporting teacher professionalism: Insights from Teaching and Learning International Survey (TALIS) 2013*. Retrieved from www.oecd.org/edu/supporting-teacher-professionalism-9789264248601-en.htm.

OECD. (2009). *Creating effective teaching and learning environments: First results from Teaching and Learning International Survey (TALIS)*. Retrieved from www.oecd.org/edu/school/43023606.pdf.

OECD. (2007a). *Taking stock of educational R&D:* Joint OECD–CORECHED international expert meeting. Retrieved from www.oecd.org/document/36/0,3343,en_2649_35845581_39379876_1_1_1_1,00.html.

OECD. (2007b). Evidence in education: Linking research and policy. Retrieved from www.oecd.org/document/56/0,3343,en_2649_35845581_38796344_1_1_1_1,00.html.

OECD. (2003). *New challenges for educational research*. Retrieved from www.oecdbookshop.org/en/browse/titles/?NAT=false&STEM=true&Q=%28SubVersionCode%2Bcontains%2Bnot%2B%28e4%2Bor%2Be5%2Bor%2Bp5%29%29&SF1=keyword&ST1=new+challenges+for+educational+research. This report has two of the five reviews of educational R&D that CERI conducted in five countries: New Zealand, England, Mexico, Denmark and Switzerland.

O'Meara, J., Whiting, S. and Suely-Maley, T. (2015). The contribution of teacher effectiveness maps and the TACTICS framework to teacher leader professional learning. *Journal of Education for Teaching*, 41(5), 529–540.

Ovenden-Hope, T. and la Velle, L. (2015). Translational research in education for knowledge mobilisation: A study of use and teacher perception in primary schools in England. *Journal of Education for Teaching*, 41(5), 574–585.

Perrin, D. (2014). Knowledge mobilisation. Roundtable Discussion. World Literacy Summit, University of Oxford.

Preston, C. (1999). Building online professional development communities for schools, professional associations or LEAs. In M. Leask and N. Pachler, *Learning to teach using ICT in the secondary school*. London and New York: Routledge.

Procter, R. (2015). Teachers and school research practices: The gaps between the values and practices of teachers. *Journal of Education for Teaching*, 41(5), 464–477.

Procter, R. (2014). Teaching as an evidence informed profession: knowledge mobilisation with a focus on digital technology. PhD Dissertation, University of Bedfordshire.

Proton Europe. (2007). Experiences on the US knowledge transfer and innovation system. Proton Europe innovation from public research. Retrieved from www. proinno-europe.eu/NWEV/uploaded_documents/US-knowledge-transfer-innovation-system.pdf. No longer available. The EU has archived the site.

Rogers, E. M. (1983*). Diffusion of innovations*, 3rd ed. New York: Free Press.

Stenhouse, L. (1975). *An introduction to curriculum research and development*. London: Heinemann Educational Books.

Training and Development Agency for Schools (TDA; previously Teacher Training Agency). (2002). Internal report: Pedagogic research submitted to the UK Research Assessment Exercise, 2001. Internal paper. London, TDA.

UNESCO. (2015). Education 2030 Framework for Action. Retrieved from www. unesco.org/new/fileadmin/MULTIMEDIA/HQ/ED/ED_new/pdf/FFA-ENG-27Oct15.pdf.

UNESCO. (2013*). Education first: An initiative of the United Nations Secretary-General*. New York: United Nations.

UNESCO. (2011a). *Report by the Director-General on Education for All Part I (EFA)*, PARIS, 26 August.

UNESCO. (2011b). *Quality educators: An international study of teacher competences and standards*. Oxfamnovib [online]. Retrieved from www.oxfamnovib.nl/Redactie/ Downloads/Rapporten/Final%20CP%20document.pdf.

UNESCO. (2009). *The teacher training initiative for Sub-Saharan Africa* (TTISSA). Retrieved from http://unesdoc.unesco.org/images/0018/001840/184060e.pdf.

US Department of Education, Institute of Educational Sciences. (2011). *What works clearing* house. Retrieved from http://ies.ed.gov/ncee/wwc /. No longer available.

US Department of Education. (2006). *The secretary's fifth annual report on teacher quality: A highly qualified teacher in every classroom*. Washington, DC: US Department of Education. Retrieved from www.ed.gov/about/reports/annual/teachprep/index. html.

US Department of Education. (2006). *The secretary's fifth annual report on teacher quality: A highly qualified teacher in every classroom*. Washington, DC: US Department of Education [online]. Retrieved from www.ed.gov/about/reports/annual/ teachprep/index.html.

Usi, M. (forthcoming). Enhancing youth education attendance in Malawi through strategy development: An analysis of strategies and challenge. PhD thesis, University of Bedfordshire/Danish International Development Agency.

Wenger, E. (1998). *Communities of practice: Learning, meaning, and identity*. Cambridge, Mass: Cambridge University Press.

Wenger, E., McDermott, R. and Snyder, W. (2002). *Cultivating communities of practice: A guide to managing knowledge*. Cambridge, Mass: Harvard Business School Press.

Younie, S. and Leask, M. (2013). *Teaching with technologies: The essential guide*. Maidenhead: Open University Press.

Younie, S. (2007). Integrating technology into teachers professional practice: The cultural dynamics of change. PhD thesis, De Montfort University.

Zeichner, K. (2008). Keynote: The third space: Where teachers and academics meet. British Education Research Association (BERA) Annual Conference, Edinburgh, BERA. Retrieved from www.bera.ac.uk/blog/2008/10/professor-ken-zeichner.

9 Reconceptualising teacher education for equitable learning outcomes: Towards a comprehensive approach

Kwame Akyeampong

INTRODUCTION

For the global education community, 2015 was significant as it marked a year for taking stock of the progress countries had made in meeting the six Education for All (EFA) goals set 15 years previously in Dakar, Senegal. What some assessments reveal is a lack of progress in achieving quality education for all, and the conclusion that much of this can be attributed to inequitable access to quality teachers and inadequate systems of teacher preparation. The setters of the EFA goals advocated policies that would ensure that teachers have developed the capacity to serve the learning needs of all students. However, the 14th edition of UNESCO's Education for All (EFA) Global Monitoring Report's analysis of teacher education policies in countries, particularly in the global South, revealed that most had not placed the preparation of teachers to serve the learning needs of students from disadvantaged backgrounds high on their education policy agenda (UNESCO, 2013/14). The report also showed that, irrespective of geographical location, students from disadvantaged backgrounds are more likely to be taught by less experienced teachers. In the global North, an OECD report also revealed that a higher percentage of more experienced teachers work in schools with more advantaged than disadvantaged students (OECD, 2013). Not surprisingly, students from disadvantaged backgrounds in many developing and developed countries have made the least progress in learning outcomes (UNESCO, 2013/14; OECD, 2010; OECD, 2015).

UNESCO's EFA Global Monitoring Report analysis described the learning gap between disadvantaged and advantaged groups within and across countries as a 'learning crisis', affecting mostly the poor, girls, and socially disadvantaged groups (UNESCO, 2013/14). Although the report focused much attention on the global South, this crisis extends to middle- and high-income countries as well. For example, the OECD's PISA data consistently show that students from poor or immigrant backgrounds lag behind their native counterparts, even though they attend schools staffed by trained teachers. PISA data on Turkey indicates that only 66% of upper-secondary students classified as poorest have acquired basic skills compared with 86% of the richest (OECD, 2014). Similarly, in Portugal only 73% of the poorest students have learned the basics of reading compared with 90% of the richest (UNESCO, 2013/14, 101). In Sweden, about 17% of first-generation immigrant students perform below proficiency level 1 on the PISA reading scale, which assesses students' ability to use reading literacy as a tool for acquiring knowledge and skills in other areas. For native students, this is about 3% (OECD, 2010).

EU policies on social inclusion stress the importance of addressing the wide attainment of diversity of school populations across EU countries (OECD, 2010), a population made up of '... increasing ethnic, cultural and linguistic diversity due to a range of political and economic factors including the expansion of the European Union and the arrival of refugees from a wide range of Asian and African countries' (Smyth, 2013, 298). The recent arrival of refugees in Europe, mostly from Syria and Afghanistan, will make this an even more pressing issue. Immigrants in Sweden, for example, make up 20% of the population, with the share from less developed countries increasing (OECD, 2015). Schools are therefore going to become more socially, economically or ethnically diverse; classroom environments and instructional relationships will also become more challenging grounds, and will place new demands that shape or constrain teachers' pedagogical choices (Gardinier, 2012) – choices that will define which students have better or worse opportunities to learn and progress in their education.

Teachers in Europe on the whole do not feel adequately prepared to teach ethnically diverse classes (OECD, 2015; Blomeke, 2012). Some systems have tried to remedy the situation by recruiting high-achieving higher-education graduates to teach in schools or areas where there is a large concentration of such students (Hambing & McCormick, 2013).

This approach suggests that what some students need in order to succeed are teachers with strong subject-knowledge backgrounds. As I argue in this chapter, the challenges are much deeper; and, besides, many education systems are simply unable to produce enough specially trained teachers or highly qualified subject graduates to meet the scale of demand (UNESCO, 2014).

So why are many disadvantaged students underachieving compared with their advantaged counterparts? The reasons and factors that produce the disparities are complex, and space limits will not permit an exhaustive exploration. Instead, I intend to focus on the role teacher education should play in preparing teachers to develop the dispositions and practices to mitigate social disadvantage on learning outcomes.

Teacher education has often come in for criticism for not doing enough to prepare prospective teachers to work collectively to improve learning or raise the achievement levels of students from disadvantaged backgrounds (UNESCO, 2013/14; OECD, 2015; Villegas & Lucas, 2002). In this chapter, I argue that rather than providing specialised programmes, or simply strengthening the pedagogical and subject-knowledge base of prospective teachers, what is needed is a comprehensive approach that articulates a vision of teacher education aimed at closing the achievement gap between disadvantaged and advantaged groups.

Teacher education in Finland is an often cited example of how prospective teachers can be prepared to improve learning for low achievers or students from disadvantaged backgrounds. Finnish teachers have managed to reduce the variance in student performance even though schools have experienced increased diversity in the student population (Sahlberg, 2011). As Niemi (2016) points out in Chapter 3, Finnish teacher education manages to prepare and support prospective teachers to develop commitments and capabilities that benefit students from different socio-economic and cultural backgrounds. Even though there are clues to how it manages to achieve this – by developing teachers' pedagogical thinking and evidence-based decision-making using a research-based approach to teacher development (Sahlberg, 2011), the principles are unclear for thinking about how teacher education could be designed to close the achievement gap. Villegas and Lucas (2002) provide some interesting insights, which I will be referring to in more detail later in the chapter.

What the research evidence makes quite clear is that students from diverse backgrounds are able to maximise their learning potential when they are taught by teachers who pay them sustained and inclusive attention, and in environments in which they feel safe, and draw on their backgrounds in the pedagogical discourse (Westbrook et al., 2013). In this chapter, I discuss some basic principles that can guide teacher education to produce teachers with a strong sense of themselves as 'agents of social justice who teach so that all learners, especially those least well served by schools, can achieve' (Spalding, 2013, 290). Two areas that need attention in teacher education are: first, teachers' knowledge and beliefs about students; and, second, how teachers interpret and respond to differences among students from various backgrounds, particularly how they are able to use differences as resources to improve learning (Villegas & Lucas, 2002).

THE IMPORTANCE OF TEACHERS' KNOWLEDGE ABOUT STUDENTS AND CHANGING BELIEFS ABOUT THEIR CAPACITY TO LEARN

Teaching and teacher behaviour are not simply the product of learning specific teaching skills. As Darling-Hammond et al. (1999) point out, when we observe teaching behaviour, we are just seeing the tip of an iceberg. Hidden from view are a range of factors that have shaped what we see teachers do or how they respond to the learning needs of different students. So what distinguishes teachers who are able to improve learning for some students and those who are less successful with others may reflect something much deeper – what they know about the backgrounds of the students they teach and how to help them succeed in education. Teachers who 'understand what is culturally relevant to their students and recognise when an existing curriculum fails to build on, or acknowledge the cultural knowledge students bring to their learning' are actually the ones with the potential to help disadvantaged students improve (Santoro, 2013, 314). Teachers without a deep appreciation of this may unwittingly amplify the effect of social disadvantage on educational performance because their behaviour and teaching decisions might reflect the cultural practices and values of particular groups of students, denying those outside these groups an equal opportunity to maximise their learning to raise their achievement levels (Richards et al., 2007). Villegas and Lucas (2002) explain that when teachers have the right attitudes and beliefs about their students they see all of them with potential:

... children who are poor, of color, and speakers of languages other than English, as learners who already know a great deal and who have experiences, concepts, and languages that can be built on and expanded to help them learn even more. They see their roles as adding to rather than replacing what students bring to learning. They are convinced that all students, not just those from the dominant group, are capable learners who bring a wealth of knowledge and experiences to school. (23)

Teacher education has to ensure that all aspects of its programmes are tuned to work towards producing teachers who are able to translate these values and attitudes into teaching behaviours that help disadvantaged students improve their learning.

Raising expectation in all teachers that they can make a positive difference is crucial. Low expectations of what teachers think they can achieve with some students often translates into low commitment to helping them overcome their learning difficulties or maximise their learning potential. The consequences for these students can be damaging. Studies have shown, for example, that the likelihood of students repeating a grade increases when teachers underrate their cognitive abilities and have low expectations of them (Torff, 2011; Goos et al., 2013). This can lead to a situation where disadvantaged students are judged as needing a less rigorous curriculum than their more privileged peers. A self-fulfilling prophecy may result: disadvantaged students then receive less challenging lessons that limit their academic growth, while advantaged students receive more challenging lessons that boost their performance. This behaviour is the classic self-fulfilling prophecy espoused in Rosenthal and Jacobsen's (1968) book: *Pygmalion in the Classroom: Teacher Expectation and Pupils' Intellectual Development*. What makes this issue so important, and therefore worth addressing in teacher education, is that teachers may not even be fully aware that their assumptions or presumptions about culturally, ethnically or linguistically diverse students can interfere with or limit the impact of their instructional practice. As Figure 9.1 illustrates, what teachers know and believe about disadvantaged students, and their attitudes to them, can work their way through to influencing their commitments, judgements and decisions and ultimately influence their instructional approaches and behaviours.

Figure 9.1 How teachers' knowledge, beliefs and attitudes might influence approaches and behaviour – adapted from Darling-Hammond et al., 1999

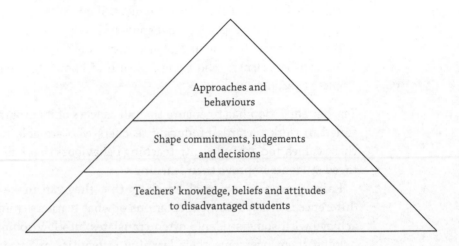

It is important to point out that teachers are not the only ones responsible for shaping the educational experiences of disadvantaged students. Inequities in schools and society and the structures and practices that perpetuate them play a big part. But my point is that teachers can and should be in the forefront of challenging stereotypes and creating learning opportunities to demonstrate that disadvantaged students, given the right conditions and support, can make similar gains as advantaged students. Lack of awareness of these issues and capabilities to address them makes it less likely that teachers will become agents of change at the school or classroom level, working to address the inequities perpetuated in schools to maintain social disadvantage (Villegas & Lucas, 2002).

Teacher education in many developing countries pays little attention to teachers' knowledge and beliefs about students and, as a result, limits the impact of teaching on some disadvantaged students, especially from poor rural backgrounds. A substantial study of teacher education known as the Multi-Site Teacher Education Research project (MUSTER), led by researchers at the University of Sussex from 1998 to 2002, found that although teachers felt that their teacher education programmes were effective in terms of the pedagogical knowledge and skills acquired, this did not translate into promoting effective learning opportunities for many students. Some teachers doubted their ability to improve the academic performance of slow learners (Lewin & Stuart, 2003; Akyeampong & Stephens, 2002). So, although teachers may feel confident in their ability to teach their assigned subjects, they may still find it difficult to act effectively based on what they know, believe and intend for their students. This problem was also demonstrated in a study of teacher education in six sub-Saharan African countries, which found that newly trained primary-school teachers did not know enough about the children they were teaching to create learning opportunities that build on the individual knowledge and experiences they bring to school (Akyeampong et al., 2013). This occurred mostly when teachers encountered children from relatively poor rural backgrounds. MUSTER researchers argued that because the teacher education systems in the countries they studied had de-contextualised effective teaching, reducing it to a set of homogenised teaching strategies, beginning teachers had not tried to know as much as possible about the children they were teaching in order to facilitate their learning. This had created a false sense of competence, with beginning teachers rarely engaging in sustained discussions with their students in order to understand how they might solve problems by drawing attention to what they already know from their own backgrounds and experiences. Instead, teachers were treating students as empty vessels (Akyeampong & Lewin, 2002; Lewin & Stuart, 2003).

These cases illustrate just how important it is for teacher education to re-examine how it defines the preparation of successful teachers, paying attention to the diversity in students' backgrounds, and how to plan instruction that has space for the different knowledge and experiences students bring into the learning environment. But, also, teachers would need to know much more about the background conditions that have produced the disadvantage and differences in some students' readiness and capacity to learn. For teacher education this means offering prospective teachers a wide range of professional-learning opportunities to help them develop a deep understanding of

> the socio-cultural factors that produce individual differences, (become) aware of educational and social issues that affect students' learning, (before learning to use) multifaceted approaches that take account of students' individual characteristics, their interests and their learning from outside school, and of their previous knowledge and individual and cultural experiences. (Florian & Rouse, 2009)

Some of this understanding will undoubtedly come from academic studies that explore the production of disadvantage, but also from field studies where prospective teachers research different types of communities to understand the different sub-cultures from which their future students come. This will raise their 'sociocultural consciousness' (Villegas & Lucas, 2002) and make their teaching more responsive to individual differences and promote their ability to work for greater equity in learning outcomes.

IMAGINING EQUITY-FOCUSED TEACHER EDUCATION FOR EQUITABLE LEARNING OUTCOMES

How should teacher education be imagined and constructed to improve prospective teachers' capacity to recognise and value differences in student backgrounds, and adopt pedagogical strategies that maximise learning opportunities and outcomes for all students, irrespective of their backgrounds? As I have argued earlier, teacher education systems should give more attention to teachers' attitudes to differences in students' backgrounds, and give conceptual coherence to the use of a wide range of learning opportunities such as coursework, reflective practice and field research to drive home the interconnectedness of the knowledge of students and pedagogical skills in the production of effective teaching for all students.

This call for preparing what some might call 'culturally responsive teachers' is not new (see Villegas & Lucas, 2002; Santoro, 2013), but in my view has become more urgent because of the widening achievement gap between advantaged and disadvantaged students in many education systems due in part to changing demographics. There are three qualities I believe teacher education should infuse in programmes to achieve a comprehensive vision of learning to teach students from very different backgrounds in increasingly diverse societies. They are based on three aspects of Villegas and Lucas's conceptualisation of culturally responsive pedagogy.

(a) The first is raising prospective teachers' sociocultural consciousness of diversity – this is an understanding

that people's ways of thinking, behaving, and being are deeply influenced by such factors as race, ethnicity, social class, and language . . .

without this insight, teachers are unable to cross the sociocultural boundaries that separate too many of them from their students. (22)

In this respect, teacher education should offer prospective teachers opportunities to study and/or research the different cultures from which students they are likely to teach come. Much of this can be done through academic studies. Santoro (2013) argues that

> unless ... programs are accompanied by academic work that engages with scholarship around [issues such as] white privilege, nationhood, the complexities of culture and ethnic belonging and culturally responsive pedagogies, they [teacher education programmes] are of limited benefit in preparing teachers to understand the complexities of their students' cultural subjectivities because they can simply reinforce existing stereotypes and attitudes about the 'cultural other'. (315)

The point is that without critically exploring the implications of student diversity on inclusive pedagogical practice, teaching may benefit some groups of students more than others.

Teacher education programmes have often neglected a related issue, which is about understanding 'who it is that is doing the knowing [of students from diverse backgrounds]' (Santoro, 2013, 316). In other words, how does it help prospective teachers see themselves in relation to their students, and to understand how being a member of a dominant cultural majority influences relations with students from a disadvantaged minority background? Helping teachers understand how their membership of a dominant majority might shape their teaching selves, their classroom practices, their relationships with disadvantaged students who may come from a different cultural background, and their expectations of these students should expose them to the impact of their own prejudices and biases. We should also add that this applies to prospective teachers who come from backgrounds similar to those of disadvantaged students or who are from a minority culture. These teachers also need to study how their own cultural identities and backgrounds shape their professional behaviours and practices, especially if they work in schools in which advantaged students form the dominant cultural majority.

Let us examine this issue further. In the case of teachers from a minority ethnic culture who teach in schools with disadvantaged students from a minority ethnic culture or background, there is the added challenge of the school curriculum. These teachers may find their practices constrained by a curriculum rooted in the dominant culture of the advantaged student, and which does not allow enough space to bring in important cultural values and examples that can make learning more meaningful for 'other' students. The same can apply in contexts where the teacher comes from a socioeconomically rich or middle-class background and is teaching in schools with predominantly poor students or students from working-class backgrounds. In a study of the experiences of minority ethnic teachers in English schools, for example, Cunningham and Hargreaves (2007) found that 'minority ethnic teachers felt that the requirements of the national curriculum hindered their ability to support the learning of minority ethnic pupils and compromised their professional expertise'. The teachers found that the curriculum had few ostensible spaces for them to draw on the culture of minorities to foster learning. Teacher education, therefore, needs to raise the sociocultural consciousness of prospective teachers, and link this to how the school curriculum through its content and illustrations might thwart or promote better learning opportunities for one group of students at the expense of other groups. Studying the school curriculum as part of teacher education for ways in which teachers can develop parallel ideas, concepts and examples to connect with diverse student backgrounds would be important.

Teacher education should also stress the significance of teacher knowledge that is personal or autobiographical and examine the influences on their own pedagogical choices, as this might reflect their own personal histories and educational journeys. This should raise their consciousness about why they may find it 'easier' to relate to and support some students and find others more challenging to deal with. Hopefully, this will teach them that a lot of this has to do with how their own personal or professional identities have been shaped. In a research study on teacher-identity formation in preservice teacher education as part of the MUSTER project, Stephens and Akyeampong (2002) found that Ghanaian preservice teachers' biographies and sociocultural histories acted as powerful influences on how they viewed effective teaching – which by and large was based on their interaction with teachers when they were students and how those teachers had contributed to their own progress in education. The teachers had gone on to construct an image of effective teaching that more or less mirrored instructional approaches that had helped them learn effectively and progress in their education. What they had not come to fully appreciate was how some of these instructional practices may not have benefitted many 'other' students. Providing space in the teacher education curriculum for critical reflection on how biographies can shape pedagogical practice will make teachers more aware of their biases and sensitive to instructional practices that might not work well for some students. As Maguire and Dillon (2001) point out,

> developing autobiographical knowledge means understanding that the way teachers teach is not only a demonstration of the skills they have learned through teacher education or 'on the job', but is also knowing how their biographies, hopes and aspirations shape their work. (8)

(b) The second is to focus attention on constructivist approaches to learning because of how these incorporate what different students bring to create meaningful learning. If teacher education is to produce teachers who deeply value what every student brings into the teaching and learning space, then it should promote instructional approaches that value the knowledge these students bring. As Villegas and Lucas (2002) argue, 'the knowledge children bring to school, derived from personal and cultural experiences, is central to their learning. To overlook this resource is to deny children access to the knowledge construction process' (25). The implication for teacher education is to develop prospective teachers' skills in how to create learning situations that make it easier for students to share their knowledge and experiences so that poor or disadvantaged students in particular can feel valued in the contribution they make to knowledge construction. But for prospective teachers to model constructivist practices for all students, they should also experience the knowledge-construction process as part of their professional learning by providing them with frequent opportunities to bring their own personal and cultural experiences into learning. What this learning experience will be saying to them is that all students, irrespective of background, have something to contribute in the construction of knowledge.

(c) The third is to develop responsive teaching practices that start with knowledge about differences in student backgrounds as the basis for developing the appropriate pedagogical response to meet different learning needs. The ability of teachers to use what they know about particular students, the cultural and personal strengths they bring to the classroom, and insights from their own personal and professional identities will be key to how they evaluate curriculum materials and vary teaching approaches to achieve more inclusiveness in learning. The goal is to ensure that prospective teachers can plan instruction that facilitates learning for all students. What teacher education should be aiming for, in effect, is to provide ample opportunities for preservice teachers to do three things:

> (a) reflect on their own assumptions and beliefs concerning the lived experiences of students; (b) test their assumptions about which pedagogical approaches work for which students; and (c) adapt, reshape and retrial teaching strategies in the light of their analyses. (Santoro, 2013, 318)

This approach to learning to teach will no doubt be demanding, requiring prospective teachers to engage in action research and other inquiry-based approaches to learning to teach, but ultimately will ensure that teachers develop personal practical knowledge of teaching that can especially benefit the disadvantaged student in all school contexts.

These three strands in my view should form an important part of the design of teacher education programmes aimed at enhancing the opportunities for students from disadvantaged backgrounds to improve their learning and close the achievement gap between advantaged and disadvantaged students.

A set of recommendations from the OECD's 2012 influential report on equity and quality in education provides insights into aligning teacher education programmes with the needs of disadvantaged schools based on the following measures:

- Including content in the curricula for teachers specialising in disadvantaged schools and students.

- Designing programmes that focus on the development of teachers' capacity to diagnose student problems and understand the context of the schools they teach at.

- Including practical field experience in disadvantaged schools as part of their teacher education; evidence shows they can then perform better as teachers. (OECD, 2012, 131)

The report also recommends that countries should consider providing mentoring to teachers in disadvantaged schools, and that schools should ensure that they combine diversified and flexible pedagogical strategies with assessment, while ensuring a curriculum with high expectations, aligned with instruction and assessment (OECD, 2012, 139, 141). While these proposals address the concerns I have raised, they seem to suggest that this is for prospective teachers who may find themselves working with disadvantaged students or teaching in areas or schools where these students are the majority. What I am advocating is for *all* teachers to develop capabilities that help to maximise learning opportunities and outcomes for all students, and that this should not be seen as a specialism for some teachers. The principles I have discussed in this chapter should be infused with every aspect of the teacher education programme so that disadvantaged students, wherever they may be found, can have access to a teacher who knows how to help them learn and raise their achievement level.

Similarly, we should not leave this to teachers from minority backgrounds who, some could argue, have a better understanding of the backgrounds of minority students, and are therefore better positioned to facilitate their learning. To do so would be to stigmatise and reinforce stereotypes of disadvantage as the 'other'. Besides, such teachers may not be sufficiently represented in teaching to meet demand. Smyth (2013) cites Scottish government demographic statistics to illustrate this point:

> In 2011 only 2% of all teachers were from a minority ethnic group, with only 1% in primary schools not being from a white ethnic group even though there were 136 languages spoken by pupils in Scottish schools with the five most common after English being Polish, Punjabi, Urdu, Arabic and Cantonese. (300)

Touching on the implications for Scotland, Smyth reminds us that

> the linguistic assumptions of teachers (who constitute the dominant ethnic majority in that context) are based on children who use English in school, go home and use English with their parents, watch English language television and read English language texts. (300)

Such a predominantly monolingual and mono-ethnic teaching workforce may find it difficult to adopt instructional practices that enhance learning opportunities for an increasingly ethnically and linguistically diverse student population.

CONCLUSIONS

A post-2015 EFA agenda that seeks to promote quality education for all students requires teachers with the commitment and capabilities to maximise every student's potential to be successful, irrespective of their social, cultural or economic background. It will not be enough to increase the supply of teaching and learning resources or trained teachers. Developing teachers' commitment and capabilities to identify and raise the achievement levels of disadvantaged students will be key. The image I have advanced for teacher education is one that provides more space to cultivate prospective teachers' self-awareness of learning to teach students from diverse backgrounds, utilising these backgrounds as a resource to tailor their teaching to meet different learning needs. Developing these capacities is not expected to be fully achieved at the preservice teacher preparation stage – that should not be the goal, but it is where it should begin. Some teacher education programmes may have indicated the need to expose prospective teachers to issues of diversity in education, but they need to go a step further to provide ample opportunities to cultivate the qualities described in this chapter. If teacher education is to prepare teachers who can teach so that disadvantaged students make significant gains in learning achievement, then its policies and practices must move towards preparing teachers who can teach students from diverse backgrounds to maximise their learning.

There are implications of what is being proposed here for teacher education policy, practice and future research. First, policies governing teacher education should demand a stronger commitment to principles of social justice, which clearly makes the preparation of teachers who can teach for equitable learning outcomes a major priority. To guide the development of policy in this direction, we should be asking: what kind of teacher do we wish to see come out of teacher education? How confident are we that prospective teachers have had the kind of teacher education that will enable them to help every student maximise their potential to succeed in education? Which elements of the teacher education curriculum demonstrate that prospective teachers will emerge with the right dispositions and competencies to improve learning for all? These are important questions that future teacher education policy should be responding to. Teacher education policy should also require accredited programmes to demonstrate how they intend to produce teachers who have the knowledge and skills to teach students from diverse backgrounds, or in challenging school contexts. Teacher education policy has to envision a new type of teacher with a professional outlook that is global, tolerant and committed to the right to quality education for all students. Obviously, these suggestions for policy will place new demands on teacher education but, as the Finnish example demonstrates, attending to these demands is what is also likely to raise the status of the teaching profession due to the high standards it sets for meeting the educational needs of all students (Sahlberg, 2010).

These proposals would also require that teacher educators receive training in preparing teachers to teach students with differing characteristics and needs. The training of teacher educators is a neglected area in many education systems. Ensuring that teacher educators have the knowledge and skills to support prospective teachers to be change agents in schools and classrooms will be crucial if plans to give teacher education this orientation are to succeed. Even after prospective teachers have been trained in how to work successfully with different kinds of students, the transition to the confident inclusive practitioner will take time. Teacher education institutions should therefore find space to work with teachers with experience of working with different students so that they can learn from their wisdom of practice.

Finally, although learning to teach students from diverse backgrounds is an area clearly needing attention, there is not much research focused on producing insights into how the teacher education curriculum can be designed to institutionalise the qualities described. We also need evidence on what actually works in terms of the professional-learning experiences that strengthen prospective teachers' commitment and ability to teach for the benefit of all students in order to close the achievement gap. We need research that also examines teacher education programmes that are making a difference in teachers' commitment and success when working with disadvantaged students. Research that explores how successful teachers teach inclusively in classrooms with students from different backgrounds is also required. In addition, research that explores the knowledge, experiences and values that students from different ethnic and linguistic backgrounds bring into school, and how teachers can identify and use them to advance learning, will produce insights into the areas that the teacher education curriculum should be including in the teacher-preparation process.

As national governments envision a post-2015 EFA that promises equitable and quality education for all, there needs to be a critical examination of the role teacher education can play in preparing teachers to achieve this goal. In this chapter, I have argued in essence for reconceptualising teacher education so that it places stronger emphasis on the development of responsive pedagogy based on a deeper understanding of student backgrounds, and the implications for pedagogical discourse.

REFERENCES

Akyeampong K., Lussier K., Pryor, J. and Westbrook J. (2013). Improving teaching and learning of basic maths and reading in Africa: Does teacher preparation count? *International Journal of Educational Development, 33*, 272–282.

Akyeampong, K. (2003). *Teacher training in Ghana – Does it count?* London: DFID.

Akyeampong, K. and Lewin K. (2002). From student teachers to newly qualified teachers in Ghana: Insights into becoming a teacher. *International Journal of Educational Development, 22*(3/4), 339–352.

Akyeampong, K. and Stephens D. (2002). Exploring the backgrounds and shaping factors of beginning student teachers in Ghana: Towards greater contextualization of teacher education. *International Journal of Educational Development, 22*(3/4), 261–274.

Blomeke S. (2012). Content, professional preparation, and teaching methods: How diverse is teacher preparation across countries? *Comparative Education Review, 56*(4), 684–714.

Burns T. & Shadoian-Gersing, V. (2010). The importance of effective teacher education for diversity. In T. Burns and V. Shadoian-Gersing, (eds), *Educating teachers for diversity: Meeting the challenge.* Paris: Organisation for Economic Co-operation and Development.

Cunningham M. and Hargreaves, L. (2007). *Minority ethnic teachers' professional experiences: Evidence from the teacher status project.* Research Report 853. London: Department for Education and Skills.

Darling-Hammond, L., Wise, A. E. and Klein, S. P. (1999). *A License to teach – raising standards for teaching.* San Francisco: Jossey-Bass Publishers.

Florian L. and Rouse M. (2009). *The inclusive practice project: Teacher education for inclusion.* Aberdeen: University of Aberdeen.

Hambing Y. and McCormick B. (2013). China: Strengthening the quality of teacher education in rural communities. In B. Moon, (ed.), *Teacher education and the challenge of development.* London: Routledge.

Niemi H. (2016). Towards induction: A case of training mentors for new teachers in Finland. In B. Hudson, (ed.), *Overcoming fragmentation in teacher education policy and practice*. Cambridge: Cambridge University Press.

Maguire M. and Dillon J. (2001). Developing as a student teacher. In J. Dillon and M. Maguire, (eds), *Becoming a teacher: Issues in secondary teaching*, 2nd ed. Maidenhead: Open University Press.

OECD (Organisation for Economic Cooperation and Development). (2015). *Helping immigrant students to succeed at school and beyond*. Paris: OECD Publishing.

OECD (Organisation for Economic Cooperation and Development). (2014). *Education at a glance. OECD indicators*. Paris: OECD Publishing.

OECD (Organisation for Economic Cooperation and Development). (2013). *TALIS 2013 Results: An international perspective on teaching and learning*. Paris: OECD Publishing.

OECD (Organisation for Economic Cooperation and Development). (2012). *Equity and quality in education: Supporting disadvantaged students and schools*. Paris: OECD Publishing.

OECD (Organisation for Economic Cooperation and Development). (2010). *Education at a glance. OECD indicators*. Paris: OECD Publishing.

Gardinier M. P. (2012). Agents of change and continuity: The pivotal role of teachers in Albanian educational reform and democratisation. *Comparative Education Review*, 56(4), 659–683.

Goodwin A. L. (2010). Globalisation and the preparation of quality teachers: Rethinking knowledge domains for teaching. *Teach Education*, 21(1), 19–32.

Lewin K. M. and Stuart J. (2003). Insights into the policy and practice of teacher education in low income countries: Multi-Site Teacher Education Research (MUSTER) Project. *British Educational Research Journal*, 29(5), 691–707.

Richards H. V., Brown A. F. and Forde T. B. (2007). Addressing diversity in schools: Culturally responsive pedagogy. *Teaching Exceptional Children*, 39(3), 64–68.

Sahlberg P. (2011). Finnish lessons – what can the world learn from educational change in Finland? New York: Teachers College Press/Columbia University.

Santoro N. (2013). The making of teachers for the twenty-first century: Australian professional development standards and the preparation of culturally responsive teachers. In X. Zhu and K. Zeichner, (eds), *Preparing teachers for the 21st century*. Berlin: Springer.

Spalding E. (2013). Social justice and teacher education: Where do we stand? In X. Zhu and K. Zeichner, (eds), *Preparing teachers for the 21st century*. Berlin: Springer.

Smyth G. (2013). Who are the teachers and who are the learners? Teacher education for culturally responsive pedagogy. In X. Zhu and K. Zeichner, (eds), *Preparing teachers for the 21st century*. Berlin: Springer.

Schleicher, A. (2012), *Preparing teachers and developing school leaders for the 21st century*: Background report for the 2nd International Summit on the Teaching Profession. Paris: OECD.

Taguma M., Kim M., Brink S. and Teltemann J. (2010). *OECD Reviews of Migrant Education*. Paris: OECD.

UNESCO. (2015). *Education for All (EFA) Global Monitoring Report. Education for All 2000–2015: Achievements and challenges*. Paris: UNESCO Publishing.

UNESCO. (2013/14). *Education for All (EFA) Global Monitoring Report. Teaching and learning for development.* Paris: UNESCO Publishing.

UNESCO. (2012). *Education for All (EFA) Global Monitoring Report. Youth and skills – putting education to work.* Paris: UNESCO Publishing.

Villegas A. M. and Lucas T. (2002). Preparing culturally responsive teachers – rethinking the curriculum. *Journal of Teacher Education,* 53(1), 20–32.

Westbrook J., Durrani N., Brown R., Pryor J., Boddy J. and Salvi F. (2013). *Pedagogy, curriculum, teaching practices and teacher education in developing countries.* London: Department for International Development.

Index